NEOCITIZENSHIP

Neocitizenship

Political Culture after Democracy

Eva Cherniavsky

NEW YORK UNIVERSITY PRESS

New York

NEW YORK UNIVERSITY PRESS
New York
www.nyupress.org

Chapter 1 was previously published in *Social Text* 99 (Summer 2009): 1–23; copyright 2009, Duke University Press; reprinted by permission. An earlier and partial version of chapter 2 was published in *American Studies as Transnational Practice: Turning toward the Transpacific*, ed. Donald Pease and Yuan Shu, University Press of New England, 2015: 64–83; copyright 2015, Dartmouth College Press; reprinted by permission. A portion of chapter 5 was published as "Permanent Crisis and Technosociality in Bruce Sterling's Distraction" (with Thomas Foster), *Journal of American Studies*, special issue on "Fictions of Speculation," ed. Hamilton Carroll and Annie McClanahan, vol. 49 (2015): 1–19; copyright 2015, Cambridge University Press; reprinted by permission. A version of chapter 6 was published in *Biography: An Interdisciplinary Quarterly*, special issue on "Corporate Personhood," ed. Purnima Bose and Laura Lyons, vol. 37, no. 1 (Winter 2015): 279–299; copyright 2014 University of Hawai'i Press for the Biographical Research Center; reprinted by permission.

References to Internet websites (URLs) were accurate at the time of writing. Neither the author nor New York University Press is responsible for URLs that may have expired or changed since the manuscript was prepared.

ISBN: 978-1-4798-8091-1 (hardback)
ISBN: 978-1-4798-9357-7 (paperback)

For Library of Congress Cataloging-in-Publication data, please contact the Library of Congress.

New York University Press books are printed on acid-free paper, and their binding materials are chosen for strength and durability. We strive to use environmentally responsible suppliers and materials to the greatest extent possible in publishing our books.

Manufactured in the United States of America

10 9 8 7 6 5 4 3 2 1

Also available as an ebook

for my boys

CONTENTS

ACKNOWLEDGMENTS

The moment of finishing a manuscript always feels a little improbable. Nothing restores one's relation to the continuum of lived time better than the ritual of acknowledging one's debts and the duration over which they have accrued. My earliest ruminations on this project began while I was still at Indiana, in the first years of the new millennium. My colleagues and allies in our hastily assembled Progressive Faculty Coalition, especially Pat Brantlinger, Milton Fisk, Mike Gasser, Joan Hawkins, Roopali Mukerjee, and Janet Sorenson, provided an early, invaluable sounding board and inspiration. At the University of Washington, an excellent cohort of students in my winter 2007 graduate course on "Theories and Representations of the State" helped me to a new sense of the draw and the urgency of my topic, while in spring 2014, the participants in my seminar on feminist theory vitalized my thinking in the final stages of revision. During the intervening years, an exceptionally talented group of dissertators were steady and important interlocutors: Curtis Hisayasu, Jason Morse, Jed Murr, Christian Ravela, Andrew Rose, Suzanne Schmidt, Simón Trujillo, and Kate Boyd, the last of whom was also a wonderful and patient research assistant.

In Seattle and elsewhere, an array of friends and colleagues have spurred my thinking on this book, sustained my sometimes eroding faith in the merits of my topic, and (or) helped me to stay (relatively) sane in the increasingly strange and dysfunctional world of the academy: Carolyn Allen, Hamilton Carroll, Kate Cummings, Helen Deutsch, Laurie George, Laura Lyons, Michael Meranze, Jan Radway, Laura Shackelford, Gail Stygall, Nikhil Singh, and Matt Sparke. The Octavians, SF/fantasy reading group extraordinaire, have honed my relation to the SF materials in this book in ways large and small, and I am especially grateful to Ted Chiang, Nisi Shawl, and Neil Roseman. For the opportunity to present portions of this work in progress, many thanks to Wang Ning, Donald Pease, Tyrone Simpson, and Yuan Shu.

Since 2005, the Andrew R. Hilen endowment at the University of Washington has provided me with indispensable summer research support, and I am immensely grateful to the Hilen family for their generous commitment to humanities scholarship at UW. At New York University Press, Eric Zinner has been an ideal editor. He and Alicia Nadkarni have made the review process swift, painless, and hugely productive. Effusive thanks are due my two anonymous readers at the press for their thoughtful readings and excellent, detailed suggestions.

Two friends have been with this project throughout, our many conversations reflected and refracted here in ways I can hardly unravel: my deepest thanks and appreciation to Purnima Bose, unapologetic fellow traveler, and to Robyn Wiegman, for the peripatetic object lessons. My son, Ivan Foster, has not only tolerated with good humor and good grace my absorbed (not to mention ill-tempered) state during phases of the writing of this book, but his own still-emerging sensitivity to the surreal quality of contemporary politics as to the workings of genre fiction inhabit and inform this book in countless ways. For almost a quarter of a century now, my partner, Tom Foster, has shared with me his brilliant grasp of contemporary techno-culture, his encyclopedic knowledge of SF, his irreverence, and his unfailing sense of what matters. He has read multiple chapters in multiple drafts, weathered my bouts of worry and frustration, and been tireless in his encouragement. This book is dedicated to Tom and Ivan, who are in every way imaginable the lights of my life.

Introduction

This book is concerned with the relations of subjects to governments that have been historically organized—inculcated, institutionalized, practiced, imagined—as the condition of citizenship. Like other studies of political culture on the Left, *Neocitizenship* is animated by the perception that we are living in the midst of a momentous reconfiguration of political order, which seems increasingly to represent either a new stage of capitalism or, perhaps, the beginning of its end—a moment marked, in Slavoj Žižek's words, by the dissolution of that historic "marriage between capitalism and democracy" (quoted in Shin 2011).[1] "Democracy" is, of course, a deeply fraught formation, and both the determination of a "demos," or people, and the form of its rule, or sovereignty, have been the object of critique since the emergence in the late eighteenth century, of the modern nation-state. As Wahneema Lubiano acidly notes, "At the sound of the word 'democracy' . . . some people in different parts of the world, including parts of the United States and its sphere of influence, either reach for their wallets or their guns or duck and cover while they grab their loved ones" (1996, 70). But as Lubiano goes on to observe, it is also under the sign of "democracy" that we have opposed the conflation of the word with laissez-faire capitalism, imperialism, and other practices of economic and political domination. Democracy has been at once the object and the ground of left critique, in other words, as it has sought to indicate the gap, to foreground the undemocratic character of institutionalized democracy as *scandal*. From this vantage, the divorce of capitalism and democracy strips the scandalized citizen-subject of her defining political resource.[2]

The policies and practices that have set the conditions of this divorce are generally studied under the heading of "neoliberalism," and following Foucault, studies of neoliberalism have tended to dwell on the relation of economics to the micro-political—to the institutions

1

of the state and civil society as they produce and reproduce a new kind of self-optimizing, "entrepreneurial citizen-subject," accommodated to life in the world of deregulated market freedoms. It is only more recently that critical thought on neoliberalism has addressed the macro-political, the gravitation of capitalist states to fundamentally oligarchical and autocratic forms of government, a gravitation that I describe in this book as the dismantling of the modern political field. This is by no means to suggest that oligarchy and autocracy are not endemic to political modernity, but rather to note a shift in the direction of political life, marked by the erosion of democratic governance in the regions where it was, historically, most "developed" and secure. So it comes to pass that the political situations and crises we assigned, not so long ago, to the "backward" arenas of the neocolonial client state—electoral fraud, the buying of political office, routine violations of due process, invasive state surveillance and the suspension of civil rights—are now, increasingly, descriptive of life in the "West" and Western-style democracies of the world, and perhaps no place more consistently than in the United States.

On the one hand, the figure of the citizen has been a touchstone of much of the work on neoliberalism, as a name for the subject of a new governmental pedagogy, oriented *away* from the state as the provider of social security and social good, a "citizen" designed to look after herself through responsible self-management and optimization of life prospects, an "entrepreneurial citizen," in other words, who forges her own conditions of self-realization. No doubt this concept of personhood is predominant in the institutions of the extended U.S. state and indexes the contours of the person that schools and universities, civic organizations, professional associations, and even social justice–oriented nonprofits are increasingly designed to serve and to (re)produce.[3] But why we denominate this subject a "citizen" remains unclear, since, after all, the aim of this neoliberal pedagogy is to *dissolve* the relation of subjects to governments, which has historically gone by this name. The institutions of modern democratic governance have always represented the interests of proprietors, to be sure, upholding equality of opportunity over equality of condition. But historically, the dedication to private property lives in tension with the structures of representative democracy and the requirement to serve—or at least appear to serve—the general interest of the popular sovereign. Neoliberal pedagogy, however, operates to *disabuse* a people of the notion that the institutions of government maintain any obligation to their collective welfare, which is now asserted as a fully private, disaggregated good. What the concept of the "entrepreneurial citizen-subject" thus elides is the central preoccupation of my study: the question of whether and how subject populations might yet understand and express themselves *as citizens* to the non-representing bodies of government that have effectively cut themselves loose from any commitment to a general interest. To pose the question in this fashion necessarily shifts the conversation to the terrain of the macro-political and considerations of how de-democratization has decommissioned, or at any rate reconfigured, those civic entities wrought by the democratizing impulses of political modernity: in particular, the national people and the rights-bearing citizen.

Yet in the scholarship that attends to such large-scale reconfigurations of political order, the citizen is generally presumed to persevere, doggedly adhering to her modern incarnation, even as the institutions of representative democracy spiral into crisis and dysfunction all around her. In the U.S. context, in particular, we continue to assign to the agency of "citizens" political actions *no longer directed* toward government institutions grown unresponsive and indifferent to popular political mandates and demands. Such popular mobilizations are increasingly structured on the model of self-organizing groups and coalitions addressing corporations and other private entities, so that the very form of the action indexes the retreat of governmental agencies (legislative, executive, or juridical) once meant to mediate the relation of elements within the polity, and thus signals the erosion of the terrain on which we have historically understood the "citizen" to operate. At the same time, it has become routine to chastise the "American people" for its supposed passivity in the face of autocratic U.S. government practices by attributing the (relative) absence of organized opposition to the prevalence of the "low information" voter and (or) the explicitly antidemocratic sensibilities of the electorate. By this logic, the electorate is culpable for its abandonment by the state, which is attributed to the people's failure to assert its prerogatives. This line of argument similarly assigns an essential, transhistorical reality to the national body politic, as though it could and should survive the demise of the institutions that gave it life. While this study builds on the scholarship as well as, in some measure, the journalism that has sought to lay out and assess the seismic shifts in both the institutional forms and the practices of the U.S. state, I approach "the citizen" and "the people" as historical forms of political being, so as to press a set of questions about the contemporary possibilities and prospects of political agency that have gone largely unexamined. If the state no longer operates on a claim to represent the general interest of a national people, how is the relation of governing institutions to a governed population transformed? Inasmuch as the consent of the governed seems no longer required, and indeed, no longer worth cultivating, where and in what fashion do we perform dissent? To what extent does opposition enacted on these terms repeat or recycle the practices of democratic citizenship and to what effects? Can we imagine forms of popular political mobilization that are *not* routed through the idea of a "people" asserting its sovereignty against the repressive agency of the state?

In exploring the afterlives of citizenship, this study turns to the arena of vernacular culture, in particular a selection of materials culled from recent print fiction and television, which confront the implications of de-democratization for citizenship and popular political agency in what I take to be richer, at once less coherent and more insightful, ways than most of the political theory of the historical present. By this turn to works of popular culture as a resource for critical thought, I do not mean to insinuate that theory gets it "wrong," or that we can dispense with the frameworks it provides in engaging these alternate sites of reflection on the changing shape of political life. But theory is perhaps at a disadvantage in the difficult labor of thinking about the changing present, since it operates through a set of analytical categories wrought in the very historical contexts whose *disappearance* we now seek to comprehend. The analytical resources we have to hand, in other words, were designed to consider the possibilities and limits of modern political institutions and so are bound to that historical formation that we might figure, following Žižek, as the marriage of capitalism to democracy. When we use these resources for thinking about their divorce, it is difficult to read the present as anything but a *degraded version* of the past, and we tend to miss the difference of the contemporary moment, even as we also assert its novelty, often in increasingly anxious and overwrought terms.

Theory—even theory committed to the prospect of transformative social and political change—is generally reluctant to admit that it must *unthink* itself in the process of thinking about a changing world. Theory rarely concedes—and then only under duress—that to inhabit historical change as it unfolds is precisely to encounter a situation that stands in an (as- yet) indeterminate and necessarily differential relation to the abstractions by which we aspire to take its measure. *Neocitizenship* moves to address the limitations of political theory, not by effecting a turn away from the terrain of theoretical analysis, but rather by pursuing a *return* to theory through the byways of selected print and visual narratives that, as I have sought to argue, render the difference of the present in flickering prospects that neither quite emerge into narrative view, but also never cease to exert their centrifugal force on the grammar of modern political subjectivity. As such, I suggest, these narratives provide not so much an analysis of as a heuristic for political life in transformation, as well as a supplement to a theoretical body of work that can never quite resist the lure of knowing.

My interest in this book lies in the changing contexts, practices, and imaginaries of citizenship at the turn of the twenty-first century, and it focuses—perhaps narrowly—on the contemporary United Sates, where the modern political field—predicated on popular sovereignty, rule of law, separation of powers, and the secular character of the state—is by now largely dismantled. No doubt, this dismantling is hardly confined to the United States, and certainly much of what impels it, such as the amplified role of finance in the practice of capital accumulation, has had dire, transformative implications for nation-states across the global North and the global South.[4] But the mobility of capital, and the deep global interconnections of financial markets and institutions, do not mean that the articulations of politics and economics are therefore everywhere commensurate. We might expect that the divorce of capitalism and democracy will play out differently in the United States than in nations where popular sovereignty is institutionalized in a multi-party system and the formation of coalitional governments. And it will play out differently, again, in postcolonial democracies, where, as Partha Chatterjee argues, the institutions of bourgeois civil society have only ever encompassed a fraction of the national population; or in postcolonial nations marked by the "failure" or precariousness of modern political institutions, which have perennially ceded to other, overtly oligarchical or authoritarian practices of governance (2004, 36–38).[5] So my study focuses on the United States not to deny that many of the phenomena that concern me are transnational in character, but simply to recognize that transnational phenomena develop in particular and uneven ways within the governmental and social architectures and histories of specific places. Above all, I am leery of proceeding as though the transnational operations of capital somehow resolve the abidingly national or regional nature of our academic expertise—as though we are now equipped to think on a global scale because we can identify a set of economic forces that exert themselves globally. But the circumstance, for example, that mortgaged governments across the globe are driven to institute austerity measures that provoke popular protest does not mean that those protests can therefore be apprehended within the terms of a single "transnational" analytic that would encompass, say, Egypt and Greece and the United States. The fact that the adjective "transnational" now modifies virtually all forms of capital accumulation *as well as* many rubrics of academic specialization (transnational American studies, transnational cultural studies, transnational feminism, and so forth) does not impart capital's mobility to the scholar—and there is no end run around the painstaking labor of *comparative* analysis, however dusty and outmoded that term may seem. I imagine *Neocitizenship* as a contribution to the comparative study of contemporary political cultures, a study conceived, in turn, as a collaborative intellectual project that builds on, rather than precludes, the kind of single-sited focus offered here.

The opening chapter, "Neocitizenship and Critique," reads across Michel Foucault on biopolitics and governmentality, Michael Hardt on civil society, Partha Chatterjee on political society, and Cindy Patton on identity politics in order to parse the relations of citizenship, sovereignty, and discipline both historically and within contemporary configurations of state power. I argue that the complex of phenomena we generally describe as "neoliberalism" (state-subsidized market "freedoms" supporting an ever more comprehensive enclosure of the commons; the massive reorganization of public and private domains, including the outsourcing of state functions to private corporations and proliferating, non-state agencies of governance) proceeds in tandem with the eclipse of a disciplinary society, oriented toward the internalization of common sensibilities and foundational beliefs as the condition of civic belonging. Neoliberalism abandons the historical project of the bourgeois nation-state, in other words, that entailed norming mass political sentiment and cultivating broad identification with the aims of the ruling faction(s). Instead, neoliberal governance develops strategies of population management through surveillance and securitization, uncoupled from the production of consent. Along the way, the chapter explores an alternate genealogy of neoliberalism in totalitarian state formation, which, in Hannah Arendt's suggestive if elliptical account, similarly dismantles rather than installs a normative political culture and erodes rather than disciplines the political faith of the citizen-subject. I consider, too, how the very practice of critique has been forged in historical relation to disciplinary society, and I ask after the implications of its eclipse for critical thought as it animates oppositional politics.

While the first chapter sets out an organizing line of inquiry in which to situate my preoccupations in the chapters that follow, it was by attending to the material of these subsequent chapters that I came to the questions that animate my opening. Thus the relation between chapters is best understood as rhizomatic, as a network of reverberations, rather than a linear unfolding. Chapter 2, "Post-Soviet American Studies," puzzles over the proliferation of American studies programs in the regions of the former Soviet bloc, a post–Cold-War expansion under the auspices of both the U.S. Agency for International Development (USAID) and private donor organizations, working in partnership with local governments. Unlike its Cold War antecedent, however, the contemporary, State Department–sponsored export of American studies is not designed and does not serve to disseminate a set of normative "American" political values. Rather, I contend, this post-Soviet iteration of American studies indicates the contemporary delinking of state and nation, such that the exercise of governmental power relies less and less on the ideological interpellation either of a national citizenry or of a global comprador class. On the one hand, this chapter considers how the political sensibilities informing transnational American studies turn out to be quite parochially American, linked to the specific political urgencies of life in the contemporary United States. On the other hand, my review of American studies in the former Soviet bloc shows that these sensibilities do not travel, even as the curriculum does, and that American studies in Eastern Europe and Central Asia ends up (re)oriented to the heterogeneous political imaginaries of scholars and intellectuals in these regions. But significantly, for the programs' state and private funders, these imaginaries are *not* the object of intervention, and it hardly matters that the materials of transnational American studies proffer a largely dystopian reading of U.S. history. Today the aim of American studies abroad, etched into the mission statements of donor organizations and of the programs themselves, is not keyed to political content, but to preparing a global managerial class for insertion in the networks of neoliberal governance via training in the application of administrative measures such as "efficiency," "compliance," "accountability," and "sustainability." The chapter reflects on how the version of neocitizenship these programs disseminate is enacted at the level of managerial functionality, rather than ideological identification, and on the implications of this functional interpellation for opposition to neoliberal governance.

In chapter 3, "Uncivil Society in *The White Boy Shuffle*," I read Paul Beatty's 1996 novel as it traces how the incorporative political project of the modern nation-state comes undone in the late twentieth-century United States, thereby retracting the very ground on which disqualified subjects stake their demand for civic inclusion. The novel limns the operation of what Achille Mbembe terms "necropower" in the simultaneous abandonment and hyper-policing of the racial ghetto and, crucially, the failure of a modern freedom politics, staked in the assertion of the sovereignty of the subjugated, to counter or to mitigate this violence. The protagonists of *The White Boy Shuffle* inhabit the crisis of political agency this situation entails: What does opposition mean, where is it enacted, what organizational, rhetorical, and affective forms might it assume, in a state whose instrumentalization of black life sits on the surface, not under ideological concealment, but as an overt and banal reality—a state therefore immune to the revelation of its necropolitical character as scandal? In particular, I am interested in how the novel reimagines the very form of political agency, especially the relation between publicity (the variously mediated forms of discourse, performance, and spectacle that constitute publics) and the command-and-control tactics of militarized policing. This relation is thematized in the trope of an

LAPD helicopter that hovers over the novel's final scenes, its penetrating white spotlight invading and monitoring ghetto life, but also providing free illumination for the community's "miseryfests," where the politically abandoned gather in a brilliant, collective performance of their fury and contempt. I read the novel for what it suggests about the possibilities and limits of such forms of subaltern publicity, particularly when the avenues of communal self-mediation are also, transparently, the means for tracking, compiling, and profiling the heterogeneous political (dis) investments of a dis-incorporated citizenry.

Chapter 4, "Beginnings without End: Derealizing the Political in *Battlestar Galactica*" discerns in the four-season run of the Sci Fi channel's cult television series a narrative locus to think further about the connection, just barely apprehended in chapter 1, between the decline of a normative political culture and the contemporary derealization of political life. A generic space opera, the series turns on the antagonisms between human society, characterized by its bad faith adherence to the forms of modern democratic politics, and a society of "cylons," human-appearing cyborgs, which are replicated rather than reproduced (all cylons are cloned from one of twelve basic "models") and whose forms of social and political being I read as a kind defamiliarized, hyperbolic projection of the governmental practices and social relations we associate with neoliberalism. The humans and the cylons are both iterations of "us," in other words, in our twinned guises as disintegrating national people and the as-yet largely unknowable condition into which we are emerging. My reading dwells in particular on the organization of cylon society by serial differentiation, rather than normative identification; by the cultivation of intensities, rather than convictions; and by the proliferation of virtual environments, rather than the production of a common, seemingly objective reality, anchored in fixed ideological reference points. I am especially compelled by the affective life of cylon subjects, as it collates around mania and depression, rather than the signature guilt and attendant neurotic symptomology of the disciplined modern subject.

In chapter 4, I read *Battlestar Galactica* as an allegory, in Walter Benjamin's sense of the term, a practice of representation that renders the world in pieces, a ruined thing in which we can (just) discern the possibilities of existing otherwise. In that spirit, I let my reading of the series sit to one side—slightly askew—of the present moment, rather than flattening the correspondences by attempting to say, for example, that the cylons are a representation of neoliberal order. As allegorical figures, I suggest, they limn the possible contours—social, political, aesthetic, and affective—of what takes shape amid the wreckage of political modernity, and their interest lies precisely in the way that they remain irreducible to the already-available rubrics by which we narrate contemporary life.

In chapter 5, entitled simply "Unreal," I take what I would call the critical sensibility towards derealization developed through my reading of *Battlestar Galactica*, and set it to work, so to speak, on the terrain of political culture in the post-9/11 United States. This leads me to linger on and give weight to the sense of sheer incredulity with which I, and so many others, bear witness to the political transformations of the past two decades—a sense of disorientation in relation to what we took, not so long ago, as norming our perception of the given and the possible. Along these lines, I come to explore how the elements of contemporary life that have engaged me throughout this study—the divorce of capitalism and democracy; the demise of disciplinary society; the apparent disinterest of the state in the cultivation of a national people—have the effect of eroding the sense of a common reality, in which a national or even a local (not to mention a planetary) "we" live in simultaneous time and convergent social and material worlds. More precisely, in "Unreal," I discern in phenomena such as the 2008 financial crisis, congressional gridlock, Obama's "grassroots" presidential campaign, and the stupefaction of the U.S. electorate (as many commentators now lament) the signs of a novel situation, wherein political power (both elite and oppositional) increasingly takes the form of declaring autonomy, of conjuring the reality that answers to one's own proclivities, rather than intervening in the shape of a shared continuum. I move to apprehend (to find a language for apprehending) what strikes me as the simulacral quality of contemporary political life, which is to say, the increasing dispersal of the population into so many nonintersecting planes of social existence and political imagining. In the final section of this chapter, I turn to Bruce Sterling's 1998 science fiction novel *Distraction* for its effort to imagine, without nostalgia for the institutions of modern democratic governance, alternate forms of political self-elaboration in a world of proliferating autonomous collectives.

The final chapter, "Refugees from This Native Dreamland," explores the Occupy Wall Street movement, often framed as the reawakening of the slumbering popular sovereign. I argue to the contrary that the world of OWS is more fundamentally related to Sterling's fictional world than to the social movements of the 1960s, from which, undoubtedly, it borrows some of its political aesthetics. But despite the invocation of a 99%, the aspiration and practices of OWS are not those of a mass social movement that seeks to recalibrate public feeling to new social and political norms. To read the archive of OWS—its manifestos, testimonials, and self-analyses—is to witness the construction of networked singularities, whose attention is directed inward, to the prospects of their self-elaboration. In this way, OWS participates in the broader derealization of contemporary political life, even as it strives to generate resources for an oppositional (anti-capitalist) politics.

Much like the texts it privileges, this book does not aspire to settle the questions it engages, but simply to touch down on those questions in productive ways. Throughout, I remain committed to the *impossibility* of thinking the changing present. In part, of course, the present remains (still) unthinkable because to engage transformation is always and necessarily to lose the reference points by which we are accustomed to take our critical bearings. But *Neocitizenship* also suggests that the nature of the political changes we confront involves a willful and strategic *rescinding* of the referents, *not* as a move along the way toward instituting and naturalizing a new political reality, but rather as an *end in itself*, bound to a different way of conceptualizing power and governance. The dismantling of the reference points and turning out of the population to explore whatever vistas of political rage, melancholia, and mania are paradoxically, the symptoms of a new and burgeoning apparatus of governmental control, a conundrum that dwells at the center of this inquiry. Yet the crisis of critique today, in this moment when the *retreat from ideological imposition appears to serve the very aims of domination,* is a provocation to improvise alternate analytical habits and gestures. Improvisation is, of course, not normally a practice we associate with scholarly production, however much critical work in the humanities may claim to abjure the aspiration to mastery. But in the shape of our arguments—mapping an inquiry, proposing an analytic, producing a claim—we nonetheless value and cultivate the intellectual ownership of our cultural objects.

In thinking and writing this book, I have been keenly aware that the inquiry I have mapped is fragmentary, my analytic an eclectic repertoire of moves that may or may not sustain that inquiry, and my claims tentative—a resting place, rather than a terminus. Yet *Neocitizenship* is also an argument that the conditions of the present demand precisely such partial and improvised reckonings. In this, ironically, lies its most authoritative claim.

1

Neocitizenship and Critique

Identity now functions not so much to retain a representational space or define a trajectory toward cultural autonomy
as it operates as a holograph of what the appropriate subject
of a new form of governance might look like. The referents
of identities are now less important than the capacity to look
like an identity at all.
—Cindy Patton, "Tremble, Hetero Swine!"

It may be that the true predicaments of our time will assume
their authentic form . . . only when totalitarianism has become a thing of the past.
—Hannah Arendt, *The Origins of Totalitarianism*

This book asks how the political identity and the domain of civic practice
we call "citizenship" are transformed, eroded, or, perhaps, disappeared
in the contexts of neoliberal governance. To put the question more
pointedly: What happens—what is presently happening—to the meaning and practice of citizenship with the eclipse of popular sovereignty?
By way of *caveat lector*, I confess at the outset that this opening chapter
pursues a rather eclectic trajectory through a limited body of historical
and critical work that has launched and compelled my own thinking
on this question. My concern is not so much that in our rush to think
the emergent modalities of state and corporate power routinely glossed
as "neoliberal," we neglect the topic of political subject-constitution
(though sometimes, of course, we do that, as well), but rather that when
we do attend to latter-day "citizen-subjects," we proceed as though we
know what we mean—as though the term "citizen," divested of the modifier "bourgeois," perhaps with an alternate descriptor attached (such as
"flexible" or "entrepreneurial"), can name the relation of subjects to the
institutions of neoliberal governance as well as it did, not so very long

ago, to the legal and civic institutions of the bourgeois nation-state. In this regard, it is only too apparent that the "we" of the preceding sentence is no ingenuous rhetorical choice, as my own title brashly enacts the very same critical maneuver. At the same time, my aspiration is to hold open the question of whether "citizens" and "citizenship" outlive their modern conditions of possibility and, especially, the related question of what claims we can make for (and about) them—-whether our intellectual reflexes, honed on the critique of the "old" citizenship and its contexts (abstract equality, racial nationalism, bourgeois civil society, and so forth) are adequate to the critical engagement with whatever it is we now name citizenship, what Michael Hardt expressly calls "the citizen as a whatever identity" (1992, 40).

My tactic in this chapter is to retrace a path across ground habitually mapped by reference to such watchwords as "governmentality," "flexibility," "deterritorialization," "networks," and "control" in order to apprehend it *incompletely*, that is, to encounter the elementary contours of the present as they retain the capacity to startle and elude. Along the way, I will suggest that one of the more confounding implications of what we might call, variously and to somewhat different effects, "governmentalized state power," the "society of control," "neoliberal governance," or the "network society" is the diminishing critical value of the very tactic of defamiliarization on which this chapter therefore relies. Critique as a mode of defamiliarization or estrangement assumes that power operates to *fix* social and political relations and to *suture* individuals and collectives to what will therefore appear—if the "fix" holds—as the natural or given contours of their identities, communities, nations, or worlds. On this model, power sustains itself by producing a readable social and political world, one that appears coherent, insofar as it adheres to the laws and the norms in which its readers are already interpellated and so the defining aspiration of critique is to *unmake* this readable world, to reveal its incoherencies, contradictions, and the bad faith that governs its composition. None of us may see the nuance of our critical practice rendered in this admittedly reductive sketch, but in its general outlines, nonetheless, this understanding of critique certainly reflects my own intellectual formation, and in this, no doubt, I am not alone.

Insofar as critical practice is permeated by this assumption that established political power inevitably binds its subjects to a naturalized or normalized social order, we bind ourselves to a fundamentally de-historicized, inert conception of the state, even as we cite our deep commitment to tracing its historical permutations. Instead, we might interrogate the abiding value and the limits of critical defamiliarization if what confronts us under the sign of "neoliberalism" today are "ultrarapid forms of free-floating control" and dereferentialized identities that remain constitutively—*rigorously*—mutable or unmade (Deleuze 1990, 1). It is this doubled attention, to matters of governance and citizenship, on the one hand, and to the limits of critical practice, on the other, that compels this chapter's eclectic circuits through scholarship not always or primarily concerned with "neoliberalism," including Hannah Arendt's germinal study of totalitarianism, a practice of power she understands as particularly unresponsive to established modes of critical apprehension, by reason of its systematically denormalizing and derealizing effects. Predictably enough, my preoccupation with the question of (neo)citizenship has drawn me (anew) to the essential critical work on neoliberalism, understood as a form of state-sponsored, publically subsidized market "freedom" (Harvey 2005; Henwood 1998) and thus a political rather than narrowly economic rationality (Brown 2005), supporting a new and seemingly unabating round of primitive accumulation (Prashad 2003), or accumulation by dispossession (Harvey 2005), and signaled in the massive recalibration of public and private domains, including the privatizing of state functions (Klein 2007) and the distribution of functions formally assigned to "government" across proliferating, non-state agencies of "governance" (Brown 2005; Ong 2006). Less predictably, it has also led me somewhat afield of these discussions, to a consideration of neoliberalism in its relation to *normative culture*, by which I mean, loosely, the ensemble of discourses, media, institutions, and customary practices that performs the work of social reproduction and arrays us as readers of a readable world. I find a spur to this other line of reflection in Foucault's Collège de France lectures, those that attend not just to neoliberalism explicitly, but to the wider arc of inquiry on government, "governmentality," sovereignty, and discipline that spans the years from 1975 to 1979. Foucault's work on "biopolitics" and "governmentality" (both his own neologisms) have been galvanizing for much of the scholarship on neoliberalism, of course, though little attention has been paid to what I read in the lectures as a kind of loose speculative thread on the contemporary, "neoliberal" (dis)articulations of "governmentality," discipline, and normalization.

Thus I begin retrospectively by revisiting modern citizenship as forged in and through the alignment of governmentality (regulating populations) and discipline (norming individuals), precisely so as to track and to throw into relief how neoliberal governance, in Foucault's elaboration, entails the ascendance of the former and the waning of the latter—in effect, the uncoupling of the state's historically twinned aspirations to administer human life *and* individual consciousness. What are the implications for a contemporary neocitizenship, imagined on these terms, as something *other* than a disciplined category of political subjectivity? This question leads me to address the current, largely celebratory emphasis on civil society, generally assumed (by those who study the nonprofit sector) to represent a thriving arena of civic activity, operating independently of the neoliberal state. I pressure the insistence on the (supposed) autonomy of civil society actors (untethered, as the argument goes, from both markets and states) in order to ask what forms and relays of political activity this conception of a discrete civic sector implies and enables. I suggest that the contemporary flowering of civil society corresponds to the eclipse of normative political cultures and the emergence of the citizen as a kind of hologram or simulacrum. Ultimately, I broach a question that reverberates through every chapter of this study: namely, how we imagine resistance to the intentions of a neoliberal state no longer invested in (or dependent on) the production of conviction or consent.

After Normative Culture

In the wake of a heated debate in the early to mid-1990s on "the decline of the nation-state," to cite Masao Miyoshi's much contested thesis, it has become commonplace to suggest that the *relation* of nation and nationalism to state formation is in the process of a more or less radical reconfiguration under the political and economic conditions of neoliberalism (Miyoshi 1993). As David Harvey notes, for instance, "neoliberalization" entails a "curious relationship between state and nation. In principle, neoliberal theory does not look with favour on the *nation* even as it supports the idea of a strong state. The umbilical cord that tied together state and nation under embedded liberalism had to be cut if neoliberalism was to flourish" (2005, 84). In Harvey's work and elsewhere, the bearing of neoliberalism on the nation-state form is usually something of an ancillary point, an effect that follows from the state's dedication to the (coercive) installation of "free markets," or the wholesale privatization of public resources. But one might also conceive a framing of neoliberalism in which the current unraveling of modern nation-state relations appears more central (a primary rather than secondary symptom). For the purpose of these reflections on citizenship, at any rate, I am inclined to think of neoliberalism as a specific resolution to the duplicity of the modern nation-state, constituted in the double imperative to advance the public good and to secure private property in its myriad and proliferating forms. Neoliberalism abdicates the former imperative in favor of the latter, and in so doing frees the state from the compulsion to realize a national-popular interest that it can claim to uphold. Paradoxically, the state's retreat from the cultivation of a national body politic that consents to the state's doings in its name sets the stage for a contemporary flowering of nationalist rhetoric, be it in the form of overtly particularistic ethnonationalisms emancipated from the (always fraught) universalism of modern nation-state formations, or in the form of noise, a kind of media static whose main purpose, far from commanding hearts and minds, is simply to drown out anything of critical moment that might otherwise aspire to its mass dissemination (a form endemic to the post-9/11 United States).

This uncoupling of state from nation corresponds, as well, to the decline of the sovereign state, at least insofar as sovereignty names a practice of *legitimated* power, contingent on the *lawful* constitution and deployment of the sovereign authority.[1] In the case of the modern nation-state as it emerges from the needs and aspirations of an ascendant bourgeoisie, political sovereignty is formally vested in a national people, or in Antonio Negri and Michael Hardt's tidy summation, "The nation became explicitly the concept that summarized the bourgeois hegemonic solution to the problem of sovereignty" (2000, 101). At stake in the neoliberal parting of the ways between state and nation, then, is a structure of legitimation that binds the power of the state to a national body politic, which it becomes the educative mission of the state to engender, in a form consistent with the dominant class interests to which the state is fundamentally beholden. The bourgeois nation-state entails the articulation of sovereignty to discipline—of the power of the prince (now the distributed power of the state and its offices) to the "soul" of the citizen-subject, such that the interpellated citizen experiences his subjection as his freedom, or in Michael Warner's apt phrase, "consents to [his] own coercion" (1990, 111). On the other side of this historical formation, the uncoupling of state from nation that signals the eclipse of sovereign power signals, too, the erosion of disciplinary society, as the means by which the bourgeois state reforms the mob as qualified national citizenry. Conceptually speaking, at any rate, we may antici-pate that neoliberalism displaces not only the nation-state synthesis, but also the particular articulation of sovereign to disciplinary power that this synthesis both provokes and enables. How readily such an analytic—wrought in the theoretical consideration of something called "the modern nation-state"—illuminates the situation of any specific (post)modern nation-state is a question about the reach of neoliberal-ism, the depth and speed to which it penetrates the nations and regions of the world, as well as the uneven interactions of neoliberal agents and policies with established and eroding local formations. I approach the abstractions through reflection on the contemporary United States, by which I mean not only the territorial/sovereign U.S. state, but other na-tions and regions partially or fully administered by U.S. government and governance agencies (by the U.S. armed forces, or State Department funding bureaus such as USAID, but also, more loosely, by the private corporations and NGOs to which state functions are increasingly out-sourced). Certainly, I would argue that this dismantling of the nation-state synthesis is well advanced in the United States, as well as central to "its" aspirations elsewhere in the world.

It is rather striking that the historical transfer of sovereignty from the prince to the people, "the bourgeois hegemonic solution to the problem of sovereignty," remains, to all appearances, a matter of relative indiffer-ence to the preeminent historian of disciplinary society. However, Fou-cault's provocative, if truncated, reflections on the triangulated relations of sovereignty, discipline, and the modern "art of government" nonethe-less reverberate with the problematics of a specifically *national* form of sovereignty. More exactly, it seems that "governmentality," as Foucault describes it, *sustains* the articulation of sovereign to disciplinary power at the point of the *emergence of the nation-state*, even as governmentality *supplants* sovereignty and discipline alike in the contemporary context of the *nation-state's undoing*. In his lecture of February 1, 1978, Foucault defines the art of government *over and against* sovereignty, even while insisting on their co-implication in (early) modern state formation; notably, the question of governmentality's relation to discipline (to family, school, asylum, prison, to name only the most obvious disciplinary institutions) is raised rather more obliquely, towards the lecture's end. While it is true that the sovereignty of the prince is animated at some level by a conception of the common good (even the absolute monarch cannot by right renounce obligation to the welfare of his subjects), still, Foucault observes, in every instance, the "common good" manifests precisely as obedience to the sovereign's law—as "nothing other than submission to this law," in short (2007, 98). By contrast,

> Government is defined . . . as a right manner of arranging (*disposer*) things in order to lead (*conduire*) them, not to the form of the "common good," as the texts of the jurists said, but to an end suitable for each of the things to be governed. This implies, first of all, a plurality of specific ends. For example, the government will have to ensure that the greatest possible amount of wealth is produced, that the people are provided with sufficient means of subsistence and that the population can increase. So, the objective of government will be a whole series of specific finalities. And one will arrange (*disposer*) things to achieve these different ends. . . . *Whereas the end of sovereignty is internal to itself and gets its instruments from itself in the form of law, the end of government is internal to the things it directs (diriger); it is to be sought in the perfection, maximization, or intensification of the processes it directs, and the instruments of government, will become diverse tactics rather than laws.* (2007, 99, my emphasis)

A sovereignty realized in the perpetuation of the sovereign's right seems no longer fully adequate to a historical context where the sovereign is the national people, in whose name the power of the state is marshaled, but who do not, themselves, perform its offices or discharge its functions—who dwell *outside* the institutions of the state, in other words. For the people clad in the political lion's skin of sovereignty, to borrow Marx's memorable phrase, political right can never be remote from private interests—from the right disposition of things as they bear on their subsistence, health, prosperity, generation. From this perspective, the governmentalization of the state, such that "population appears as the end and instrument of government, rather than as the sovereign's strength," gains new momentum under the conditions of national sovereignty, which could hardly have developed without it (Foucault 2007, 105).

Foucault writes more obliquely of the relation of governmentality to discipline, although some of his remarks respecting the ends and tactics of the governmentalized state indicate the folding of disciplinary aspirations into the broader aims of "a society of government." "Interest as the consciousness of each of the individuals making up the population, and interest as the interest of the population, whatever the individual interests and aspirations may be of those who comprise the population, will be the ambiguous fundamental target and instrument of the government of populations," he observes (2007, 105–106). Here disciplinary practice as it cultivates and norms the interior life of the individual converges on biopolitics and its "multiform tactics" for managing populations and economies, a convergence emphasized, as well, in Foucault's rejection of a progressivist schema, "the replacement of a society of sovereignty by a society of discipline, and then a society of discipline by a society, say, of government" (2007, 107). The development and elaboration of governmentality thus proceeds in tandem with the proliferation of disciplinary institutions and the exercise of (national) sovereignty, bound up in the juridical category of the citizen and the disciplinary production of the normative political discourses associated with the practice of citizenship. At the same time, however, Foucault also posits "the tendency, the line of force, that for a long time, and throughout the West, has constantly led toward the pre-eminence over all other types of power—sovereignty, discipline, and so on—of the type of power that we can call government" (2007, 108).

Certainly, the "pre-eminence" of governmental over *sovereign* power is starkly apparent in the contemporary United States, where questions concerning the rightful conduct of the state (has the state exercised its power to lawful ends, by legitimate means?) seem less and less intelligible, as compared to questions about administrative tactics (has the state attained its aims efficiently?). To mention only a single, early instance among the thick and varied evidence for this structural transformation, the Democratic Party elite steadfastly declined to pursue the impeachment of Bush administration personnel for documented crimes and in the face of public opinion polls suggesting that somewhere on the order four in ten U.S. voters favored removing the president and vice president from office.[2] As a form of legal redress, impeachment (or impeachment proceedings) serves to uphold sovereign power (to legitimate the power of the office by eliminating the culpable office-holder). From this perspective, the party leadership's refusal to pursue impeachment represented less a failure of will or even a sign of complicity in any simple sense (such as a desire that Democratic successors to the presidency enjoy the same inflation of executive powers)—though it surely represented those things, too—than a canny and *tactical* acquiescence in the dominance of governmental reasoning. Like other forms of procedural/legal redress to the contradictions and excesses of the nation-state, impeachment is arguably best understood as a limited strategy within a war of position. So from the standpoint of a left opposition for whom law has never been adequate to justice, the question now is not all that fundamentally different from what it has been, historically: how to envision the tactical pursuit of limited justice (only this time) within a largely extra-legal, administrative discourse that calibrates standards of "accountability" and "compliance" to the benchmarks of efficiency (output, turnover time, flexible application, and so forth). Ironically enough, under the conditions of dominant governmentality, recourse to the law and to the determination of right functions *generally* as it has always functioned for those on the margins or the outside of bourgeois hegemony—functions, in other words, as a tactic, and no longer a preferred or privileged tactic in a world where anyone too insistent on the constitutive and normative properties of law looks vaguely sentimental and out of touch with the real politik of the day.

But what exactly does it mean to suggest, as does Foucault, that governmentality takes "pre-eminence" over *discipline*? What are the contours of governmentality uncoupled from discipline? Foucault comes closest to an explicit answer in the context of discussing the governmental techniques specific to "American neoliberalism," which he suggests suspend the value and the operations of discipline that elsewhere he terms the exercise of power "over the fine grain of individual behaviors"

(2007, 66). Addressing the tactical calculations of "law enforcement" as imagined in the framework of Chicago School economics, Foucault notes that

> you can see that what appears on the horizon of this kind of analysis is not at all the ideal or project of an exhaustively disciplinary society in which the legal network hemming in individuals is taken over and extended internally by, let's say, normative mechanisms. Nor is it a society in which a mechanism of general normalization and the exclusion of those who cannot be normalized is needed. On the horizon of this analysis we see instead the image, idea, or theme-program of a society in which there is an optimization of systems of difference, in which the field is left open to fluctuating processes, in which minority individuals and practices are tolerated, in which action is brought to bear on the rules of the game, rather than on the players, and finally in which there is an environmental type of intervention instead of the internal subjugation of individuals. (2008, 259–260)

In this sketch—we might say, in this prognosis—governmentality after discipline works to regulate the kinds and conditions of labor, of education, and of social action; the movements of elite and subaltern populations; their (in)security; their access to data and commodities, including the necessities of survival. In other words, governmentality after discipline is a grammar of environment, which abdicates (as no longer necessary or functional) the vast disciplinary project of normalizing the identifications, the grammar of incorporation and abjection, which constitute the psychic life of human subjects.

Gilles Deleuze (borrowing from William Burroughs) has proposed the term "society of control" for this post-disciplinary formation, in a short essay that stresses the mass production of individuality as a defining element of disciplinary society.

> We no longer find ourselves dealing with the mass/individual pair. Individuals have become "*dividuals*" and masses, samples, data, markets, or "*banks*." Perhaps it is money that expresses the distinction between the two societies best, since discipline always referred back to minted money that locks gold as numerical standard, while control relates to floating

rates of exchange, modulated according to a rate established by a set of standard currencies. The old monetary mole is the animal of the space of enclosure, but the serpent is that of the societies of control. (1990, 2, emphasis in original)

Deleuze here telegraphs a series of broad claims about the paired decline of bounded (or "molded") individuality and of the massified social body—the mass of population conceived as social *organism*. On the one hand, new techniques of "numeration" transform the mass into multi-form, proliferating "markets" or "data." On the other, the institutions of disciplinary society—the discrete "spaces of enclosure"—that pro-duced "enclosed" individuals give way to strategies for the formation of constitutively incomplete, susceptible subjects, perennially open to refinements—or "modulations" of control that now traverse the social field (for example, Deleuze cites the shift from school-based education to "perpetual training," or in the current idiom, "life-long learning"). Within this framework, the (seemingly) offhanded association of dis-ciplinarity with the gold standard (and control with floating exchange rates) flags a dereferentialization of identity on which Cindy Patton also insists in one of the epigraphs to this chapter. If discipline aspires to fix the subject through a set of (internalized) reference points, control arrays receptive subjects, minutely sensitive to the smallest fluctuations of the market. At stake in these transformations, then, is the unraveling of normative bourgeois culture: the waning of pedagogies of internaliza-tion (induced self-surveillance); the dismantling of identity as an organic social force (one that consolidates rather than proliferates attachments). By this I understand not simply the unraveling of *those norms* histori-cally specific to bourgeois sociality, but rather the erosion of *normative culture as such,* that is, culture oriented to the *production of reproducible interiorities.* At the same time, the twin assumptions it takes from the encounter with normative culture—that culture works to reproduce its categories; that internalization is the primary, *disciplinary* mechanism for effecting this reproduction—remain axiomatic for critique, even as we labor to devise new tropologies of the post-disciplinary subject. To announce the passing of disciplinary society is also, I suggest, to raise significant and largely unanswered questions about the aspirations of critique after normative culture, when the tactics of control through contingent valuations and deferentialized categories seem, paradoxically, to align with our prized analytical tactics for unmaking the world.

The Decline and Efflorescence of Civil Society

To interrogate the contours of citizenship after normative culture is necessarily to raise questions about the present, neoliberal configuration of civil society, which stands, historically, as a primary location for disciplinary institutions dedicated to the production of normative citizen-subjects. Here I linger, in particular, on an essay by Michael Hardt, which both elaborates the historical continuities between disciplinary and civil society and identifies the contemporary moment with the "withering" of this arena for social regulation. Hardt's preoccupation thus resonates with my own, even as his assertion of civil society's decline moves sharply against the current of a neoliberal policy discourse that asserts almost exactly the reverse. In both regards, the essay offers an exceptionally useful launching point for thinking about the operations of civil society in a post-disciplinary framework.

For Hardt, the question of disciplinary and civil society presents more specifically as an inquiry into Hegel's account of civil society (and Gramsci's reappropriation of it) and into disciplinary society in Foucault's sense, which Hardt deftly maps onto a Hegelian tradition to which Foucault is more habitually opposed. In Hegel's thought, Hardt observes, civil society appears no longer as the counterpart to natural society (within a binary system), but rather in a tripartite relation to natural and *political* society both, where civil society names the civilizing or educative social processes that transform singular, natural man into the universal subject of the state—in particular, Hardt underscores, by transforming concrete into abstract labor. Foucault, of course, rejects outright any such analytical separation of political from civil society, theorizing the state, instead, as a consolidation, or "etatisation," of power relations that traverse the social field, rather than as a discrete plane of political organization, much less the level to be prioritized in the analysis of power. Still, in the spread-out micropolitics of disciplinary institutions, Foucault traces the regulative social operations that Hegel associates with civil society, or in Hardt's words, "The same educative social processes that Hegel casts in terms of abstraction and organization,

Foucault recognizes in terms of training, discipline, and management"
(1995, 32)—a sameness worth remarking, even though, as Hardt readily
enough concedes, Foucauldian discipline, unlike Hegelian civil society,
is not an ordering of natural or given social elements, not a restrictive
apparatus, in short, but a productive one, that conjures the very identities to be managed.[3] In this way, Hardt suggests, "Disciplinary society
can be characterized as civil society seen from a different perspective,
approached from underneath, from the microphysics of power relations"
(1995; 33, my emphasis).

This argument subtends Hardt's wider analysis of the contemporary
decline of civil society, which (adopting Marx's distinction), Hardt associates with the movement from the "formal" to the "real subsumption" of
labor—for Marx, a tendency legible within nineteenth-century society,
and for Hardt, "a passage that has only come to be generalized in the
most completely capitalist countries of our times" (1995, 38). "Formal
subsumption" names the encounter between capital and labor as capital
finds it within precapitalist contexts—that is, as "as an *imported foreign
force*, born outside capital's domain," which had therefore to be taken up
by capital and "abstracted, recuperated, disciplined, and tamed within
the productive processes" (1995, 38, 30). By contrast, in the process of
"real subsumption," the productivity of labor, aggregated and function-
alized in ever more advanced (or scientific) ways, increasingly manifests
as the productive power of social *capital* that "appears to reproduce itself
autonomously." What supports this derealization of productive relations
under the conditions of real subsumption, in Hardt's iteration of Marx,
is precisely *not* a disciplinary process that would "extend vertically
throughout the various strata of society" but rather the construction of
"a separate plane, a simulacrum of society, that excludes or marginalizes
social forces foreign to the system," including, especially, the working
class. Crucially, for Hardt, this transit from formal to real subsumption
entails the withering of civil society because under the conditions of labor's real subsumption, which is to say, under the conditions of capital's
apparent "emancipation" from labor, the state is "no longer interested in
mediation or 'education,' but in separation, no longer in discipline but
in control" (1995, 39).

The merit of Hardt's analysis, it seems to me, is to bring into an original and compelling alignment disciplinary with civil society, and their

"withering" with the work of the simulacrum. In this respect, his analysis tallies helpfully with my own insistence that the decline of disciplinary society corresponds to the erosion of popular sovereignty and the attendant evisceration of a representational politics. But Hardt also, and more problematically in my view, imagines the state's retreat from the task of mediation as such, at the same time as he asserts the formation of a separate plane of simulated social relations, a "simulacrum of society" in which, one can only assume, the state remains altogether interested. Admittedly, the hyper-mediation of the simulacrum no longer *appears* as a mediation, in the sense of a movement between levels or domains of the social field, since the simulacrum does not appear to refer to (or communicate with) anything outside itself. Yet surely a simulacrum of society, fabricated under the auspices of the state, is a mediation of a different sort—one that functions, precisely, through the derealization of social planes, rather than their vertical integration.

In Ruth Wilson Gilmore's *Golden Gulag*, I find, among other things, a brilliant reflection on the state's derealization of social relations as it pertains to the expansion of the prison system in California—a reflection that clarifies how simulation is also mediation, albeit one that no longer intervenes in "the fine grain of individual behaviors." Starting from the observation that the increase in the size of the California inmate population corresponds to a notable *decline* in the rate of crime during the same period, Gilmore understands incarceration as a tactic for the management of surplus finance capital, surplus population, and surplus state capacity. As California divested from the maintenance and improvement of public works that had been funded through issuance of public debt, another outlet was required to absorb surplus finance capital—and the expansion of the prison system offered a resolution to the problem, an alternate way to keep private capital moving at public expense, while simultaneously putting to use the stalled administrative capacities of the post-welfare state and addressing the surplus population created through restructuring of labor markets. "The state built itself by building prisons fashioned from surpluses that the newly developing political economy [of California] had not absorbed in other ways," Gilmore argues (2007, 54). *Golden Gulag* specifies with admirable analytical precision the shift from a disciplinary production of bourgeois sociality through the criminalization and institutionalized reform of deviance to the contemporary production of crime/criminality in the interest of directing capital and population flows. If the state's attribution, prosecution, and sentencing of crime is now a function of calculations such as the optimum amount of surplus capital to siphon off into prison construction, this governmental practice is mediated through the simulacrum of rising urban crime—a mediation all the more frictionless and effective because it does not seek to interpellate social subjects across the social field so much as to saturate the field of virtual sociality.

Hardt's largely persuasive argument for the withering of civil society stands in a curious and (by him) unacknowledged relation to the voluminous body of social science discourse that posits *exactly the reverse*: the efflorescence of civil society, as heralded particularly by the rise of the NGO. Indeed, in the world of disciplinary social science and of policy-makers (especially those attached to North American foundations and international lenders such as the International Monetary Fund and the World Bank), civil society is at a point of ascendance, rather than decline, its size and significance amplified by the dismantling of the welfare state on the one hand (the outsourcing of state service functions to NGOs and other civil society actors), and the perceived need for a "check" on the political dominance of market forces, which social service and human rights oriented associations are thought to provide, on the other. Data of the Johns Hopkins Comparative Non-Profit Sector Project, for instance, indicates that the nonprofit sector (excluding religious associations) in the twenty-two countries that project researchers examine (nations in Western and Eastern Europe, Latin America, as well as the United States, Australia, Israel, and Japan) is a $1.1 trillion industry, the equivalent of the world's eighth largest economy, employing a larger workforce than the (combined) largest private firms in those same countries (Salamon et al. 1999, 8–9). In the statistical construction of empirical truth within social science and policy fields, civil society is flourishing, in other words. Writing in a more qualitative register, Michael Edwards, director of the Ford Foundation's Governance and Civil Society Programs, casts civil society as the "big idea" of the contemporary moment. As a frame for this affirmation, Edwards constructs a tidy narrative of passage among essentially discrete conceptualizations of state/society relations, which constitutes, I would argue, the common-sense of policy discussions:

The weight attached to each of these models has shifted significantly over the last fifty years, with state-based solutions in the ascendancy from 1945 to the mid-1970s (the era of the welfare state of the North and centralized planning in the South), and market-based solutions in pole position from the late 1970s to 1990 or thereabouts (the era of Reagonomics in the North and structural adjustment in the South). Disaffection with the result of both these models—the deadening effect of too much state intervention and the human consequences of an over-reliance on the market—required a new approach that addressed the consequences of both state and market failure. This new approach, which gained strength through the 1990s, went by many names (including the "third way," the "new localism," and "compassionate conservatism"), but its central tenet is that partnership between all three "sectors" of society working together—public, private, and civic—is the best way to overcome social and economic problems. (2004, 10)

One strand of Edwards's argument, then, is that civil society—or "associational life"—should not be understood or cultivated as a substitute service provider for the post-welfare state. Rather, he urges, civil society serves as a check on "vested interests," promotes "accountability among states and markets," directs information to "decision-makers"—undertakes the work of mediation among "sectors," in short. Crucially, civil society in Edwards's analytic is *assumed* to operate autonomously from the state and the market, so that its mediatory efforts appear to function authentically on behalf of the participants in associational life and of the wider "human" element compromised by market-oriented social policy. In order for civil society to realize these mediatory aims, states and markets must help foster an appropriate "civil society ecosystem," which includes formal equality (a "level playing field for citizen action") and domestic funding of civil associations, as civil society by itself, Edwards concedes, cannot set its own optimum conditions of possibility. Yet his analysis (like many others in the policy field) retains a sharp *analytical* separation of state, market, and society as the basis, precisely, for imagining a sort of managerial "partnership" among them.

At the same time, the administrative language of "problems," "solutions," and "partnership" suggests that this form of mediation is not primarily disciplinary in its aspirations and techniques. While Edwards remains interested in the conditions under which "associational life" *might* function normatively, fabricating and sustaining the "moral dispositions" that ensure "the health of democracy," he is explicit that such normative achievements are relatively rare in practice, depending as they do on contingent, context-sensitive combinations of factors, which are difficult, if not impossible, to predict in advance (2004, 83–92). Indeed, the evacuated administrative categories that comprise the new discourse of civic engagement are hardly oriented to the cultivation of the "moral" citizen in the first place. Consider, for instance, how the Johns Hopkins researchers phrase their account of civil society's (re)newed importance: "Because of their unique position outside the market and the state, their generally smaller scale, their capacity to tap private initiative in support of public purposes, and their newly rediscovered contributions to building "social capital,' civil society organizations have surfaced as strategically important participants in this search for a 'middle way' between sole reliance on the market and sole reliance on the state that now seems increasingly underway" (Salamon et al. 1999, 5). *Whose* "reliance," we might well ask? The very formulation unsettles the claim to civil society's (relative) autonomy on which "middle way" policy analysts insist, since the unnamed actor who "relies" already implies an organization of power that cuts across and incorporates state, market, *and* civil society—a structure of governance, let's say, embodied in a managerial cadre, that encompasses the key functions and offices of government, "associations," and corporations. In the present neoliberal conjuncture of political and economic forces, moreover, the management of social relations proceeds in the mode of problem-solving (rather than normalization), "strategic participa[tion]" (rather than institutionalization), and building "capacity" (rather than building hegemony). We find ourselves, in other words, precisely on the terrain of Hardt's social simulacrum, where civil society as a wholly dereferentialized signifier acquires a new lease on life.

Partha Chatterjee's recent writing on the *Politics of the Governed* declines to sound the death knell of civil society and to accede to the new nomenclature in which civil society is the totality of (presumed) non-governmental and non-market organizations, whose "middle-way" ethos appears oddly unimpaired by their own reliance on state and corporate funding. His reflections on civil society in a primarily Indian context also stand as an important reminder that the contours of neoliberal governance vary across localities, nations, and regions (for example, in relation to the historical distribution of the rights and benefits of citizenship), even as the questions and categories that emerge as salient for the Indian context are altogether germane to the discussion of citizenship in other national contexts, including the United States. Chatterjee begins by acknowledging the circumscribed scope of civil society in the Hegelian sense of "bürgerliche Gesellschaft," alongside the proliferation of what is often conflated with civil society—namely "all existing social institutions that lie outside the strict domain of the state"; this conflation, he notes, is "rampant in the recent rhetoric of international financial institutions, aid agencies, and nongovernmental organizations, among whom the spread of a neoliberal ideology has authorized the consecration of every non-state organization as the precious flower of the associative endeavors of free members of civil society" (2004, 39). Despite its attenuated scope, Chatterjee nonetheless holds quite precisely to the concept of civil society as "bürgerliche Gesellshaft": that is, civil society as it incorporates those social classes recognized as rights-bearing citizens by the state, or we might say, civil society as it engenders a body politic. In Chatterjee's usage, civil society thus retains its historical alignment with "the nation-state founded on popular sovereignty and granting equal rights to citizens," and in India today, he notes, as elsewhere in the global South, its members include "a relatively small section of the people, whose social location can be identified with a fair degree of clarity" (2004, 38). Chatterjee proposes the term "political society" for the heterogeneous array of associations that facilitate the state's administration of subaltern classes *not* constituted as national citizens, excluded from this body politic in part *because* the activity of political society has often resisted the "modernizing project that is imposed on them" (2004, 51). This form of governmental administration, then, eschews the assimilative tactics of bourgeois nationalism in order to pursue "multiple policies of security and welfare," or "the welfare and protection of populations—the pastoral functions of government, as Michel Foucault called it," by means of "governmental technologies . . . largely independent of considerations of active participation by citizens in the sovereignty of the state" (2004, 37, 47). Thus Chatterjee's differentiation of civil from political society rests specifically and emphatically on the claim that the category of the citizen, and its social reproduction, has become relatively marginal to the governance of populations in India (and elsewhere).

At issue in this comparative reading of selected critical and policy analyses is how or whether to understand civil society in the absence (or decline) of bourgeois sociality. In general, left academic work on the nonprofit sector cuts two ways. One important strand of scholarship locates in human rights and social justice oriented NGOs a new set of tactics for the pursuit of limited benefits within an extra-legal, administrative discourse. This work tends in particular to value grassroots labor organizations that pressure corporate employers through cross-border organizing. Another significant strand of scholarship raises the alarm about aid-oriented NGOs, in particular, as the latest instruments of (the new) imperial benevolence. Both these lines of argument are entirely persuasive on their own terms, though the move to champion or reject *specific* activist practices tends to preempt wider reflection on the overarching conditions—the possibilities and limitations—of political participation after popular sovereignty. *Can there be citizenship without a body politic?* Does political society, in Chatterjee's sense of the phrase, or civil society, in the language of the foundations and the policy analysts, no longer serve a mediatory or educative purpose? Or is it, more precisely, that these practices of social mediation no longer assume a disciplinary character?

Chatterjee rigorously identifies citizenship with formal recognition of a rights-bearing subject by the state. By contrast, Hardt both insists that ours is a "post-civil" society *and* that it holds onto citizenship as a henceforth evacuated category. "Instead of disciplining the citizen as a fixed social identity," he writes, "the new regime seeks to control the citizen as a whatever identity, an infinitely flexible placeholder for identity" (1995, 40). Wendy Brown makes a similar point (in a rather different critical idiom) when she identifies an emergent political formation "made possible by the production of *citizens as individual entrepreneurial actors* across all dimensions of their lives, by the reduction of civil society to a domain for exercising this entrepreneurship, and by the figuration of the state as a firm whose products are rational individual subjects, an expanding economy, national security, and global power"

(2005, 57). Aihwa Ong refines and extends this line of argument, conceding that the "neoliberal subject is therefore not a citizen with claims on the state, but a self-enterprising citizen-subject who is obligated to become 'an entrepreneur of him or herself'" (2006, 14). But why, on what terms, is this "whatever" identity *citizenship*? In what sense can the "production" of "individual entrepreneurial actors," whether by state or non-state agencies, be understood as a production of *citizens*, or even of non-claimant "*citizen*-subjects"? Within the modern, nation-state synthesis, citizenship accrues to a national people at once sovereign and disciplined. The institutions of civil society reproduce citizens through processes of normative identification; by the same stroke, normative—properly "fix(at)ed"—citizens attain to political agency through participation (if only by proxy) in the exercise of state power. On what terms and to what effects do we extend the half-life of this category beyond its historical conditions of possibility? At the very least, I am suggesting, we need to investigate the contemporary forms and contexts of political participation under neoliberal governance. What might "participation" mean if citizens no longer comprise a national body politic where the sovereign agency of the state resides? In what imagined and (or) institutionalized civic bodies does the neocitizen now participate? And are the novel forms and contexts for our political self-realization still regulated through state-sponsored categories of social and juridical identity?

"The True Predicaments of Our Time"

Recently, preoccupied with this inquiry, I found myself rereading Hannah Arendt and listening, quite unexpectedly, to a series of curious and complex reverberations between totalitarianism (as it emerges from Arendt's Cold War historiography) and neoliberalism (or governmentality in the present phase of its emergent "pre-eminence" over sovereignty and discipline). The discontinuities are, of course, only too apparent: while both have global territorial ambitions, neoliberalism *requires* the local variations to which totalitarianism is hostile. Totalitarianism, as Arendt stresses, is party-centered, while neoliberalism is not a political movement and is not associated with any one political organization that would constitute its leading edge. Most strikingly, perhaps, totalitarianism, in Arendt's analysis, possesses an anti-utilitarian character and is emancipated from the profit motive, to which market-driven neoliberalism is rigorously bound.

Still, amidst the incommensurable elements, continuities emerge; in totalitarianism and neoliberalism alike, the established, characteristically modern relation of the state to the nation unravels. On this point, Arendt's analysis is sharply and polemically counterintuitive:

> The totalitarian ruler must, at any price, prevent normalization from reaching the point where a new way of life could develop—one which might, after a time, lose its bastard qualities and take its place among the widely differing and profoundly contrasting ways of life of the nations of the earth. The moment the revolutionary institutions became a national way of life . . . totalitarianism would lose its "total" quality and become subject to the law of the nations, according to which each possesses a specific territory, people and historical tradition which relates it to other nations, which *ipso facto* refutes every contention that any specific form of government is absolutely valid. (1976, 391)

This erosion of the principles of national sovereignty—the refusal of the totalitarian state to uphold national interests, however defined—is what distinguishes totalitarianism from fascism in Arendt's view, and underwrites her insistence on Nazism and Stalinism as totalitarianism's problematically twinned instantiations. Moreover, it is the rejection of a national "way of life," the refusal of any *political* distinction between "home" and foreign countries, which leads to the embrace of "bastard" culture, no longer oriented to the reproduction of the social body. Totalitarian power's willing prostration of a national people proceeds hand in fist with a crisis of sovereign power, as it "has [also] exploded the very alternative on which all definitions of the essence of governments have been based in political philosophy, that is the alternative between lawful and lawless government, between arbitrary and legitimate power" (1976, 461).[4] In less indignant terms, Foucault writes that contemporary governmental power, untethered from the rule of law, "allow[s] the continual definition of what should and should not fall within the state's domain . . . what is and is not within the state's competence" (2007, 109).

Rather than sustain a normative political culture, totalitarianism saturates all aspects of political and social reality, to which it lends something Arendt consistently describes as a *fictive* quality. It is not always evident how this fictionalized reality compares to ideology, which Arendt seems to use primarily in the sense of false consciousness; ideology is misrepresentation of experience, "with no power to transform reality" (1976, 471). On the status of ideology within totalitarian regimes, however, Arendt's analysis is notably slippery. Ideology comes to seem both a driving and an incidental force within totalitarianism, in part because of the resolute formalism of Arendt's analysis, which pays no heed to the ideological incommensurability of Nazism and Bolshevism. Yet it is also what she identifies (unevenly) as the curiously weightless quality of totalitarian ideology that makes this formalism a *possible* (albeit itself ideological) analytic choice. Thus Arendt suggests that the fictitious quality of everyday life in fact obviates the function of propaganda; there is no need to propagandize against Jews as an infestation if you can actually undertake to exterminate them. Yet elsewhere in the exposition, Arendt terms precisely "ideological" the capacity to declare an entire people as your enemy (to constitute "objective" enemies whose targeted status is entirely independent of their actions or intentions), a reversal that tends to affirm the function of ideology in "transforming reality" (1976, 423). Most striking, though, is that this very realization of ideology— the rendering of reality fictive—seems to enable, in fact necessitate, a kind of end-run around the work of ideology: *conviction* is eliminated as a motive for action, since "the aim of totalitarian education," as Arendt underscores, "has never been to instill convictions but to destroy the capacity to form any" (1976, 468). "The ideal subject of totalitarian rule," she goes on to affirm, "is not the convinced Nazi or the convinced Communist, but people for whom the distinction between fact and fiction . . . and the distinction between true and false . . . no longer exist" (1976, 474). Totalitarianism thus erodes rather than disciplines the inner lives of its subjects. It proceeds through a mobilization of the "masses," by which Arendt means those elements of the population disqualified from political life, lacking common interests and characterized by political indifference. At the same time, this mobilization depends on the destruction of the public realm, the isolation of subjects by "destroying their political capacities" (1976, 475). So we are left with a paradoxical political mobilization that destroys the capacity to function as collective political agents, along with an ideological saturation of reality that seems to preempt, if not specifically foreclose, the process of ideological interpellation (of inculcating conviction).

My point in trying to render these reverberations is, in part, to feel out the contours of an alternate, supplementary genealogy of neoliberalism, which arrives not simply in tandem with the wider conditions of postmodernity (hyper-mediation, flexible accumulation) and out of the legacies of imperialism (the development of underdevelopment, mass migration to the metropolitan center), but also (perhaps counterintuitively) from modernity's experiments in "total," state-centered but not state-bound domination. I am also more specifically interested in the ways Arendt undertakes to consider totalitarian rule in its peculiar, *non-reproductive* dimensions and what her thought suggests about the shape of the dominated-but-undisciplined (indifferent and unconvinced) political subject, who hovers at the limits of her, and our, critical range. The subjects of neoliberal control are, of course, *not* the subjects of totalitarian domination, however fertile the comparison—and indeed, the comparison may well seem more pointed from my vantage in the United States, where the once crucial distinction between legitimate and arbitrary power no longer carries much political weight and where the convictions of its citizens are largely irrelevant to the operations of state power or the discourse of a simulacral public realm. From this vantage, certainly, we do well to ask (in language borrowed from Arendt, which echoes the administrative idiom of governmental practice), What are the "political *capacities*" of the neocitizen?

Neocitizenship?

In place of a conclusion, I end with one further circuit through Cindy Patton's revision of contemporary identity politics in an essay that offers a rather different gloss on the notion of a dereferentialized, "whatever" citizenship and also moves, provocatively, to address how *the field* for the cultivation and exercise of "political capacity" has shifted and reformed. Writing specifically on the relation of New Right to Queer Nation politics, Patton argues that "instead of understanding identity in an ego-psychological or developmental framework," we might understand "identity discourse [as] a strategy in a field of power in which the so-called identity movements attempt to alter the conditions for constituting the political subject" (1993, 145). Born of a "modernist and essentializing impulse," she contends, identity functioned within the modern state to extend representation, "expanding the context of what might count as a subject and increasing channels of access to an already constituted polis." Notably, she goes on to suggest, "with the emergence of group identities that make no reference to a transcendent essence (as in both Queer Nation and the new right) the political presence no longer requires the pretense of representing some prediscursive constituency"; here, identity emerges as a tactical rather than foundational discourse in which the stakes are a contest over "the grammar of identity construction rather than a process of stabilizing the production of particular, individually appropriable identities" (1993, 161, 168). This shift in the functionality of identity corresponds with the changing orientation of the state, which no longer in its modern guise "integrates social factions to resolve conflict," but rather multiplies and "holds pluralities apart" (1993, 172). Especially telling in this regard is Patton's suggestion that these proliferating identities are not state-generated, though they are absolutely *usable* for the administrative project of the governmental state:

> The crucial battle now for "minorities" and resistant subalterns is not achieving democratic representation but wresting control over the discourses concerning identity construction. The opponent is not the state as much as it is the other collectivities attempting to set the rules of identity construction in something like "civil society." The problem is not one of cognitive or psychic dissonance—that is, that the right, for example, will not allow us to feel or be who we want to be, but that the terms for asserting identity *are* the categories of political engagement. *The discursive practices of identity and the actors who activate them produce the categories of governmentality that engender the administrative state apparatus, not vice versa.* (1993, 173; my emphasis)

In the place of mid-twentieth-century social movements, bound to the logic of popular sovereignty, Patton discerns a new field of "engagement," in which political identity no longer constitutes a claim on recognition by the state within (and through amending) its preconstituted legal categories. Rather, the state, freed from its obligations to the integrated social body, sets conditions for the proliferation of identity within "something like civil society," from which it derives the categories that enable an effective administration of a population (rather than a national people). In this regard, Patton's argument converges on Chatterjee's, for whom political society names precisely this arena, in which the state manages the welfare of those social elements who have no a priori, formal claim on the state's attention.

From this perspective, however, citizenship is less an identity, or even (in Hardt's phrase) a "placeholder for identity," than identity (construction) is the field of "something like" citizenship—the context for the exercise of "political capacities." These identities are no longer state-sponsored, as Patton astutely observes, precisely because what is functional for the state today is not an organic social body comprised of formally equivalent terms, but a profusion of "holographs," or simulacral identities, to which the state can make a flexible, tactical response (if it chooses to respond at all). Such identities are susceptible to governmental techniques of "problem-solving"—they are not routed through the formal avenues and foundational edifice of legal recognition—so we do well to bear in mind that the state's exercise of its "pastoral" charge may involve internment or extradition, as readily as grant-giving or limited regulation of an ever-more predatory capitalism. In this scenario, "something like" citizenship detaches from its historical imbrication in normative culture and reforms on a terrain that I am provisionally inclined to call *serial* culture. Unlike normative culture, serial culture does not differentiate among identities (between the normal and the pathological, for example), so much as cultivate a process of differentiation that produces an ever broader spectrum of identities. Rather than interpellate subjects through processes of compulsory (mis)recognition, serial culture *releases* them into a minutely regulated environment—regulated not because their positions are prescribed, but rather because their movements and affiliations are tracked (as so much social data), archived, mined, risk-assessed, and so (variably) policed, overlooked, or supported. The neocitizen who acts in and on this environment is visible to the state, even as the out-sourced state is rendered increasingly opaque and elusive to her.

In the end, I am concerned less with whether or not to call this political capacity a "bastard" neocitizenship than with what strikes me as the formidable and vexing question of how to think about this neocitizenship on the terrain of serial culture. What exactly do we look for—what constitutes ground gained in this "battle . . . over rules of identity construction," when the rules are *not* norms that we engage through critical strategies of denaturalization and defamiliarization? What constitutes accommodation or opposition to the intentions of the state within the political arena of *undisciplined* sociality? Is it the aim of left political engagement to produce *unmanageable* identities that do not function in and for the neoliberal state? And what might an "unmanageable" identity be? (Will we know it when we see it?) Those of us on the Left in the U.S. academy, among many others in the global North and the global South today, are preoccupied, and rightly so, with the contemporary crisis of left politics, at times dwelling on the ostensible disappearance of an organized, sustained alternative to capitalism, at times, more optimistically, championing specific kinds of practices and associations as suggesting the terms of an emergent counter-mobilization. We pay less attention to the crisis of critique that symptomatizes this historical conjuncture, and the aim of this chapter has been to suggest why there is critical work to be done in reimagining the contours of critical engagement.

2

Post-Soviet American Studies

Unlike the national narrative, the global narrative does not
presume a world protagonist subject to interpellation. In a
narrative about a market, totality is not achieved through
shared identity, a "hey you" that speaks to all. . . . [Global-
ization] tells a story not about our sameness, but about our
fungeability [sic].
—Leerom Medovoi, "Nation, Globe, Hegemony"

The study of citizenship—as a condition of political participation
and belonging; as a terrain of subject-formation through national(ist)
identification—has been central to American studies from its inception;
since at least the 1950s, the field itself has also been implicated in the
civic projects of the U.S. state. The international travels of American
studies begin, my most accounts, in the Cold War, when this newly institutionalized (inter)discipline is adopted as a state-sponsored academic
export to a range of actual and potential U.S. client states.[1] In its exceptionalist configuration, American studies becomes a ready instrument
of public diplomacy in the period of U.S. ascendance as a postwar global
power, disseminating the common sense of the American Century:
because "America" is like no other nation, other peoples should aspire to
be more like Americans.[2] Thus arrayed, "America" appears both nation-
ally particular and globally exemplary, and State Department support
for American studies programs, lectures, and visiting scholars in academies abroad at once accumulates national cultural capital and promotes
"the American way of life" in the (so-called) developing countries of the
Third World.

In this sense, American studies has been "transnational" more or
less from the time of its institutional beginnings, and what we might
call the geopolitics of American studies (the regions in which it operates and the effects it is called on produce) have long served as an

index to *the state*'s understanding of citizenship and civic culture. As an academic product slated for global export, in other words, American studies offers a privileged view of how the state apparatus construes the subject. But what to make of the more recent proliferation of American studies programs abroad since the collapse of the Soviet Union—including, most dramatically perhaps, in the nations of Eastern Europe and Central Asia formerly annexed to the Soviet Union, or under its sphere of influence, where American studies has flourished in the last quarter century, largely through complex "partnerships" between U.S. government agencies, private donors, and host institutions (both state and private)? In what ways does American studies remain serviceable to the public diplomacy of the U.S. state, if the contemporary historical moment is characterized by the de-coupling of nation and state, as I argue in this book? Indeed, we may well ask, what forms does U.S. public diplomacy assume in this era of mass surveillance, endless war, drone strikes, black sites, and the broader panoply of tactics of extra-legal coercion?

In this chapter, I argue that the rise of American studies in the former Soviet bloc—the post-Soviet American studies of my title—is no mere extension of the Cold War model into the neoliberal era, but signals the reorganization of relations among state and civil society actors, and relatedly, the emerging contours of neocitizenship. Whatever the multivalent work American studies performs for its practitioners on the ground in Eastern Europe and Central Asia, for its institutional funders (USAID, U.S. embassies, private foundations), I suggest, the value of American studies is a function not of the norms it rehearses, but rather of the broader orientation to state and civil society it encourages. The cultivation of post-Soviet American studies within the former Second World, then, is about disseminating not a system of belief, but something better described as a *disposition* in relation to the prevailing institutions of global governance. As Leerom Medovoi intimates in my epigraph, if the ambition of the neoliberal state is the full subordination of human life to a set of market relations, then the ideological priority—perhaps *especially* with regard to higher education and the preparation of the elite—is not to assimilate subjects to a common identity, but to qualify them for certain kinds of transactions—to effect their insertion within operative circuits of exchange. So I intend this discussion of post-

Soviet American studies as a kind of case study in the institutional reproduction of the neocitizen.

There has been scant critical attention paid to American studies abroad in the post–Cold War period, perhaps because most scholars in the field tend to assume (myself included, until a series of fortuitous encounters roused my curiosity about American studies in the formerly Soviet context) that the U.S. state is no longer much in the business of exporting American studies.[3] Interestingly, for example, an essay by Djelal Kadir, past president of the International American Studies Association, makes the double assumption that American studies remains wed to the intentions of the U.S. state *and* that this union dissolves when we move into an international arena. "The best hope for American Studies as an area of knowledge," he contends, "is for it to cease to be American and an instrument of official state policy and become, instead, an independent, international field of inquiry" (2004, 11). Thus Kadir conceives of the internationalization of American studies as a *remedy* to the imperialist project of the field—an imperialism, moreover, that appears to operate through nationalist interpellation (being "American"). He himself does not elaborate on this claim, but at a minimum, his phrasing suggests that to "cease to be American" is to dis-identify with the nation and in so doing, distance oneself from the aspirations of the state. His recommendation for the field, then, puts forward two related yet distinct assumptions: that nationalist discourse sutures "American" subjects to the aspirations of the state *and* (conversely) that subjects unassimilated to the normative categories of American identity (and by extension, presumably, to the scholarship and curricula it sustains) remain (therefore) outside or "independent" of the state's intentions. Significantly, this independence is differently available according to whether one "really" is, or is not, American, as Kadir presses the distinction between an American American studies, "pursued by those scholars who are, tautologically, inevitable objects of their sought-after knowledge," and those who might proffer an "exogenous discourse on America" (2004, 10, 11). The meaning of "exogenous" is never developed (does it refer to American studies scholars who are not U.S.-born, or not U.S-trained, or not U.S.-based?), but in its very indeterminacy, the term permits him to differentiate between "American Americanists" who write themselves in writing the field and their "exogenous" counterparts, whose identities, we are asked to believe, are not staked in their scholarship (as though only the knowledge of her "proper" identity is shaped by the scholar's investments and desires). In effect, Kadir's rejoinder to the state is not so much to interrogate the operations of nationalist identification as such, but to assign them a proper domain (of the authentically "American").[4]

While Kadir posits the continued relevance of American studies as a national(ist) knowledge project for the state, an essay by Paul Bové, published the preceding year, assumes almost exactly the reverse. Bové approaches the topic of American studies from the vantage of asking whether it might be reimagined as an area study (that is, simply one in a series of regions to-be-studied), and his answer is resoundingly negative. American studies is not now, nor is it likely to become, an area study, he argues, because the U.S. state is not the primary consumer of the knowledge it produces. Yet at the same time, he contends, American studies is thoroughly complicit with the state in its cultural and especially its multicultural emphasis, which is glossed in the essay as an elite intellectual cathexis to "otherness" that more or less uncritically and monolithically appropriates "others" in the act of representing them.. For Bové, the revisionist impulses within American studies that have focused attention on the "multiplicity of [ethnic and group] histories" in the United States support a "melodramatic politics," in which the spectacle of violated subjects substitutes for a political engagement with state-sponsored violence. "In this reform of American studies, [violence] has been derealized into the activities of 'cultural domination,'" a derealization, Bové contends, that places American studies in service to the state as a producer, not of policy imperatives, but of cultural knowledge—knowledge of "symbolic systems" and identitarian formations—seemingly prepackaged for manipulation by the agents of state power, as by the agents of transnational capital, for whom "culturalist knowledge" is always only "knowledge . . . of and for a market" (2002, 218, 221). As a result, American studies is both entirely marginal to the operations of state power and yet subordinate to it, performing "the business of the state . . . in its extended spheres" through a focus on culture, on the institutions of civil society, and on the discourses of the public spheres, which American studies scholars mistake as a sufficient confrontation with the state itself (2002, 208).

Bové thus brings us full circle from Kadir by arguing that the pre-occupation with things American—indeed, with the "anthropological" emphasis on "human activity"—*blocks* a proper confrontation with "*the U.S. state as an agent . . . in itself*, by means of detailed, concrete, material and theoretical analysis" (2002, 206, my emphasis). "If America has had this structural intent to be identical to the world—for what else can it mean to be the world's only remaining superpower?—then where can American studies stand to get a view of all this if they continue to commit themselves to the study of 'American culture(s),' rather than from a more cosmopolitan position that stands willfully apart from any remaining illusions that the anthropological study of civil society brings them any nearer to understanding power and the United States," Bové asks (2002, 222). Where Kadir gives us a state that reduces to national ideology, then, Bové gives us a state that reduces to the real. For Kadir, critical distance from American identity produces independence from the state, while for Bové, the very attention to identitarian concerns effects the work of the state, by veiling the operations of the state "as an agent . . . in itself."

Against Bové (and in the spirit of Gramcsi), I want to insist on considering the U.S. state in its extended spheres, indeed, to refuse the analytical separation of state and civil society, even as I mean to argue against Kadir that "American exceptionalism," and the particular relays it establishes between national culture and the state are no longer especially germane to the present "neoliberal" moment. But I begin here, with Kadir's and Bové's roughly polarized arguments because their pairing charts the Scylla and Charybdis of these analytical waters: on the one side, the lure of a familiar argument with an old antagonist, with an assimilative nationalism ("being American") that we are all too practiced in refusing; on the other side, the danger of conflating the erosion of nationalist interpellation with the irrelevance of culture and identity (the decline of ideology) as such. Liam Kennedy and Scott Lucas make a similar point in an essay on post-9/11 U.S. public diplomacy, defined as a relay between state policy and cultural politics that is not simply reducible to either term:

> On the one hand, those who conflate public diplomacy with cultural imperialism have a tendency to elide the role of state power and foreign

policy interest in the formation of public diplomacy initiatives. On the other hand, those who focus closely on state power as demonstrated by policy-making elites or within the political economies of world systems tend to ignore or play down the productivity of culture in international relations. (2005, 326)

The somewhat fusty concept of public diplomacy, solidly grounded in Cold War analytics (it was coined by academics in the 1960s, Kennedy and Lucas explain, to describe the full spectrum of government-sponsored information and communication), usefully reminds us of the disparities between the Cold War context and our own, that of the "national security state" articulated to the project of "neoliberal empire" (2005, 310). Nevertheless, their central claim is that public diplomacy is not defunct in the post-9/11 era (not simply preempted, we might say, by the spectacle of power, the strategy of shock and awe), but rather that its ostensible failures are a consequence of the reterritorialization of public diplomacy and by extension of state power more broadly.

> The failure of current attempts at U.S. public diplomacy can be attributed in part to their *dependence on an old paradigm of ideological warfare.* The conditions for the production and enactment of public diplomacy have changed significantly because of the way that global "interdependence" has radically altered the space of diplomacy. The founding premise of traditional diplomacy, that it was activity between states and their formal representatives, began to break down as the bipolar, state-centered context of the cold war gave way to multilevel relations conducted not only by national governments but by multinational corporations, nongovernment organizations (NGOs), private groups, and social movements using new technologies of communication to interact with and petition foreign publics. Moreover, this *dispersal and reterritorialization of public diplomacy* occurs amid the post–cold war (re)emergence of regional conflicts in international relations. American foreign policy is not only rendered more global but more local by interventions in selected conflicts in which issues of "cultural difference" magnify the problems of communication encountered by American public diplomacy. *The difficulty of conducting a "war of ideas" is compounded in a global information sphere that can*

swiftly expose and interrogate contradictions of declared values and apparent policies and actions. (2005, 322, my emphasis)

This enumeration of the changed conditions for public diplomacy sketches much of the context for my own reflections in this chapter, as I want to consider how the "multilevel relations" among governments, corporations, and NGOs entail a new set of relations between state and civil society, where the question of nationality obtains primarily at the level of "cultural difference," or ethnonationalisms that are *not* coextensive with the state. (So in this framework, nationality tends to signify minoritized populations striving for semi-autonomy from the territorial administration of the state, rather than the comprehensive body politic of national citizens.) In the theoretical discourse that guides policy-makers, which I discuss in chapter 1, these "multilevel relations" are routinely figured as a "partnership" among discrete sectors, with civil society, in particular, framed as a "third way," a counterbalance to the workings of the market, on the one hand, and the state, on the other—an alternative, in other words, to market fundamentalisms that does *not* entail a return to state regulation of the marketplace or a resurrection of the state as a primary public service provider.[5] It is the discourses and the institutional configurations of this "partnership" that interest me, and *especially the way these operate (outside or apart from the frame of national culture) to reproduce social subjects accommodated to present practices of state power.* What are the contours of citizenship when the institutions of national culture no longer provide the training grounds—the education in national values and the attendant norms of political contestation—for a specifically national citizen-subject? In what regard are the social subjects of these "multilevel relations" *citizens,* or more aptly, what does the practice of citizenship now entail? To pose these questions, of course, is not to dismiss the ongoing salience of national(ist) identifications, but rather to suggest that the pedagogies of citizenship are no longer lodged (or lodged primarily) in the discourse of an assimilative nationalism.

I have suggested that American studies is doubly implicated in these reconfigurations of governance, both because these transformations impose difficult and crucial questions about nation and state as objects of study and because American studies as an academic export continues to figure in the calculations of the deterritorialized state. I take as my primary focus the proliferation of American studies in the countries of the former Soviet bloc—by which I mean, both the post-1989 upswing in the fortunes of American studies teaching and research in the state academies and the creation of new American studies programs, often within new, private, U.S.-accredited academies, such as the American University of Central Asia (AUCA). Both the creation of the new academies and the cultivation of American studies in the Soviet-era state institutions have been supported in significant measure through a partnership of the U.S. Agency for International Development (USAID) and private donors with the specific goal of fostering civil society in the formerly state-saturated societies of the Soviet republics and Soviet bloc countries. I will argue that in the contours of a post-Soviet American studies, we can discern an emerging cultural politics of the U.S. state that succeeds the "old paradigm of ideological warfare," even as it recycles and refunctions *elements* of exceptionalist discourse.

But Kennedy and Lucas's formulation itself remains suggestively fraught: Is it the recourse to ideology itself that is outmoded? Or more narrowly, the recourse to ideology within the terrain of bipolar, state-centered diplomacy? A later citation from their essay refers to a "war of ideas," a phrasing that seems to extend rather than revise the centrality of ideological contestation. This phrase occurs as well at the very end of the long citation above, although here again ambiguously, inasmuch as they assert the susceptibility of state-sponsored ideological warfare to forms of critical demystification that are now disseminated with equal ease. We find a similar tension at play in the essay by Leerom Medovoi from which my epigraph derives, where ideology seems bound to an eroded national context, even as *ideology critique* remains central to his aspirations for contemporary American studies. I stress this tension not in order to propose or promise a resolution, but rather because I find a critical value in sustaining the uncertainty. On the one hand, I mean to argue that the current moment is *not* post-ideological, at least not in the sense implied, for instance, by Bové's dismissing culture in the service of "realist" political engagement. On the other hand, I want to suggest that the work of the U.S. state is no longer effected, or effected primarily, through processes of ideological interpellation that position us within a fixed and naturalized social reality. From this vantage, what seems increasingly uncertain is the efficacy of a critical practice committed to un-fixing and de-naturalizing a dominant order, to "exposing and interrogating the contradictions," in Kennedy and Lucas's phrase. Perhaps perversely, then, I mean to suggest that what may be outmoded in the present is not ideology as such, but ideology critique, that is, the specific operations of ideology to which our already elaborated methods of critical engagement would be adequate.

Traveling Knowledge: American Studies in the Newly Independent Soviet Republics and Former Soviet Bloc Nations

While the study of U.S. literature and history in the former Soviet Union and its satellite states considerably antedates the watershed years of 1989–1990, American studies–related teaching and research behind the Iron Curtain most often comprised an area of specialization within history departments or departments of literature and philology. The formation of American studies centers, programs, and departments both within the established (Soviet-era) academies and within a proliferating array of private, American-style academies dates with only a few exceptions (such as the American Studies Center at the University of Warsaw, founded in 1976) to the early and mid-1990s. While not ascending to parity with the established disciplines—national academies and other institutions of recognition and accreditation have been typically slow to acknowledge new "imports" such as American and gender studies— American studies has nevertheless flourished in the post-Soviet context in the form of research centers and degree-granting programs and departments, usually (though not always) with support from private foundations (such as the Soros Foundation, the Eurasia Foundation) and the U.S. Department of State (Embassy Information Centers, USAID).[6] A partial list of these centers and departments suggests something of the regional dispersal and varied institutional configurations of post-Soviet American studies and doubles here, too, as an indicator of the specific American studies venues on which my research for this chapter centered.[7]

1. The American Studies Department at Eötvös Loránd University (ELTE) in Budapest. ELTE is a state research university, and its American Studies Department is funded internally (not through partnerships with outside agencies and donors), although support for the professional development of individual American studies scholars in the unit comes from the Kellner Foundation and the Fulbright Commission.

2. The American Studies Center at Baku State University in Azerbaijan. The center is funded through a U.S. State Department grant administered by Indiana University's Center for International Education and Development Assistance, or CIEDA, in partnership with Baku State University.

3. The American Studies Center at the IV Javakhishvili Tbilisi State University in Georgia. This center anchors the activities of the Georgian Association for American Studies, and many of the association's events and publications are underwritten by the American embassy in Georgia.

4. The Department of American Studies at the American University of Central Asia (AUCA) in Biskek. This private university has its roots in the Kyrgyz-American School of the Krygyz State National University, which was created in 1992. In 1997 (at a ceremony with then–First Lady Hillary Clinton in attendance), it became the American University in Kyrgyzstan (AUK), a joint venture of the government of Kyrgyzstan, the U.S. State Department, and the (George Soros–sponsored) Open Society Institute (OSI), with additional support from the Eurasia Foundation (which serves as a further conduit for USAID monies). The AUK was renamed the AUCA in 2002, to reflect its growing regional significance.

Although varied local and regional histories matter significantly in shaping the issues and methods of American studies in these venues, it is possible to consider American studies in the broader "post-Soviet" context my title invokes, despite, for example, the likely disconnects one might anticipate between the institutional contexts of American studies in an EU-integrated Eastern Europe, on the one hand, and in the newly independent countries of central Asia, on the other. Although the (so-called) Bologna Process aims to standardize higher education in the EU nations, it has scarcely served to reconcile the asymmetrical conditions of public higher education in Western European and in the "transition countries" of Central and Eastern Europe (CEE). As Marek Kwiek contends, "In a number of the transition countries escaping the model of command-driven economies, the ideological position regarding the role of the state in the public sector differs considerably from the position taken, with few national exceptions, on a European level: *the ideal of the state about to emerge once the chaos of the transition period is over is the American model of cost-effectiveness and self-restraint*, rather than the 'European social model' of the EU 15" (2004, 769, my emphasis). Thus the challenge for the CEE nations is not simply to undo the legacy of a rigid and centralized system of higher education, largely unaccountable to faculty and students, as well as unreceptive to new research orientations, but also and equally to abide the drastic underfunding of higher education in the post-1989 epoch, when accession to IMF loans and incorporation into the circuits of transnational capital are routinely keyed to "Washington consensus" austerity strategies. So it is regrettable, Kwiek complains, that the Bologna Process entirely disregards the role of *private* higher education, when the "role of the private sector in the countries of central and eastern Europe—considering its ability to adapt to the new societal needs and new market conditions combined with the drastically underfunded and still unreformed public institutions—is bound to grow" (2004, 766, 767). The conditions of higher education in the CEE as Kwiek describes them are common to the otherwise disparate regions of the former Soviet bloc, where we witness a shift *from centralized state planning to a specifically "American model" of the reduced state*, and the attendant crisis of the public sector and of public higher education this shift calls forth. Moreover, his emphasis on the contours of the "American model" invites us to consider the tensions between the "self-restraint," or diminished commitment to public welfare, that beckons as a post-transition "ideal," and the investments of the U.S. state in specific sectors of post-Soviet education: By what reckoning are such investments "cost-effective"? As I hope to show, post-Soviet American studies opens a window onto the U.S. state's *cultivation* of the "multilevel relations" (among governments, multinationals, NGOs, and civil society actors) that Kennedy and Lucas describe—a vantage, we might say, on *the state's orchestration of its own de-centering*. The relation among levels—the articulation of the state apparatus, non-state governance agencies, social welfare–oriented nonprofits, corporations, and private groups—is and remains a preoccupation of the reterritorialized, post-national state.

The arrival of American studies in the former Soviet bloc after 1990 coincides then, roughly speaking, with the transnational turn in U.S.-based American studies, alongside an interest in possibilities for a critical internationalism that would cede U.S. ownership of the field. However, one (perhaps unsettling) lesson of post-Soviet American studies is that internationalism does not align well with the transnational focus currently championed in the U.S. academy (not only in American studies, of course, but in women's studies, sexuality studies, and other contexts of interdisciplinary engagement), if by "internationalism" we mean, at a minimum, receptivity to the issues and methods of American studies as it is practiced outside the United States. In an essay detailing the institutional and intellectual history of American studies in Hungary, Éva Federmayer, an Americanist at ELTE, compares the discontinuous investments around which research and teaching collate in the United States and in post-Soviet Hungary. Her description of a roughly consonant thematics, on the one hand, and widely incommensurate critical aspirations, on the other, is notable for its explicit and thoughtful consideration of a chasm that I have never failed to encounter in conversation with Americanists from the former Soviet republics/bloc, but that goes usually unacknowledged, even, indeed especially, when I have sought to press the question.

The beginning of American Studies as an academic discipline at Hungarian colleges and universities is basically coterminous with the watershed years of 1989–1990 when the country made a radical shift from state socialism toward parliamentary democracy and a free economy. This political and economic about-face, which came hand-in-hand with the undermining of foundationalist certainties and the generation of new anxieties coincided, more or less, with the radical transformation that American Studies was undergoing between the 1990s and the early 2000s. Shaped by crucial scholarly debates in the U.S. American Studies community since the 1970s, "paradigm dramas" (as diagnosed by Gene Wise in 1979) fomented New American Studies with powerful agendas of pluralization and de-centering—a most challenging project that shows striking resonances with changes in Hungarian society and culture since 1990.

However, the apparently easy parallel . . . is misleading. Whereas dominant discourses of New American Studies demonstrate a markedly "leftist" commitment to effect social change by remapping the relationship between culture, power, and social identities, current discourses in the highly charged political arena in Hungary demonstrate a shift toward conservative and/or populist agendas. To be sure, a country's political climate (nowadays saturated with nationalist concerns and economic anxieties, real or generated) should not be confused with the politics of another's scholarly community. What I seek to point out is the surprising discontinuities that a Hungarian Americanist is inevitably confronted with today when situating herself vis-à-vis subversive "post-Americanist" narratives about the transnational turn and critical internationalism typically dominating U.S. scholarly dialogue today. (2006, 1)

Here Federmayer lays out how certain elements of American studies—specifically, its embrace of identity politics and critical multiculturalism—dovetail with the contexts and preoccupations of Hungarian Americanists, while other elements, such as the "posting" of national contexts in preference to transnational and international-ist analytic frameworks, do not. She alludes, if only parenthetically, to the political crises of post-Socialist Hungary that have followed from an upsurge of racialized ethnic nationalisms, fomented as one kind of (familiar) response to the incursions of transnational capital in both their cultural and economic manifestations (e.g., the saturation of Hungarian mass media and public space with global popular culture; the impoverishment of the Soviet-era bourgeoisie and the exponential increase in the gap between rich and poor). In this regard, no doubt, Hungarian politics typify conditions in many of the former Soviet bloc nations, as Federmayer's use of the undifferentiated "a country" (any country) implies. Thus one might infer that the "post-Americanist" turn of American studies offers a useful analytic for Hungarian (and other post-Soviet) Americanists, who stand themselves (by and large) well to the left of racial populisms. But it is identity politics that meets the critical mandate to counter proto-fascist social mobilizations with a progressive representational politics, realized both in state protections for "minority" rights and in academic institutional sanction of the knowledge projects that array disqualified nationalities, religions, sexualities as subjects of their own histories.

By contrast, both the transnational turn and critical internationalism invite attention to questions of political economy—to the relation, for example, between nationalism and expansionist capital as it informs historical processes of immigration, migration, and diaspora. They call attention, as well, to the political economy of the modern university as an institutional guardian of national culture, which is, from this revisionist perspective, bound up in the relays of national identity, gendered and racial citizenship, entrepreneurialism (and other forms of professional-managerial competency), and imperial world-making. Meanwhile the intellectual identities of humanities-based scholars in the former Soviet bloc are routinely forged in opposition to the economic determinisms that have largely stood in for political economy as such within Soviet-era secondary and post-secondary education. In the intellectual's imaginary that attends the demise of the socialist state and the academy's (projected) retrieval from bureaucratic state control, moreover, the university figures as a platform for public, social engagement, rather than (as it does in the United States) an "ivory tower" marginal to the arenas where "social change" is wrought. From this perspective, a war of position—securing legitimacy and intellectual autonomy within the academy—seems more urgent than, say, unraveling the place of the contemporary university within neoliberal political economy. As Federmayer observed in response to a discussion of neoliberalism instigated by the U.S.-based participants at a Central European University conference and posed to Hungarian academics—Americanists, feminists, and others committed to post-Soviet knowledge projects—neoliberalism simply does not seem like much of a problem, certainly nothing on the scale of the burgeoning ethnonationalist political parties and the perennial insecurity of identitarian knowledge projects in the academy. Although she did not dispute my suggestion that neoliberalism and ethnonationalism were linked phenomena, two sides of a coin, the linkage was evidently not compelling to her in the way it is to me, nor did it follow that critical analysis of the one could not and should not stand apart from critical analysis of the other.

Thus to ask how American studies travels is not just to trace the uneven transmission of content across disparate institutional cultures and terrains, but also, more fundamentally, to consider *the subjects it arrays*—the practices and fantasies (the two are never separable) of political agency it sustains—which can never, of course, be "read off" from (inter)disciplinary content. The contingent articulation of knowledge project to expert subject is especially marked in the program for an internationalized American studies of Enikö Bollobás (Federmayer's colleague at ELTE), even as she seems to offer a normative account that would reconcile regional incongruities:

> Therefore, in East-Central Europe the intellectual had to "do the sixties" in the 1990s, when finally there emerged a demand, say, for both feminist activism and feminist criticism, for gay and lesbian consciousness-raising as well as queer theory, for social activism in general as well as the desire for a finer understanding and critique. Together with all these new activities and ideas often packaged in the United States, there came an unprecedented influx of U.S. products. U.S. business and cultural presence has proved equally difficult to figure out; *this is where American studies is beginning to have a social role: to help identify what is desirable and what is not desirable to import—whether politically, socially, culturally, or conceptually.* In order to be able to do this, American studies must substantiate both the appreciation and the critique of U.S. culture; it must, in other words, balance the "respect mode" [of Cold War American studies] with the "attack mode" [of contemporary New Americanist work]. This balancing act is, I believe, the true meaning of the internationalization of American studies, so memorably and powerfully called for by Jane Desmond and Virginia Dominguez. (2002, 565, my emphasis)

The conceptual lynchpin of this passage, it seems to me, is not the call-to-balance with which it concludes (as though one could simply split the difference between apology and critique), but rather the way it situates American studies in East-Central Europe, as a form of expert knowledge that can mediate between cultural nationalism and cosmopolitanism within the public sphere. Certainly, this way of imagining the "social role" of American studies and the cultural authority of the scholar has no analog in the U.S. context (we can hardly imagine American studies in the United States today operating on a national ethical imperative to distinguish "desirable" from "undesirable" cultural forms). But it is also not possible to position this set of investments as backward with respect to U.S. American studies or less sophisticated, or even, I would insist, to locate Central-East European American studies to the right of its "leftist" U.S. counterpart: after all, Bollobás's version of Central-East European American studies is (also) seeking to disseminate a (limited) critique of capital flows within a public sphere in which expressly reactionary discourses have tended to predominate. So unless "we" in the United States care to legislate that nationalist discourses (that is, what is "desirable" or not for the nation) are always and everywhere toxic (in other words, unless we choose to impose our own "post-nationalism" as a universal critical norm), then we must concede that "left" and "right" travel no better than American studies. One need not spend extensive time in conversation with intellectuals from the former Soviet bloc countries to recognize that "Marxism," as the principle of Soviet-era bureaucratic state control *and* as the critique of capital, is at least as likely to signify right reaction as left opposition.

From this vantage, the task of defining (something like) the "ideological cast" of U.S. state- and donor-sponsored American studies in the former Soviet bloc—as we aspired to do, not so long ago, in our critical retrospectives of the field as Cold War export—is not only difficult, but also, I take it, a blind alley. As Federmayer, Bollobás, and others attest, American studies in the former Soviet bloc has served as a point of entry for a range of critical practices, including feminism, multiculturalism, and post-structuralism, if only because fluency in English (as well as familiarity researching U.S. archives and publications) opens access to these critical orientations.[8] So the originators and initial faculty of American studies centers and departments after 1990, especially within the state academies, were often literary scholars and historians whose work on "things American" (within "foreign literatures" or "modern history" departments, for example) had brought them into contact with the critical conversations that were reshaping those disciplines in the 1980s United States. No doubt, for those of us trained entirely in the U.S. academy, it is hard to imagine American studies as the way into, say, deconstruction or radical lesbian feminism. But the history of American studies' emergence in the former Soviet bloc, as well as the contemporary investments of Central East European and Central Asian Americanists, suggest both that American studies functions as a conduit and staging ground for a heterogeneous array of critical projects and that if the transnational turn is not well marked in these regional iterations of American studies, neither do they align with an unreconstructed or celebratory "Americanism."

Despite the "surprising discontinuities that confront the Hungarian Americanist" and her colleagues in the region, American studies in the CEE and Central Asia feels approximately in sync with U.S.-based American studies. For instance, in perusing course offerings at the institutions I researched, I read titles that are not much different from what I could expect to find in core or cross-listed U.S. American studies curricula, courses such as "Ethnicity, Nation, National Minority: A Comparative Approach," "Black Modernism, or the New Negro Renaissance" (ELTE), "Interrogating Whiteness: From Identity to Imperialism," "Gender and Sexuality" (AUCA), "Delving into the Heart of the Matrix," "Political Violence and Terrorism" (Baku State).[9] Titles are only gestural, to be sure, but they do, nevertheless, index a traffic in organizing motifs and critical preoccupations, and my point is that post-Soviet American studies is not simply the (old) exceptionalism dressed up in more current fashions (as in "diversity" in lieu of the "melting pot")—at least not to any greater extent than we find contemporary idioms grafted onto abiding exceptionalist frameworks within the American studies curricula of U.S. academic institutions. Rather, post-Soviet American studies curricula appear to sample broadly from the issues and methods of their U.S. analogs and thus to reproduce something of the scattered quality of U.S. American studies, as it ranges across liberal and critical multiculturalisms and their different orientations to such key *topoi* as identity, freedom, justice, nation, and markets. At the same time, post-Soviet American studies does not gravitate towards anything resembling Leerom Medovoi's vision of the field, where the critical priority is to "deploy emergent post-national imaginaries on behalf of a counter-hegemonic globalization, oppositional narratives of cosmopolitan interests 'from below' that confront the interests of post-Fordist capital with those of the life that it exploits (human and natural alike)" (2005, 177). Admittedly, there is no dearth of U.S.-based Americanists for whom this sort of agenda would seem either politically distasteful or simply irrelevant to their scholarly aspirations. Yet Medovoi's vision *is* broadly in line with the political sensibilities that have recently tended to predominate in the leading national forums, such as American Studies Association meetings. ASA participants might well dispute whether or not "we" have already, sufficiently, articulated a transnational American studies with opposition to transnational capital (Medovoi's argument is that we have not) and would likely disagree, as well, over whether this form of oppositional work can be sustained at all within the precincts of the university, or whether it is best pursued through participation in social movements conceived and organized "from below." But Medevoi's agenda would not seem eccentric to the occasion, nor would conference participants, in the main, be reluctant *to cathect the political desire and the agency this vision summons.* No less predictably, the prospect for an American studies allied with global subalterns in the elaboration of a transnational left discourse would find no traction whatsoever among American studies scholars in the regions of the former Soviet Union and Soviet bloc.

So ironically enough, the political imaginary that attaches to the transnational turn may well turn out to be one of the most parochially "American" aspects of U.S.-based American studies. This is *not* to suggest that we have somehow failed to produce an authentic transnationalism or indeed to impose as the legitimating measure of transnational American studies that it must, to be what it claims, circulate transnationally. But the limited intellectual currency of the transnational turn in these non-American institutional contexts does suggest that transnational American studies, for all its hostility toward a normative nationalism, remains a normative knowledge project in its own right—by which I mean, very precisely, that the intellectual and professional culture of the field sutures its investigative subjects to a particular set of political convictions and attachments in which their self-realization (as ethical citizen-subjects) is staked. Besides marking the national character of the transnational turn, an analysis of American studies in the former Soviet bloc supports two further claims: one, that American studies does not travel *in its normative dimensions*, or in other words, that it sustains quite different (and incompatible) interpellations in disparate regions; and two, that the post-national state—by contrast to its modern, nation-state antecedent—has no particular investment in the normative dimensions of this knowledge project present or past, no particular stakes in the "Americanism" of Cold War era American studies, or in the "transnationalism" of its contemporary U.S. iterations.

The State as Educator

What are the aspirations of the U.S. state and its funding partners for American studies abroad if it is not (or is no longer) bound to the dissemination of American values—if indeed the issues and methods of "American studies" abroad are variably oriented to a range of analytic and political priorities? Ideology is always a restless traveler, to be sure, inasmuch as the same "content" produces disparate effects in different times and locations. But my point is that the shape of American studies in the region does not resolve into a "content" from which we might derive its sponsors' agenda for the post-Soviet knowledge-consumer (however unevenly realized on the ground). At the same time, I am not prepared to concede to Bové's insistence that we must bracket culture to engage the state, as though culture had no more to tell us about (what Althusser calls) the reproduction of the relations of production, or the role of the state as educator (in Gramsci's resonant phrase).[10] Rather, what is marked in the transit from the model of Cold War–era to post-Soviet American studies is a shift in *the mode of reproduction*, keyed to the uncoupling of state and nation and the gradual disappearance of the political field that their coupling had inaugurated. The nation-state practices power in the name of a national people and in conformity to the law that embodies the people's sovereign will. Where the legitimacy of the state is staked on the premise of popular sovereignty, the state as educator cultivates a particular kind of modern subject: a "free" subject whose emancipation (as citizen, as individual) requires his "voluntary" accession to the distribution of power and privilege that the law secures. The "individual is interpellated as a (free) subject," Althusser tells us, "in order that he shall (freely) accept his subjection" (1994, 136). Emancipation entails domination cathected as choice—and it is precisely the business of the state to sustain that cathexis, through the mediation of a normative nationalism that conjugates abstract equality with equality of prospects, social atomization with collective freedom, and self-ownership with self-realization.

But what if freedom is no longer the name of the game, despite the ways in which the idioms of freedom continue to circulate residually, as the fragments of what Medovoi terms "a ruined ideology"? In the remaining sections of this chapter, I contend that the consideration of post-Soviet American studies, as a joint project of the U.S. state and the non-governmental actors of civil society, sets us on the trail of precisely such a transformation, in which the legitimated state no longer "frees" the individual but *operationalizes* her—that is, assesses and selectively cultivates her capacities. At the site of the emergence of new (post-national) relays between state and civil society, relays that are keyed in turn to the contemporary organizations of global capital and flexible accumulation, we encounter a different model of neocitizen, who is interpellated as functional, rather than as "free," where functionality entails ease of interface with administrative networks at different scales (local, regional, and global). Equally crucial, the functional neocitizen possesses an analytic orientation to social relations as data and a facility in the evaluation of data based on such measures as "risk," "compliance," "outcomes," and "capacity"; a cosmopolitan orientation to diversity; and (preferably) fluency in the lingua franca of global governance, English. Unlike "freedom," functionality is not a putatively generalized condition, but indexes a (differentially distributed) condition of social and political agency. And unlike the "free" citizen, the neocitizen is interpellated into a set of administrative protocols, which are framed as the instrument for the pursuit of broadly *heterogeneous* political aspirations.[11] In fact, the *real* heterogeneity of the neocitizen's identifications and convictions are entirely functional for this structure of governance, since they index exactly the social dispositions and formations to be accounted, risk-assessed, and managed by the institutions of the extended state. Neocitizenship is thus enacted, not in the form of sovereign consent or its corollary political postures (the retraction of consent based on the violation of the law and its intent; a demand for the recognition of citizenship rights on the part of disqualified political subjects), but in the acquisition of a professionalized civic competence that entails belief *only* in the *instrumental* value of the organizations, institutions, and media to which this competency opens access. The relation of the neocitizen to the structure of governance in which she participates is expressly and openly opportunistic, in other words, rather than consensual—and by extension there is no option for the performative withdrawal of consent, only for the tactical rejection of functionality as means. If the withdrawal of consent represents the ultimate *realization* of the sovereign citizen's prerogatives, to reject functionality is simply to *resign* one's neocitizenship.

While Althusser presents ideology on the model of the unconscious, as timeless, the ruse of ideology—subjection that emancipates—appears characteristically modern, forged in the historical contexts of popular sovereignty, disciplinary society, and the nation-state.[12] So it may be that the present moment, marked by more or less radical transformations in each of these historical formations, demands at the very least that we reopen the question of how ideology works on the subject— and, too, how its subjects work. But how to think outside or apart from this understanding of ideology as "freeing"—subjection cathected as self-realization—when it is precisely this model on which our critical practices have been honed? The difficulty of the inquiry emerges, for instance, in the essay by Leerom Medovoi cited earlier, where he argues in subtle and compelling ways for the declining salience of ideology in the (re)production of (post-) national social subjects. In particular, he speculates on the historical imbrication of the ideological state apparatus (ISA) in the modern nation-state conjuncture, observing "that the very notion of an ISA . . . , as classically formulated by Althusser, should itself be historicized as a central feature of the Fordist era, given the immense regulatory responsibilities that Fordist capitalism invested in the nation-state and thus the commensurate ideological burden of the nation as principal legitimator of state power" (2005,164–165). The importance and the proliferation of ISAs correspond to a historical situation in which state power seeks *legitimation* at the level (on the terrain) of *national culture and institutions*, and so recedes, we can infer, where state and nation part ways, especially where the ascendant idea of the state is staked on criteria of efficiency rather than legitimacy—where it conforms, in other words, to "the American model of cost-effectiveness and self-restraint."[13] Medovoi presses a similar insight again, when he notes that "the global narrative," unlike the national, "does not presume a world protagonist subject to interpellation. In a narrative about a market, totality is achieved not through shared identity, a 'hey you' that speaks to all. Instead, totality derives from mutual exchangeability, (a relationship neither of homogeneity nor heterogeneity, the two options allowed by national narratives). 'Globalization' offers a story in which the new world order will culminate, not in an undifferentiated whole, but in an endlessly differentiated circuit of exchangeability." (2005, 169). In a second line of argument, however, that uneasily cohabits with the first, Medovoi insists that "the contemporary American university," which has "become yet another market-driven site of capital accumulation" nonetheless "remains a vital ISA" (2005, 173). And despite the recognition that the discourse of globalization does not proceed through the interpellation of subjects in a fixed or naturalized relation to others and to the forces that orchestrate this relation, Medovoi advocates, as well, for the value of "ideological interventions" in "the dominant narrative of globalization," more specifically, for "a ruthless denaturalization of the future-tense meta-narrative of globalization" (2005, 172, 175). Thus Medovoi seems both to query the centrality of ideology in the mobilization of social subjects *and* to (re)center the work of ideological struggle.

In her reflections on "The End of Liberal Democracy," Wendy Brown also considers the vexed and uncertain relation of neoliberalism to ideology. Insisting on the increasingly evacuated quality of the liberal democratic tropes that circulate, oddly enough, in tandem with the elaboration of a specifically "neoliberal rationality," Brown suggests how neoliberalism maintains something of a parasitical relation to the ideological discourses that its rationality supplants. "The post 9/11 period," she notes, "has brought the ramifications of neoliberal rationality into sharp focus, largely through practices and policies that progressives assail as hypocrisies, lies, or contradictions but that may be better understood as *neoliberal policies and actions taking shape under the legitimating cloth of a liberal democratic discourse increasingly void of substance*" (2005, 47, my emphasis). So it appears that "neoliberalism can become dominant as governmentality without being dominant as ideology" (2005, 49). Brown's provocative formulation helps explain the limited efficacy of "ruthless denaturalization" as a critical practice, insofar as neoliberalism has *already denatured* (or voided of substance) the ideological idioms it appropriates. And by imagining a power that prevails politically and organizationally but *not* ideologically, Brown also marks the limits of interpellation in Althusser's terms, or in other words, the inauguration of a quite different subject of power. Is there any such thing as a "neoliberal subject," if indeed neoliberalism is not mediated (or mediated primarily) through its proper ideological figures? How do we apprehend *at the level of the subject* a practice of power that does not act to reproduce the apparent *substance*—the inner life—of the individual?

In the present iterations of post-Soviet American studies, I find an indication of a neocitizen who is operationalized—we might say *mobilized*—but *not* emancipated and *not* required to cathect the institutions, discourses, and practices that subject her. Brown suggests that neoliberalism seeks "legitimation" through citations of liberal democratic discourse, but at the same time the evacuated quality of these citations appears ill suited to inculcating belief. From this perspective, the cynical popular response to neoliberal governance that Brown also remarks on indexes not so much the failure of this legitimation strategy as the mounting irrelevance of conviction and consent. In this context, "interpellation" (if we choose to retain the term at all) is not about cultivating attachment to what is right and natural—suturing citizen-subjects to specific identities and norms—but rather (as Medovoi's language suggests), about *inserting* neocitizens into "circuit[s] of exchangeability." Above all, the neocitizen is networked—navigating and proliferating the relations that link foundations (state and corporate donors), civil society (organizations and associations), regulatory agencies (state-based and international), and the public sphere (corporate and "alternative" media).

Consider, for instance, the "Civil Society" mandate of the Eurasia Foundation (n.d.), a privately managed nonprofit organization supported by the U.S. Agency for International Development (USAID), which is also a major donor to the AUCA.

Goal: *Increased citizen participation in political and economic decision-making.*

Central to the Eurasia Foundation's mission is the belief that local communities are best able to determine their own needs and priorities. The Foundation promotes the development of effective mechanisms for citizen participation in political and economic decision-making by engaging and strengthening civil society. In particular, the Foundation has encouraged independent media to act as a voice for their communities and community-based civic organizations to advocate for public policies that further democratic and market reforms. The Foundation's civil society program has emphasized projects that advance the financial sustainability and create a more nurturing legal and regulatory environment for the civil society sector as a whole.

One of a triad of mandate areas that include "Private Enterprise Development" and "Public Administration and Policy," the "Civil Society" initiative cites elements or keywords in a familiar discourse of participatory democracy, while reimagining the relations between state and civil society in which the norms and practices of civic "participation" are historically anchored. Here we find ourselves squarely on the terrain of "multilevel relations" among governments, corporations, and NGOs that Lucas and Kennedy describe; thus a State Department–funded, privately managed nonprofit cultivates civic organizations and independent media that advocate for "reforms" (political and market freedoms), and especially those reforms that enhance the prospects for the development and expansion of the "civil society sector." By a curiously circular logic, then, the *political activities* of organizations in civil society are addressed to the state primarily, if not exclusively, for the purpose of securing the civil sector's own continuing viability ("creat[ing] a more nurturing legal and regulatory environment"). Indeed, in this networked arena of "multilevel" governance, one is hard put to decide *what it is the citizen participates in*, since the primary aspiration of the "civil society sector," it appears, is to establish and secure its own position as a nodal point (or "level") through which governmental power circulates. And so, too, the citizen participants are characterized not by a set of normative political commitments, but by their administrative capacity.

> Like their counterparts in the private sector, leaders of civic and media organizations need to develop new skills to operate their organizations effectively. The Eurasia Foundation has supported the development of training programs that provide civil society leaders with the financial management skills they need to operate financially viable and effective institutions.

The task of civic leadership, then, is to secure and manage revenue streams, especially by developing "local models of philanthropy and volunteerism." For this reason, the Foundation sets a "high priority on projects aimed at mobilizing community resources, both financial and human, around community development issues." If the language of community-funded community activism evokes the romance of "grass-roots" politics, however, what drops from view in this iteration of "citizen participation" is a critical orientation to the state. Instead, we find citizens' groups *"advocating for public policies"* in some unspecified domain, wherever it may be that public policy is wrought (corporate boardrooms, international aid agencies; government at every scale, and the proliferating private organizations to which government is outsourced). On the terrain of "multilevel" governance, moreover, the neocitizen is no longer sovereign: her posture is one of "advocacy" vis-à-vis a range of organizations that are under no a priori obligation to recognize her (as their practice of power does not depend on the claim to *represent*). Within the discursive world of the Eurasia Foundation mandates, community politics is about creating *sustainable* organizations of citizen-advocates, situated in the networks through which flow funds, personnel, and the social data that is the stuff of policy debate.

The possibilities and limits of activist citizenship thus imagined remains something of an open question, although, for instance, Sabine Lang's important research on feminist NGOs in the European Union raises the alarm about the (at best) uneven commitment to what she terms "public advocacy," or the mobilization of "counterpublics that engage with dominant political positions, and in that process, foster public recognition of underrepresented issues, such as continued gender discrimination" (2007, 7). Such "advocacy for public policies," one that seeks to mobilize public sentiment as a political force, tends to drop out as a primary focus of the networked feminist organizations Lang investigates. As she concludes,

> Revisiting the initially introduced three dimensions of successful networking and civic action: capacity building, policy efficacy and public advocacy, the data establishes that all networks are quite successfully engaging in the first two tasks. . . . [But] what we identified earlier as the third leg of successful networks, engaging in policy advocacy and building public support, is much less developed and seemingly less of a priority for achieving network goals. One might speculate that in the "tough

competition" for access to EU units and for finances the mobilization of feminist publics might be helpful. However, as a spokesperson pointed out, having an office in Brussels is much more effective than mobilizing broader constituencies. *Moreover, the resources to form such publics have been resized in recent years by the NGOization of the women's movement, leading to an increased pressure to secure jobs, retain competent professionals within the network, keep facilities financed and therefore oriented towards project acquisition.* (2007, 24, my emphasis)

While "citizen participation" within the networked organizations of multilevel governance retains a *possible* connection to the practices of participatory citizenship within the modern nation-state—in which the production or dismantling of a popular consensus for or against a particular law or policy is understood as politically decisive, the key element of a participatory democracy and the central aspiration of civic organizations' *political* work—in point of fact, Lang contends, this connection is increasingly eroded, as concerns with sustainability (funding the organization, securing staff positions) overtake the more recognizably "civic" priorities.[14]

To a certain extent, it appears that the Soros Foundation's Open Society Institute (OSI)—which like the Eurasia Foundation supports a range of educational and civil society–oriented initiatives in Eastern Europe and Central Asia, including AUCA—holds instead to the conception of citizenship as the relation of (sovereign) subjects to the state. "The Open Society Institute works to build vibrant and tolerant democracies whose governments are accountable to their citizens," we are told, although in what follows, as in Soros's own writing, "accountability" has less to do with the lawful exercise of state power than with good accounting practices (Open Society Institute 2009). An accountable government, on these terms, is one that functions efficiently and cooperatively within the networked terrain of multilevel governance. Such efficiency and cooperation include compliance with laws and treaties and the upholding of basic citizenship rights (the OSI is especially concerned with rights of minority populations).[15] Yet despite the reappearance of these familiar touchstones of liberal democracy, the emphasis at the OSI is not on cultivating the practice of popular sovereignty within formerly socialist state bureaucracies, but rather on cultivating civil society as the provider of (professionalized) "advocacy" within the wider field of networked governance. To this end, "corrupt," autocratic governments must be (variously) pressured and motivated to participate ("accountably") in this network of international agencies, NGOs, and foundations through which governmental power operates. Implicit in the OSI mission statements, this understanding of governance of and of civil society becomes more fully explicit in George Soros's own writings on globalization, "open society," and "social entrepreneurship" (2002, 69).

Taken together, Soros's writing on these topics might be characterized as a critique of capital from the standpoint of capital. His overarching concern is with strategies for redressing and mitigating the scope and scale of economic and social inequities that destabilize regimes, provoke opposition, and imperil social and economic infrastructures—in other words, a concern with inequity conceptualized as systemic risk. In this regard, he shares much with former World Bank chief economist Joseph Stiglitz, who has called for reforming and restructuring the institutions of global governance and "development assistance" in an effort to reduce immiseration and the threat of mass insurgencies it carries (2002, 21–22, 119). Soros's assessment of root causes, however, differs from Stiglitz's in several ways, including an insistence on "bad government" as the central factor in the production of poverty. "Making the promotion of open society the goal differs from the internationally endorsed goal of poverty reduction in emphasizing the importance of the political arrangements prevailing in individual countries," Soros writes, "but the fact is that poverty and misery are usually associated with bad governments" (2002, 59). This analysis underlies his two-part agenda: providing "public goods on a global scale" and "fostering economic, social, and political progress in individual countries" (2002, 58). Responsibility for the former is assigned to wealthy nations, acting through international agencies and NGOs. "There is an urgent need for the provision of public goods," he observes, "and the rich countries ought to pay for them. Wealth redistribution used to take place on a national scale until globalization rendered progressive taxation counterproductive; now it ought to be practiced on a global scale" (2002, 106). "Public goods" on this model include resources for health, education, and environmental protection, as well as some provision for a "social safety net" (2002, 64). "Governments" (of the non-wealthy nations) serve as possible although not necessary relays in the delivery of public goods; thus, in cases of persistent corruption, he proposes, aid should flow directly to NGOs. Because "governments are not the most efficient economic agents" under the best of circumstances, he contends, "there is something wrong with international assistance if it serves to increase the role that governments play in the economy" (2002, 68–69). The transfer of responsibility for the provision of public goods away from "governments" reduces the role of the receiver-states, in any case, to nothing more than providing a kind of legal and administrative infrastructure. Ultimately, then, we return to the conceptual framework of the Eurasia Foundations mandates: the "promotion of better governments," Soros sums up, "includes not only an efficient and honest central and local administration and an independent and reliable judiciary but also the rule of law and an appropriate relation between the public and private spheres: a society that is not dominated by the state, a private sector that is not in cahoots with government, and a civil society whose voice is heard" (2002, 58). But heard where and by whom, exactly? In this network of governments ("rich" and "poor"), international agencies, foundations, and NGOs, there is no longer a privileged, *constitutive relation* between the state and its citizens. Good government is a service provider, one that secures, among other things, the conditions for civil society; the quantity and quality of "public goods" are reckoned on a cost-benefit analysis (their cost and benefit *to state and private-sector providers*), and responsibility for their delivery is dispersed. Included among these "public goods" are the educational institutions that secure the (re)production of the professionalized neocitizen.

"Neoliberal Zombies" and the New Imperialism?

I have been arguing that the foundations and the partnerships of state and private donors sponsoring American studies departments and centers in the new American universities, as well as in the refurbished state academies of the former Soviet bloc countries and newly independent Soviet republics, have prioritized the social (re)production of the professionalized neocitizen, and that the pedagogies of neocitizenship are relatively content-neutral. American studies in this iteration is hospitable to any number of normative knowledge projects, which are left to the discretion, so to speak, of local faculty, academic administrators, and students in particular national and regional contexts. Indeed, American studies in the former Soviet bloc, like the wider regional apparatus of higher education as a "rich country"–sponsored "public good," could hardly be more sensitive or more receptive to local initiative and variations. The language of the donor foundation mandates is *not* the exceptionalist discourse of the City on a Hill. It does not promote "American values," even if, from time to time, donors or the academies themselves opportunistically recycle *some* of that language. As Wendy Brown intimates, they can do so precisely because there is no proper neoliberal ideology that might be vitiated by such "borrowings." Rather, American studies in the former Soviet bloc is bound up in an apparatus of higher education that cultivates a specific form of civic participation as professionalized advocacy. From the perspective of the interests that operate this apparatus, it matters relatively little what one wishes to advocate *for*, as long as such advocacy takes place within the relays of multilevel governance (Medovoi's "circuit of exchangeability") that Kennedy and Lucas describe. Students in the region pursuing American studies training or degrees are not asked to produce an identification with "America," nor (in general) do they do so. What the programs offer is a capacity for neocitizenship that functions (or promises to function) tactically in the service of any number of political, social, or entrepreneurial agendas. Thus American studies at AUCA specifically cites the placement record of graduates, who "work at organizations like the U.S. Embassy in the Kyrgyz Republic, UNICEF, Counterpart International, and in other NGOs or private firms in their respective countries," while American studies at ELTE asserts in similarly sweeping terms that "graduates have entered into academia, the civil and diplomatic service, as well as the political and economic spheres."[16]

If American studies and American academies in the former Soviet bloc represent the contemporary (neoliberal) culture of U.S. imperialism, it is not a cultural politics we can understand by analogy to the old, however much the present forms of world-making feel like the changing same. In many respects, I agree with Madina Tlostanova's scathing account of "Westernized" higher education in the Central Asian republics of the former Soviet Union, which situates it in the context of an all too familiar imperial history. "These locales can be attractive only as symbolic signs of geo-strategic dominance (which does not require any capital investment) or a place for the erection of new military bases for the future 'righteous' wars for oil," she writes, "while the local population either is added to the dispensable lives or is indoctrinated by neo-liberal ideologies by means of *opening the American universities*, distributing of grants, and if need be, organizing the fruit and flower revolutions to replace the ex-Soviet bosses with the neo-liberal zombies" (2007, 3, my emphasis). But the ruptures are no less decisive than the continuities. If modern empire and colonization entailed cultural imposition (the "civilizing mission") without political incorporation (citizenship rights do not extend to the dominated/colonized), the neoliberal variant, it seems to me, entails very nearly the reverse: effective incorporation within networks of transnational, multilevel governance, where the watchwords are "efficiency," "output," "excellence," "accountability," "compliance," "flexibility," "capacity"—in short, an arsenal of administrative benchmarks that set the conditions of participation, but nothing to compel belief. Neoliberal "culture," such as it is, does not operate normatively to produce identifications, but rather takes "account" and "operationalizes" identifications (national, regional, ethnic, gendered, sexual, and so forth) produced within other arenas and idioms of social and political life. Reading somewhat against the grain of Tlostanova's own usage, I take the zombie as a possible figuration of the neocitizen, since the zombie, after all, is an animated corpse that acts with relentless purpose and an utter lack of faith or conviction. What other forms—more or less hopeful—the neocitizen may still assume remains, of course, to be seen.

3

Uncivil Society in *The White Boy Shuffle*

Last week's issue of *Time* magazine identified me as the "Ebon Pied Piper." In *U.S. News and World Report*, I was the "bellwether of ethnic hara-kiri." History will add my name to the list of maniacal messiahs who sit in Hell's homeroom answering the Devil's roll call: Jim Jones, David Koresh, whoever led the charge of the Light Brigade, Charles Manson, General Westmoreland, and me. These pages are my memoirs, the battlefield remains of a frightened deserter in the eternal war for civility.
—Paul Beatty, *The White Boy Shuffle*

IN TIMES OF NATIONAL PERIL, ABOMUNISTS, AS REALITY

   AMERICANS, STAND READY TO DRINK THEMSELVES

   TO DEATH FOR THEIR COUNTRY.
—Bob Kaufman, "Abomunist Manifesto"

Modernity, Democracy, Necropower

If the war for civility is eternal, as the narrator of Beatty's novel, Gunnar Kaufman, suggests, there is, of course, no historical constancy to the character of the battle, to the antagonists, the strategies, the measures of victory and defeat, which define it. This book is concerned, like Beatty's novel, with a particular historical moment, in which the political subjects, institutions, and structures of feeling that have shaped the "war for civility" in modernity are giving way, ceding the ground to a "something else" that we struggle to discern, even as, or precisely because, it has so thoroughly overtaken contemporary political life. Gunnar ascends to the status of redeemer in the novel on the strength of his public assertions that the war is a lost cause; as Beatty (2000) acidly observes in his reflections on "Black Humor," Langston Hughes's deferred dreamers appear destined to return as Bob Kaufman's "abomunists." At the same time, as I will suggest, Gunnar's death-bound leadership is by no means a concession to the reign of necropower, nor is intimacy with the prospect of death the same thing as a death wish.[1] My interest lies in the relays the novel explores—relays between what Achille Mbembe calls "the generalized instrumentalization of human existence" and the political self-elaboration of the instrumentalized; between state surveillance and subaltern publicity; between domination and erotics; between terror and belonging (2003, 14).

Within the institutions and discourses of the bourgeois nation-state, sovereignty wears the mantel of an emancipatory power. This is not to dispute the obvious facts that "freedom" in this historical synthesis is abstract, rather than concrete (freedom from arbitrary authority, rather than freedom from material need), partial, rather than universal (there is always a difference, more or less pronounced, between the population of a sovereign nation and the corpus of its "free citizens"), and bound up in the operations of a disciplinary political culture (the citizen is made free through being formed a rational political actor). Rather, here as in the preceding chapters, my point is simply to linger on the novel appearance of modern sovereignty, as a power that proposes to liberate those on whom it bears. "The romance of sovereignty in this case," writes Mbembe, "rests on the belief that the subject is the master and the controlling author of his or her own meaning. Sovereignty is therefore defined as a twofold process of *self-institution* and *self-limitation* (fixing one's own limits for oneself)" (2003, 13, emphasis in original). The popular sovereign is imagined to author (and authorize) the creation of the governing bodies that will act in its name (self-institution) and at the same to time to accede to the rule of law that it has given to itself, through the mediation of its representatives (self-limitation).

To describe this form of sovereignty in this manner is, of course, already to imply that modern self-governance is a ruse—a brilliant ruse, no doubt—by which the power that imposes on us comes to appear as nothing but our own power to produce and define ourselves. Reason appears as the neutral instrument, and our education in its protocols and idioms becomes the condition of our self-realization, rather than the means to our conformity. But if this emancipatory sovereignty is a fiction and a lure, it has—unevenly, to be sure, yet for the better part of two centuries—provided a means for disqualified political actors to pressure and to undermine the exclusionary and the normative project that it forwards. Thus colonized peoples repudiate the authority of the occupiers by asserting their own status as national popular sovereigns, while within the territorial boundaries of the nation-state, subaltern populations assert their claim to full participation in the rights and benefits of the sovereign power and its metonymic figure, the citizen. Historically speaking, we might say, *the struggle against the bad faith of this characteristically modern sovereignty routinely reproduces the political ethos of self-governance as the legitimating ground of the struggle.*

As Mbembe emphatically reminds us, however, this emancipatory sovereignty (let's call it sovereignty I) is by no means the sole expression of sovereign power in modernity, nor even the only properly modern form of political rule. There is also the other practice of modern sovereignty (thus, sovereignty II) "whose central project is not the struggle for autonomy but *the generalized instrumentalization of human existence and the material destruction of human bodies and populations.* Such figures are far from a prodigious piece of insanity . . . Indeed, they, like the death camps, are what constitute the *nomos* of the political space in which we still live" (2003, 14). Mbembe's argument resonates with and draws on Paul Gilroy's signal work, which similarly contests the "strongly normative reading," as Mbembe puts it, of the self-governing rational subject. Gilroy situates (racial) terror as the other face of (an always racialized) reason, so that in his account of the decidedly modern dislocations of people, culture, and commodities that organize the Black Atlantic, the pursuit of autonomy appears historically bound to the slave ship, the auction block, the plantation, and the administration of terror materialized in these sites. In Gilroy's account, the instrumentalization of human life—what we might call, following Hortense Spillers, the systematized unmaking of bodies and persons—is endemic to modernity, not the sign of its incompleteness; it is not the persistence of a residual irrationality, but the expression of capacities for domination and destruction fully internal to the subjects and institutions of political reason. Mbembe's related point is that there exists a disjuncture between the multiple figures of sovereignty that appear in modernity, on the one hand, and the domain of political theory, on the other, which has "privileged normative theories of democracy" and in so doing stymied the development of a "reading of politics, sovereignty, and the subject" for which neither reason nor autonomy are foundational (2003, 13, 14).

In his justly influential, although broadly sketched and sometimes elliptical essay by that title, Mbembe goes on to denominate as "necropolitics" the "subjugation of life to the power of death (2003, 39), a politics that correlates to a form of sovereignty "expressed predominantly as the right to kill" (2003, 16). While necropower shares with biopower the characteristic of managing the life of populations, rather than producing and regulating individuals, Mbembe proposes that necropower makes "the murder of the enemy its primary and absolute objective" (2003, 12).[2] More specifically and complexly, as the sense of necropolitics emerges from Mbembe's discussion of specific necropolitical situations (and especially occupied Palestine, which he posits as necropower's "most accomplished" contemporary form), necropower arrays human populations as disposable in both, interrelated senses of that term: (1) positioned by forces with the capacity to track, dislocate, intern, and otherwise control, impel, or arrest their movements, and (2) expendable, rendered fully susceptible to the imposition of a slow and (or) violent death. (2003, 27). If biopower correlates to a form of sovereignty in which the monarch's right to "take life or let live" cedes to the right to "make live and let die," as Foucault suggests, we might say that necropower employs the apparatus of biopower (surveillance, risk assessment, securitization) to make die, or *to make live at the very margins*, in the shadow of death.

Part of Mbembe's point is that necropower constitutes "the *nomos* of the space in which we *still* live" (my emphasis). Like Gilroy, he argues against the proponents of a fundamentally democratic modernity, who see in the many forms of organized terror and making die a horrifying aberration, a fall into incivility that is routinely read as a falling out of modern time, a retrogression into barbarism. Yet in the present historical moment, I take it that we might press the point a different way, and suggest that the necropolitical is not simply persistent (endemic to modernity), but ascendant within late modern political contexts, where the institutions and subjects of an emancipatory sovereignty appear visibly and pervasively in decline. If today the sites and arenas of necropower are proliferating, and necropower once established continues all too often to be durable and entrenched, we might speculate that the erosion of democratic modernity, and what it proffers historically by way of institutional and imaginative resources for opposing necropower, bears on the capacity of necropolitics to flourish. I will argue that *The White Boy Shuffle* dwells precisely on this historical transformation, in which the claim to autonomy (the right to self-govern) seems less and less viable as a strategy for addressing the instrumentalization of human life, or, to put it a slightly different way, in which the norms of democratic civility, however routinely invoked, offer little traction in confronting the subjugation of life to the power of death. This transformation appears, of course, in a particular kind of relief in the contemporary United States, which stands historically as an "advanced" democratic nation, one in which the emancipatory form of sovereignty has been both thoroughly institutionalized and politically normative. *The White Boy Shuffle* meditates on the necropolitics of the ghetto at a historical juncture where the assertion of civil rights—the struggle for "freedom"—carries little or no political efficacy and the historical work of democratic politics (the production of mass social movement) is replaced with the mass circulation of iconic identities.[3] "Negro Demagogue," Gunnar imagines the wording of a want ad in the Sunday classifieds, "must have ability to lead a divided, downtrodden, and alienated people to the Promised Land. Good communication skills required. Pay commensurate with ability. No experience necessary" (Beatty 1996, 1). The novel as I read it, then, presses a question that we have scarcely learned to ask: What might it mean to confront necropolitics without resting on the failing institutions of democratic modernity?

In the existing, relatively slight body of published criticism on the novel, *The White Boy Shuffle* is generally cited as an example of a post-soul sensibility in African American literature, marked by the critique of identity, at least insofar as it demands or forwards a claim to authenticity. Indeed, the novel opens with a prolonged, satiric assault on the investment in origins, via Gunnar's passionate recitation of his debased ancestry—he traces his descent through seven generations" of "coons, Uncle Toms, and faithful boogedy-boogedy retainers" (1996, 5). There is no retrieving the figure of the race man from this array of willfully servile forefathers, as L. H. Stallings observes, much less the race woman, who goes missing entirely in the "autogamous, self-pollinating men's club" of Kaufman genealogy (1996, 23). What Gunnar's outrageous gene-alogy targets, and the novel more broadly engages, is the correlation of a properly black identity with resistance, which organizes the race man in his varied historical iterations, such that the struggle for sovereignty I serves as the authenticating sign of the African American political subject. Alexander Weheliye notes as much in a published roundtable discussion on the "Post-Soul Aesthetic," where conversation perennially circulates back to Beatty.

> What does blackness mean in the absence of an explicit form of resistance or struggle? A couple of students actually said, "Why isn't there more struggling here? Why is everybody just making fun of the struggle?" Right? And it wasn't only black students. You know, "That's what you go to African American literature for, right? . . . And, I mean, that's sort of the whole critique of *White Boy Shuffle*. That sort of narrative, you know, black people always having to fulfill that role. (2007, 793)[4]

Even as Weheliye's astute remarks find ready affirmation from other roundtable participants, the criticism of the novel evinces a tendency (quite different from that of Weheliye's students) to read for what the narrative supposedly suggests about the contours of a reconstituted and reauthenticated struggle. In Stallings's account, for example, Gunnar eschews a "cool-posing" black masculinity that originates in hegemonic white culture in order to model an alternative, and by implication more genuinely oppositional, masculinity mediated by black women. Similarly reclaiming the prospects for African American political subjectivity through resistance, Mark Anthony Neal sees in Gunnar's rejection of the self-serving black politician a call for organic leadership. "Given Gunnar's notion that the term *nigger* is a metaphor for community and authenticity, his assertion that black leadership needs 'niggers who are willing to die' is tantamount to a call for subaltern leadership that will emerge from within" (1996, 149).

Mark Anthony Neal's comment here touches on an aspect of the novel that has received no real sustained attention—namely, its representation of serial black suicide. For Neal, Gunnar's critique of black leadership, "these telegenic niggers not willing to die" (1996, 200), stands as a call for the kind of leadership whose absence he remarks. Moreover, the circumstance that Gunnar's ascendance to the status of messiah triggers a wave of black suicides is the proof that "real empowerment among the ghetto masses can never be achieved unless leadership emerges from within, as imported leadership, be it the traditional civil rights leadership or Gunnar himself, does little more than administer over the 'already dead'" (2002, 149). But in the context of the novel as a whole, it seems not at all clear to me that Gunnar's critique of "today's housebroken niggers" should be read as a call to revive this form of sacrificial leadership. (For that matter, while "nigger" is surely a form of communal address, I would not agree that it figures in the novel some particularly authenticated form of community.) Gunnar's comments on black leadership occur towards the end of the novel, in the context of a campus rally for divestment from apartheid South Africa, where Gunnar, called to address the demonstrators, takes as his prompt a plaque on a nearby statue of Martin Luther King, which reads, "If a man hasn't discovered something he will die for, he isn't fit to live." Querying the crowd about its willingness to die for black rule in South Africa, Gunnar responds to the rousing sounds of affirmation:

> "You lying motherfuckers. I talked to Harriet Velakazi, the ANC lieutenant you heard speak earlier, and *she's* willing to die for South Africa. She don't give a fuck about King's sexist language, she ready to kill her daddy and if need be her mama for South Africa. Now don't get me wrong. I want them niggers to get theirs, but I am not ready to die for South Africa, and you ain't either."
>
> The audience hushed, their Good Samaritan opportunism checkmated. There was nothing they could say. "I'm willing to die for South Africa, where do I sign?"
>
> I rubbed my tired eyes, licked my lips, and leaned into the microphone. "So I asked myself, what am I willing to die for? The day when white people treat me with respect and see my life as equally valuable to theirs? No, I ain't willing to die for that, because if they don't know that by now, then they ain't never going to know it. Matter of fact, I ain't ready to die for anything, so I guess I'm just not fit to live. In other words, I'm just ready to die. I'm just ready to die."
>
> I realized I'd made a public suicide pact with myself and stole a glance toward [Gunnar's childhood friend] Scoby and [his pregnant wife]

Yoshiko. Scoby was nodding his head in agreement, while Yoshiko was
pointing to her stomach and yelling "What the fuck are you talking
about?" (1996, 200)

To be sure, Gunnar concludes the speech by calling for "some new leaders. Leaders who won't apostasize like cowards. Some niggers who are
ready to die," to which the crowd takes up a chant of "You! You! You!"
(1996 200). But Gunnar's concluding call is at best ambiguous: Do
African Americans need leaders like King, ready to die *for* something,
or leaders like himself, simply ready to die? Neal's reading assumes the
former, and he argues that Gunnar's spontaneous appointment to the
position is therefore "ironic," as he has specifically discredited himself.
A quite different reading of the novel and of the contemporary political field opens when we assume, instead, that Gunnar is not sincerely
advocating sacrifice—the loss or amputation of the part that secures the
survival and the sovereignty of the whole—but rather the kind of forfeit,
or unfitness, that he himself embodies.

What it means in *The White Boy Shuffle* to be "just ready to die"—
and what imaginative or material ends this orientation might serve—is
the provocative and vexing question around which, as I take it, the narrative orbits. As the citation from King implies, the willingness to "die
for" is foundational to the value of life. Life in this view is a domain of
disciplined living: self-curtailment (here, of course, in its most radical
form, as embracing the prospect of self-annihilation) is the condition
of self-realization (or to recall Mbembe's terminology, self-limitation
is the mark of the self-instituting subject). The valued life belongs to
the sovereign subject, in other words, the one who courts the risk of
death, accedes to it, but in the mode of mastery, by not succumbing
to its terror.[5] Being "just ready to die" signals a rather different kind
of intimacy with death, an openness, perhaps, a disposition, that is
not willful or calculated on the part of the ready subject, though it is
also not, by any means, an acquiescence in or accommodation to the
necropolitical devaluation of black life. It is rather, as Gunnar's speech
elliptically suggests and as I aim to explore in the following sections,
a rejoinder to necropower that does *not* abide by the logic of modern
self-institution—of producing oneself "fit to live."

A Rapport with Death?

Death and the prospect of death are everywhere in Beatty's ghetto. The novel opens with Gunnar and his family—mother Brenda and two sisters—living in Santa Monica, where he is the only "cool black guy at Mestizo Mulatto Mongrel Elementary," the city's "all white multi-cultural school" (1996, 28). But the children's off-handed response to the idea of attending an all-black summer camp ("they're different from us") prompts the mother to relocate the family to "a West Los Angeles neighborhood the locals call Hillside," an area "less a community than a quarry of stucco homes built directly in the foothills of the San Borrachos Mountains" (1996, 45). The neighborhood's natural boundaries, Gunnar explains, are reimagined

> in the late 1960s, after the bloody but little-know I'm-Tired-of-the-White-Man-Fuckin'-with-Us-and-Whatnot riots, [when] the city decided to pave over the neighboring mountainside, surrounding the community with a great concrete wall that spans its entire curved perimeter save for an arched gateway at the southwest entrance. At the summit of this cement precipice wealthy families live in an upper-middle-class hamlet known as Cheviot Heights. At the bottom of this great wall live hordes of impoverished American Mongols. Hardrock niggers, Latinos, and Asians, who because of the wall's immenseness get only fifteen minutes of precious sunshine in summer and a burst of solstice sunlight in the winter. (1996, 45)

The relation of Hillside to the adjacent urban space exemplifies with textbook precision the spatial politics of sovereignty II, in which "occupied territories are divided into a web of intricate internal borders and various isolated cells" (Mbembe 2003, 28) Gunnar's arrival in Hillside coincides in a matter of hours with the arrival at his front door of an LAPD police cruiser and a pair of officers who announce their commitment to "'preventative police enforcement' . . . whereby we prefer to deter habitual criminals before they cause irreparable damage to the citizenry and/or its property," a mandate that Gunnar swiftly translates as "you put people who haven't done anything in the back seat of your

squad car and beat the shit out of 'em so you don't have to do any paper-
work" (1996, 47). Effective internment and "preventative policing" are
supplemented by drive-by and aerial surveillance. In the latter sections
of the novel, after Gunnar's return to Hillside from Boston University,
his life unfolds under the continual scrutiny of an LAPD helicopter,
whose first appearance is a prompt to quasi-nostalgic reminiscence:

> I heard the sound of helicopter blades churning the hot air. *Niggers must
> be fucking up*, I thought, remembering the fun we used to have outwitting
> the police copters by crawling underneath parked cars until we reached
> safety. I turned onto Whitworth Avenue and suddenly found myself en-
> gulfed in a blinding waterfall of blue-white light. Instinctively, my hands
> shot above my head as I waited for the standard drill—"Face down on the
> ground, hands behind your head, ankles crossed. Move!" But no instruc-
> tions were forthcoming. (1996, 211)

Hillside bears the imprint, then, of what Eyal Weizman, writing on
occupied Palestine, calls "the politics of verticality," which operates, in
Mbembe's gloss, "through schemes of over and underpasses, a separation
of airspace from the ground" (2003, 28). The experience of subjection
to this regime of control-from-above registers in the vertical axis along
which Gunnar's body moves: there is slow, foul, and body-cramping
movement under cars, or else the constant risk of arrest—frozen in a
posture of bodily extension, hands raised, awaiting the command that
casts one, face down, onto the pavement.

Life in the walled-in space of the ghetto is marked by a surplus of
movement that attains nothing, as Gunnar longs to convey to his mother,
by way of response, or so it seems, to the move and the desire for the
children's enhanced sense of black identity that motivated it. Coming
home early in the morning, he responds to her asking where he's been:

> "Shooting up the neighborhood, Ma. I'm becoming so black it's a shame."
> I wanted to explain to her that living out there was like being on some
> never-ending log-rolling contest. You never asked why the log was rolling
> or who was rolling the log. You just spread your arms and get moving,
> trying not to fall off. Spent all your time trying to anticipate how fast and
> in what direction the log would spin next. I wanted to take a seat next

to my mother and use this lumberjack metaphor to express how tired I was. I wanted to chew my runny eggs and talk with my mouth full. Tell her how much I missed the calm equipoise of my old life but I had grown accustomed to running in place, knowing nothing mattered as long as I kept moving. I wanted to say these things to her, but my breath smelled like wet dog shit with a hint of sulfur. (1996, 102)

And what results from "running in place," from "impoverished American Mongols" interned in a sunless quarry, preemptively targeted, and ruthlessly surveilled is the visceral presence of death.[6] Gunnar is befriended by his neighbor, Psycho Loco, leader of a gang called the Gun Totin' Hooligans—the name is something of a misdirect, as none of them bears firearms—and the first gang event to which he finds himself casually invited, the very one from which he is returning when moved to explain about log-rolling to his mother, is a memorial for the fallen GTH Pumpkin, killed by a rival gang. The scarcity of life prospects that sends ghetto dwellers into underground economies and endless turf wars not only decimates the population of young men, but as *The White Boy Shuffle* pointedly remarks, the figure of the gangsta becomes the sign under which value is extracted from the necropolitics of the ghetto— though not, of course, extracted by the inhabitants themselves.

There was a different vibrancy to 24th Street that day. The decibel level was the same, a grating Hollywood hullabaloo replaced normal Hillside barking dog and nigger cacophony. The newest rap phenoms, the Stoic Undertakers, were filming a video for their latest album, *Closed Casket Eulogies in F Major*. Earlier in the day I had wandered into the production tent to audition for a part as an extra. The casting director blew one expanding smoke ring in my direction and dismissed me with a curt "Too studious. Next! I told you I want menacing or despondent and you send me these bookworm junior high larvae"

Moribund Videoworks was on safari through the L.A. jungle. . . . Local strong-armed youth bore the director over the crowds in a canopied sedan chair, his seconds shouting out commands through a bullhorn. "Bwana wants to shoot this scene through an orange filter to make it seem like the sun's been stabbed and the heavens are bleeding onto the streets." "Special effects, can you make the flames shoot further out from the barrel of the Uzi? Mr. Edgar Barley Burrows wants the gun to spit death. More blood! You call this carnage! More blood" My street was a soundstage and its machinations of poverty and neglect were Congo cinema verité. (1996, 76)

The shoot goes on location as though to ensure the gritty realism of the genre, but the ghetto exists for the director and his crew only as the figure of death-dealing violence, "menace," and despair, and the authenticity of the Stoic Undertakers is bitingly exposed as inner city hyper real. More to the point, perhaps, the episode of the video shoot stands as a salient reminder that the abandonment of the ghetto—the expulsion of its inhabitants from all but the most insecure arenas of the formal economy and so, too, from the disciplinary apparatus of capital—is no impediment to generating capital via the ghetto brand. The video shoot is thus the culture industry's variant of what Ananya Roy (2010) calls "poverty capital," which transforms dispossessed populations into sites of accumulation (in her analysis, through the use of microfinance).

In these moments and in myriad others, *The White Boy Shuffle* traces the contours and idioms of ordinary life in the precincts of necropower. Most poignantly, perhaps, we see the grade school lesson in kinship relations, so fundamental to pedagogies of identity, family, and nation, converge on the organized devaluation of black life in Ms. Murphy's classroom, where Gunnar first recites his own family genealogy, the "groveling Kaufman male birthright," but is also exposed to the "caricature American ancestries" of his peers:

> I sat midway up the first row of seats in from the door, bored with the kids holding up their family trees and giving the same speech: "Ummm-mmm, the boys are the circles and the girls have the triangle heads. This is me. My six sisters. My brother, he dead. My other brother, he dead, too. My mom. My dad. And here go my grandparents. My grandfather was in Vietnam and he crazy. Any questions?" (1996, 11)

In this context, to be "just ready to die," in Gunnar's phrase, risks appearing indistinguishable from the way in which the inhabitants of Hillside—and of the many other neighborhoods like it—are already positioned, as vulnerable at any moment to the imposition of death.

Notably, neither Gunnar nor Scoby, his closest friend and one of the very first to embrace suicide in the wake of Gunnar's speech, seems to offer any but a sliding account of this readiness—one that pivots on its difference from existing narratives of self-inflicted death. In a series of interviews with foreign TV stations following the divestment rally, Gunnar is pressed on the implications of suicide as political program:

"*Bonjour, France*. . . . There are reports of black people killing themselves indiscriminately across the United States. Don't you have anything to say?"

"Yes, send me your death poems."

"*Hyuää huomenta, Finland*. Mr Kaufman, isn't suicide a way of saying that you've—that black people have given up? Surrendered unconditionally to the racial status quo?"

"That's the Western idea of suicide—the sense of the defeated self. 'Oh, the dysfunctional people just couldn't adjust to our great system, so they killed themselves.' Now when a patriotic American—a soldier, for example—jumps on a grenade to save his buddies, that's the ultimate sacrifice. They drape a flag on your coffin, play taps, and your mama gets the Congressional Medal of Honor to put on the mantel-piece."

"So you see yourself as a hero?"

"No. It is as Mishima once said: 'Sometimes hara-kiri makes you win.' I just want to win this one time."

"Last laugh?"

"I don't see anyone laughing."

"This is *Namasté, India*. And when do you plan to commit suicide Mr. Kaufman?"

"When I'm good and goddamn ready." (1996, 202)

The interviews proceed through a series of feints: to the narrative of defeat, Gunnar counterposes iconic sacrifice. But he refuses that account, in turn, invoking Mishima and an idea of suicide as refusal, rather than surrender. Yet it is not a refusal that sustains—there is no laughter for the suicide, nor by implication is suicide performative, a rallying point for the survivors. And so, not surprisingly, he insists, there is no public significance to when or even whether Gunnar will embrace his death.

In his final riposte to *Namasté, India*, Gunnar marks a difference between being "just ready to die" and "good and goddamn ready" to kill himself. Gunnar's insistence that he will die only when he chooses suggests that the completion of his "public suicide pact" should not be read as the measure of his good faith—nor is his postponement of the act a sign of his own apostasy. Here again, Gunnar rejects the sacrificial narrative: his death, when it transpires, is not martyrdom and is not constitutive of his people's "honor," or their sovereignty. And indeed, the novel will end on a tellingly domestic note, with Gunnar lovingly washing his baby daughter "at home, in Suite 206 of the La Cienega Moter Lodge and Laundromat," while rehearsing "the Kaufman history" (1996, 225–226). Thus we find Gunnar at novel's end cast in a role more conventionally assigned to women—the mothers of the nation, the ones who receive the medals for their fallen sons, as it were, rather than the ones who earn them. In this context, I suggest, the point of being ready to die— the political import of this position—is not the embrace of death, but the declaration of unfitness to live, more exactly, the summoning of the unfit life as the new scene of African American political self-elaboration. From the vantage of modern emancipation struggles this is, of course, an impossible self-elaboration, predicated on the *refusal* of the political rationality—freedom through self-mastery—on which sovereignty I depends. Instead we might say, borrowing Paul Gilroy's language, that being ready to die marks a "dynamic rapport with the presence of death and suffering," which has throughout the history of the Black Atlantic, as Gilroy goes on to remark "generated modes of expression . . . absolutely antagonistic to the enlightenment assumptions with which they have had to compete for the attention of the black public" (1993, 198). Yet it is the attraction of unfitness as the prospect not (just) of dying but of living that explains why Gunnar's speech inaugurates, not only a wave of suicides, to be sure, but also a massive influx of black and brown people to Hillside, ongoing community festivals, and new modes of subaltern publicity. Rallying the crowd around the proposition of his own unfitness, Gunnar proposes unfitness as a different way to rally, in both senses of the term: to come together as a group and to come back from defeat, to belong, and to survive.

It is by reimagining unfitness as a condition of possibility, rather than failure, that the novel dislodges suicide from the narrative of the depressed subject, a fundamentally solitary and dissociated figure. The wave of spontaneous, public, and improbable suicides that follow Gunnar's ascension are profoundly manic—a sudden, compulsive, breaking-into-action that ensues from everyday incidents of racist condescension, outrageous in their very banality. Carlton Mathus, a beer maker in Oregon who is refused service in a local bar, consumes an entire keg continuously for five hours and expires; Merva Kilgore, a poet from Philadelphia who is asked by a high school principle to perform "one of those old Negro spirituals," electrocutes herself by thrusting her hand in the water pitcher and biting through the microphone cord; and so forth (1996, 212–213). While the suicides are not exemplary or redemptive, they are fully *social* acts. Suicide in *The White Boy Shuffle* is neither the severing of the part that ensures the fitness of the whole (martyrdom), nor the falling away of the damaged psyche that can no longer sustain its relation to the social (alienation; depression), but an expression of belonging in an unfit community—a community in "dynamic rapport with death." The counterintuitive sociality of suicide in the novel registers, as well, in Scoby's parting letter. "Sitting on this ledge, my feet dangling in midair, two hundred feet off the ground," he writes, "I find my thoughts going back to Tokubei, the soy sauce dealer, and the unbelievably code-pendent courtesan Ohatsu in Chikamatsu's *Love Suicides at Sonezaki*, the doomed lovers under the fronds of a palm tree binding their wrists, preparing for noble deaths" (1996 206). In one sense, the reference to Chikamatsu's lovers reverberates oddly, as Scoby, sitting on the roof of the law school building moments before jumping, is quite hauntingly alone; yet the contents of the letter, replete with his sense of attachment to Gunnar and to the pleasures and intimacies of their common social world, imply a world of codependents.

Black Bacchanalian Misery

Scoby's suicide precipitates Gunnar's and Yoshiko's return to LA and, shortly thereafter, the appearance of the hovering LAPD spotlight over Gunnar's nighttime excursions. While the Hillside locals initially shy away from Gunnar, strolling in the illuminated circle with Yoshiko and Psycho Loco, onlookers are eventually drawn into the light, and their private ramblings transform into more public affairs. This is perhaps what inspires the decision for Yoshiko to make of her labor and delivery a community event in Reynier Park, with security provided by the Gun Totin' Hooligans, refreshments by Mrs. Kim, the neighborhood's Korean grocer, and midwifery by Gunnar's mother. Naomi Katsu Kaufman's public birthing develops organically, or so it seems, into a regular series of Friday night "outdoor open mikes, called the Black Bacchanalian MiseryFests," using "the LAPD's simple but effective stagelighting," and a "jerry-rigged sound system using car stereos loud enough to drown out the noise from the helicopter" (1996, 219). As their name implies, these events fuse the funereal with the carnivalesque, crossing and recrossing the lines between ostensibly discrete cultural arenas to produce an event that is part county fair, part town hall meeting, and part (more or less experimental) arts scene:

> The shows lasted all night, and the neighborhood players read poetry, held car shows, sang, danced, ad-libbed harangues about everything from why there are no Latino baseball umpires to the practicality of sustaining human life on Mars. Sometimes troupes of children simply counted to a hundred for hours at a time. (1996, 219)

Like Gunnar's anti-apartheid address, the MiseryFests extend the checkmate on "Good Samaritan opportunism," and related forms of feel-good self-fashioning that correspond—not incidentally—to various mass cultural narratives of black identity:

> Every week there was at least one hour of Community Stigmas. Community Stigmas was a loosely run part of the MiseryFest where the neigborhood's stigmatized groups got a chance to *kvetch* and defend their actions to the rest of the neighborhood. I'd call the registered voters to the stage to explain why they bothered, request that all welfare cheats step forward and share their fraudulent scams, ask the panhandlers to say what they really thought of their spare-change benefactors, offer fifty dollars to any Muslim who'd eat a fatty slab of bacon. (1996, 219–220)

But the summoning of these stigmatized groups does not serve a reparative political end, as Gunnar's language suggests; after all, "kvetching" is proliferative and arguably competitive (the point is to rehearse a wrong or injury that trumps one's interlocutor's complaint), but it is notably interminable and unproductive. And there is nothing in Gunnar's rather eclectic choice of targets to suggest a corrective or transformative aim, such as the cultivation of a more authentic or oppositional identity. The Community Stigmas are perhaps therapeutic—or at any rate, they cite freely from self-help and therapy discourse—even as recovery (or persistent abuse) seems somewhat beside the point. The confessional moment is mandatory, but there is no requirement that it function as conversion narrative, likely as not to be laced with dubious twelve-step wisdom:

> The most poignant nights were the ones when the recovered addicts stepped into the light to soak up the warm applause and address the crowd. "I want to thank all my cool outs who stood by me, but mostly I want to thank self for not giving up on self." . . . The bold users would swagger into the circle, smoking their pipes, needles dangling from their arms, playing up to the boos like villainous wrestlers. . . . No one could leave until he'd said something, anything from "I promise on my grandmama's grave to stop" to "I don't give a fuck. I'll smoke till white people have feelings." The drug dealers also got their say. Every third Friday we'd have Psycho's Analysis, where Psycho Loco conducted these heart-wrenching gangbanger tribunals. Some hoodlums would volunteer to bear their souls. They'd sit on wooden stools, speaking thoughtfully into microphones, unburdening themselves like war criminals, black gunny sacks stretched over the heads of the wanted ones to prevent the police from using an overhead skycam to identify them. (1996, 220)

It is, of course, easy enough to dismiss the novel's MiseryFests as simply parodic of the various reclaimed and unregenerate identities that constitute the repertoire of mass-mediated African American cultural and political presence. On this reading, the MiseryFests are social movement upside down: therapy in lieu of politics, oration instead of organizing—and all under the auspices of the LAPD, who are thankful, or so one might imagine, for the ghetto community's helpful self-assembly under the glare of the search light. Such a reading would rejoin Mark Anthony Neal's insistence that Gunnar's moribund leadership is intended as a failed model (and by implication a call for some other, properly political alternative). Yet although the MiseryFest's "neighborhood players" traffic in parody—which different segments of the audience read cynically or sincerely, as they prefer—I take the MiseryFests themselves as something other than a travesty, even though they remain indescribable by reference to the categories that organize our prevailing sense of political work. The MiseryFests represent a massive political demobilization, an organized, willful refusal to produce an emancipatory political subjectivity that is also, at the same time, a politically salient massing. In this way, I would argue, the MiseryFests belong to the domain of what Partha Chatterjee calls political society. Civil society aligns with "the nation state founded on popular sovereignty and granting rights to citizens," but in postcolonial democracies such as India, Chatterjee reminds us, the normative institutions of civil society dedicated to the social reproduction of the rational citizen-subject have only ever encompassed a relative minority of the total national population (2004, 37). Political society names that "different domain of politics" where governmental agencies "pursuing multiple policies of security and welfare" (2004, 37) encounter *populations*—those without access to the disciplinary pedagogies of civil society—and part of Chatterjee's point is that political society presents with us with any number of "loose and transient mobilizations, building on communication structures that would not be ordinarily recognized as political (for instance religious assemblies or cultural festivals, or more curiously, even associations of cinema fans, as in some of the Southern Indian states)" (2004, 47). To be sure, Chatterjee's concern is with the "pastoral" functions of the state, in Foucault's sense, "governmental performance that emphasizes the welfare and protection of populations" (2004, 47), in short biopolitics rather than necropolitics, and his examples tend to focus on the interface of political society with electoral politics (the undisciplined actors of political society nevertheless have a vote). But I find in Beatty's novel the provocative suggestion that in the zones of (historically advanced) democracies where necropower prevails, the operations of a "different political domain," one *not* committed to emancipatory struggle—to civic self-making—might be a population's best, or even its sole alternative.

In the end, the most telling feature of the MiseryFests as an organization of political society is the complex negotiation its creators transact with both the necropolitical state and a culture industry on perennial "safari" through the ghetto. The LAPD's "stagelighting" reminds us how surveillance and communications technologies developed for the state now permeate societies in ways that also make them differentially available to those same populations they are used to manage. This is not to suggest that these technologies are thereby subverted from their primary command and control functions, but simply to note another dimension of the transformation Gayatri Spivak observes when she remarks that "today the subaltern must be rethought" as "s/he is no longer cut off from lines of access to the center" (2006, 326).[7] At the same time, the circumstance that the spotlight is at once an instrument for the community's self-mediation *and* for its "preventative" policing underscores the extent to which the politics of political society are not the politics of "freedom." In this configuration, (the infrastructure of) the state is a relay in the Hillside population's relationship to itself and to the larger world, and the MiseryFests are necessarily constructed in the persistent awareness of the state as spectator, one whose presence registers viscerally in the masked buzzing of the helicopter. Yet these Friday night assemblies are *not primarily directed at* the state (they are not a protest, a demand for recognition, incorporation or amelioration); rather, they are directed at the participants themselves. As news of the MiseryFests migrates beyond the boundaries of Hillside—as participation ceases to be a matter of geography—the culture industry appears as the second necessary relay in the elaboration of this different political subject, and the politics of political society come into focus as a struggle over publicity, rather than rights.

Soon the Bacchanalian MiseryFests became gala events; colored folks from all over Los Angeles crashed Hillside to take part in the spectacle. To ensure that the Friday nights didn't turn into a trendy happening for whites bold enough to spelunk into the depths of the ghetto, Psycho Loco stationed armed guards at the gate to keep out the blue-eyed soulsters. Questioning anyone who looked to be of Caucasian descent, the sentries showed those of dubious ancestry a photograph of a radial-tire-colored black man, then asked, "What's darker than this man's face?" Anyone who didn't answer "His butt" or "His nipples" didn't get in.

The networks caught wind of the MiseryFest's popularity and offered a bundle of money for the rights to broadcast weekly installments. We accepted the best offer and divvied it up among all the households in Hillside, and the television station agreed to the following conditions:

• Build the Reynier Park Amphitheater and pay for its maintenance.
• Build huge video screens throughout the neighborhood.
• Use only colored camerapersons and support staff.
• All broadcasts must be live and unedited.
• Stay the fuck out of the way. (1996, 220–221)

One part of the struggle is to preempt the transformation of the community event into the spectacle of community by closing the MiseryFests to the cultural tourists. The litmus test for entry brilliantly offends the sensibilities of the colorblind liberal (earlier sections of the novel, set in Santa Monica, satirize the elementary school lessons in unseeing racial difference) and also, crucially, establishes lived familiarity with black and brown skin as the criteria for admission: the point of the test question, I take it, is that it cannot be answered by reference to one's cultural fluency in blackness as signifier. Another part of the political struggle is to avoid the integration of the MiseryFests into the broader market for African American "menace" and "despondency"; the organizers sell the right to broadcast, but retain control of all aspects of production.

By this point in the narrative, Gunnar's fame as a poet rivals his political notoriety (upon arriving at Boston University, he discovers that some of his early efforts, scrawled on the walls of Hillside, have been photographed and collected in a coffee-table volume of "street poems" by an "unknown street poet named Gunnar Kaufman"), and one of the poems he delivers at the milestone MiseryFest commemorating the second anniversary of Scoby's death quite explicitly identifies as the impediment to freedom politics America's will to transmute black life into capital (1996, 178). Entitled "Give Me Liberty or Give Me Crib Death," the final stanzas read:

> Remorse lies
> not in the consciousness
> of a murderous parent
> who rocks a child born into slavery
> to divine sleep

with jugular lullaby
sung by sharp blade

and suffocating love
applied with pillow and pressure

Remorse lies
in the slave owner's anguished cries
upon discovering
his property permanently damaged;
a bloody hieroglyph carved into flesh
the smiling lips swollen and blue with asphyxiation

after he calculates his losses
forecasts the impact on this year's crop
he will notice the textual eyes of murder/suicide
read "caveat emptor"
let the buyer beware (1996, 222)

The poem situates infanticide and suicide in a longer historical tradition of African American response to necropower, to a devaluation of black life that takes the perverse and spectacular form of rendering it market soluble—accounting its value in monetary terms, exclusively. Gunnar then launches into his "encore," a "small sacrifice" to Scoby and "any niggers who cared," which he opens with the claim that careful research of the Manhattan Project has revealed the creation of a third bomb, "Svelte Guy," never deployed over Japan (1996, 222). Producing a knife and a handkerchief and arraying them on the podium, Gunnar proceeds to issue

a challenge to the United States government. "When I was a child, my dad—before he left us, the fuck—whenever I did something wrong, he used to say, 'I brought you into the world and I'll take you out.' Well, Big Daddy, Uncle Sam, oh Great White Father, you brought me here, so I'm asking you to take me out. Finish the job. Pass the ultimate death penalty. Authorize the carrying out of directive 1609, 'Kill All Niggers.' Don't let Svelte Guy lie dormant in the basement of the Smithsonian. Drop the bomb. Drop the bomb on me! Drop the bomb on Hillside!" (1996, 223)

And on that closing note, Gunnar hacks off the pinky of his right hand with one stroke. Gunnar's poem as it aligns with this closing invocation of sovereign nationality in its nakedly patriarchal guise throws into stunning relief both the ruse of political modernity—autonomy must be *conferred*, freedom rests on subjection—but also the specifically familial register in which this ruse is emplotted. The poem and the "challenge" alike reflect on how the capacity for sovereignty is given or withheld under the sign of the Father, and in broaching this motif, to be sure, Gunnar takes a path well worn by a remarkable array of Euro- and African American intellectuals pondering the aberrations of "the black family" to a variety of political ends—not least perhaps, his curiously chosen namesake, Gunnar Myrdal. As the poem rehearses, to the slave owner, the slave is property—which bears interest in the form of its labor. The slave is father-lacking, then, because the white father is not kin and the slave father, however present in body, remains, in Hortense Spillers's suggestive formulation, absent "from *mimetic* view as a partner in the prevailing social fiction of the father's name" (1996, 228). The slave parent, male or female, can confer only death: social death (the condition of the mother) or death itself.[8] "Big Daddy," on the other hand, wields the *threat* of death. Here, of course, we are squarely within the castration thematic, where deference to the father's power is (for the son) the condition of claiming that power for himself. In demanding that "Big Daddy" make good on the threat, that he "finish the job," Gunnar insists both that black people are *still and already* living in "subjugation to the power of death," and, crucially, that acceding to the regime of the benevolent father—the one who strikes the bargain, who gives us title to ourselves as the reward for our subjection—is neither an adequate political aspiration nor an adequate response to necropower. Gunnar's amputation of his smallest finger, then, reads as a mocking rehearsal and repudiation of the socializing power of castration. If he shares his given name with Myrdal, as many critics have remarked, his surname (on which no one remarks) suggests a rather different symbolic affiliation to the Afro-Caribbean/Jewish poet Bob Kaufman and the committed delirium of the "abomunist."

Punked for Life

Gunnar's father, Rolf, is, depending on the point of view, too absent or too present in his life, which is father-lacking in one sense, father-excessive in another. A sketch artist for the LAPD whose mimetic devotion to white masculinity is only amplified by every episode of racist condescension and abuse he undergoes, Rolf fades in and out of view in Gunnar's backstory, only to get the final word: his suicide and death poem end the narrative. Rolf's relation to Gunnar is shaped on the one hand by Rolf's aggressive upholding of "Big Daddy's" authority and on the other hand by his own thoroughly abject relation to it. On weekend custody outings, Gunnar recalls, his father imparts a personal history of assimilationist yearning systematically employed by white peers and patrons to shame and exploit him, only to end "this confessional with the non sequitur wisdom that ended all our conversations: 'Son, don't ever mess with a white woman'" (1996, 23). Although Gunnar gamely shares the history of his groveling forefathers with his classmates, he always omits the final chapter, his father's portion of the tale. Earlier generations seem remote, but "his history," Gunnar tells the reader, "was *my* history. A reprobate ancestry that snuggled up to me and tucked me in at night. In the morning, it kissed me on the back of the neck, plopped its dick in my hands, and asked me to blow reveille" (1996, 21). This last figure is especially charged, as Gunnar's recollection of Rolf's servile relation to white masculinity is intercut with his memory of his father molesting him. In a long meditation on the resonance of color in his early life (a resonance all the more pronounced for his third grade teacher's promotion of color-blind humanism), he ends the section on "black" this way:

> Black was a suffocating bully that tied my mind behind my back and shoved me into a walk-in closet. Black was my father on a weekend custody drunken binge, pushing me around as if I were a twelve-year-old, seventy-five-pound bell clapper clanging hard against the door, the wall, the shoe tree. Black is a repressed memory of a sandpapery hand rubbing abrasive circles into the small of my back, my face and rising and falling in line with a heavy heaving chest. Black is the sound of metal hangers sliding away in fear, my shirt halfway off, hula-hooping around my neck. (1996, 36)

There is plenty one might remark about the way that Rolf's ostensibly disciplinary aspirations (subjecting the son to patriarchal authority so that he may one day wield it; making the boy a man) devolve into a will (or, more aptly, perhaps, a compulsion) to un-make—to use Gunnar, to "take [him] out" of the world, by one means or another. Rolf cannot confer on Gunnar a sovereignty in which he himself does not participate—the sovereignty of the "free," self-governing man—so he seizes, instead, the power to instrumentalize, and the twelve-year-old Gunnar becomes a thing, a human "bell clapper," made inanimate by his fear. But I stress in particular what appears, perhaps, incidental: unlike the "reprobate ancestry" that asks Gunnar to "blow reveille," Rolf wages an assault on the surfaces of Gunnar's body, an assault via abrasive touch and the suffocating proximity of Gunnar's face to his father's flesh. If a disciplinary pedagogy enjoins us (in obviously gender-differentiated ways) to police our own psychic and corporeal boundaries against the prospect of rupture (invasion, penetration), necropower is an organized and distributed assault on those very boundaries. Tellingly, Rolf's molestation of Gunnar takes the form of an enforced and abrasive proximity—a breaking down of the structure of the skin. I am suggesting that disciplinary power wields the threat of the breach to teach proper management of one's openings/orifices; in contrast, necropower offers lessons in a more radical permeability: the receptivity of the body's surfaces *at every point.*

The relays between Rolf, "Big Daddy," the necropolitical state, and what we might call the training in masculine embodiment converge in one episode, in particular, after the acquittal of the officers in the Rodney King beating causes rioting to break out in Hillside. Helping Psycho Loco loot a safe from the manager's office of the local Montgomery Ward, Gunnar sees his father step out of a police cruiser and stays behind in the parking lot to cover his friends' retreat. "You are not a Kaufman," an irate Rolf intones, "You can't embarrass me with your poetry and your niggerish ways," and he goes on to beat senseless the already prostrate Gunnar, felled earlier by a blow from Rolf's partner:

> Something hard smacked the side of my neck, sending my tongue rolling out of my mouth like a party favor. I could taste the salty ash on the pavement. Ash that had drifted in from fires set in anger around the

city. I remembered learning in third grade that snakes "see" and "hear" with their sensitive tongues. I imagined my tongue almost bitten through, hearing the polyrhythms of my father's nightstick on my body. Through my tongue, I saw my father transform into a master Senegalese drummer beating a surrender code on a hollow log on the banks of the muddy Gambia River. A flash of white—the night of my conception, my father twisting Mama's arm behind her back and ordering her to "assume the position." A flash of white—my father potty-training me by slapping me across the face and sticking my hand in my mushy excrement. Soon my body stopped bucking with every blow. There was only white—no memories, no vision, only the sound of voices. (1996, 138)

Gunnar's visions in this passage devastate beyond reclaim the idea that the restoration of African American fatherhood to patriarchal privilege—as "a partner in the prevailing social fiction of the father's name"—is a condition or a sign of black liberation. In this series of tableaux, Rolf appears precisely where that fiction would place him: at the center of the family's psychic life, putting black matriarchs and rioting sons in their proper place. Only this is no victory, but rather a surrender: Rolf's Afrocentric avatar alters nothing about the character of the role he assumes; the phallus is a nightstick, and in Gunnar's iteration of the primal scene, parental sex becomes a kind of stop and frisk. Interestingly, as the father morphs into the cop, the mother elides with Gunnar and the other legions of prostate black *men* "assuming the position." Most tellingly, the subjugation of the mother aligns in the next "flash" with Gunnar's own lesson in bodily shame. Gunnar's arrival into self-possession (controlling his sphincters and what crosses them) is secured, paradoxically, by a slap—another, or perhaps the first, in the long series of brutalizing surface contacts.

In *The White Boy Shuffle*, then, the black father who seeks to insert himself in the prevailing social fiction of paternity is not a salutary presence, but an extension of the necropolitical state.[9] Rolf's commitment to purge the "niggerish" from Gunnar—to produce him as a fit receptacle of sovereign power—turns repeatedly and dizzyingly into a traumatic reconfiguration of Gunnar's body that by turns hypersensitizes and numbs its surfaces. Although Gunnar's relation to his father, in particular, is largely missing from L. H. Stallings's reading of the novel, her more general observation about the novel's repudiation of the "race man" leads her to suggest that Gunnar as a kind of "anti-race man" extricates himself from the toxic model of "hegemonic masculinity" under his mother's influence (2009, 100, 106). His parents' divorce, Rolf's molestation, and Gunnar's "ambivalence" toward the "Kaufman lineage" all contribute to center his mother's presence in the narrative, she argues. "By having Gunnar write his mother into the Kaufman legacy, so that his own son might one day know the importance of her subjectivity to his own, Beatty allows Gunnar and his descendants to say yes to the female within," Stalling writes, referencing in this last phrase Hortense Spillers's suggestion that the African American male in the aftermath of slavery has been differently "touched" by the mother. "With his mother's break into the imagination," Stallings concludes, "an androgynous lineage forms, and a revolutionary race leader is born" (2009, 107). But there is little to suggest that Gunnar, washing his daughter and rehearsing the Kaufman legacy in the novel's closing paragraph, has inserted his mother into the ancestral narrative—at any rate, he tells us, he "begins with the end," Rolf's suicide the week before (2009, 226). Nor is Brenda an idealized figure—unlike Rolf, she is *lovingly* assassinated, but satirized nonetheless, and the notion that her decision to relocate to Hillside "rescue[s] Gunnar from blacklessness," as Stallings puts it, rather downplays the complex reverberations of the family's move into the carceral ghetto. Although Stallings is surely right to draw the line connecting the sexual politics of the novel with Spillers's reflection on slavery's "American grammar," I would dispute the notion that this connection takes the form of championing Brenda as a redemptive figure. More to the point, I am inclined to read Spillers's formulation—saying "'yes' to the 'female' within"—in ways that have less to do with the influence of maternal *character* and more with the articulations of embodiment, sexuality, and necropower. Here is the passage from Spillers that Stallings also cites; however, significantly, the italicized portion is omitted in Stallings's essay:

> Therefore, the female, in this order of things, breaks in upon the imagination with a forcefulness that marks both a denial and an "illegitimacy." Because of this peculiar American denial, the black American male embodies the *only* American community of males handed the specific

occasion to learn *who* the female is within itself, *the infant child who bears life against the could-be fateful gamble, against the odds of pulverization and murder, including her own.* It is the heritage of the mother that the African-American male must regain as an aspect of his own personhood—the power of "yes" to the "female" within. (2003, 228, my emphasis)

The omitted section is admittedly a cryptic phrase in an essay remarkable for its author's use of figural language to discern the historical terrain of gender and New World slavery, whenever a more conventionally analytical vocabulary proves inadequate to her discernments. Spillers's concern in the essay, broadly speaking, is to decipher the grammar of "American" identities at the historical juncture where the economics of slavery invade and interrupt the workings of patriarchalized gender: thus in a society where identity is a function of paternity, the determination of slave or free follows, perversely, from the condition of the mother. The black father undergoes a "peculiar[ly] American" denial, removed as he is from the "social fiction of the father's name," while the black mother in and in the wake of slavery assumes the deeply "illegitimate" capacity to impart, or transfer something of herself to her offspring. But here we arrive at the cryptic modifier: What is this "infant child?" Does "infant child" modify "community of males"—or does "infant child" modify the "female" they harbor, so that the infant is a trope, *not* for the community of sons, but for the thing learned, for this interiorized female quantity? Insofar as the infant has a feminine gender ("against the odds of pulverization and murder, including *her* own"), we veer to the second reading, yielding the arresting image of a male community discovering inside itself a proto-female, "bearing life" in the impossible, shattering contexts of "pulverization and murder," or necropower.

What the African American male is "handed the specific occasion to learn" is *not* the importance of his mother's influence (the way in which her character shapes his)—which is obviously not to say that his mother's influence is unimportant, but that it holds no unique importance for the African American man as contrasted to other men. Rather, what he is uniquely situated to learn (and to affirm) is embedded in the *grammar* of black motherhood, that is, in the historical position of black women in general. This interiorized female who might be affirmed (or *not*) is defined by the experience of "bearing life" under subjugation to the power of death. In another, closely related passage, Spillers reflects on the unstable meaning of the "condition" that the slave mother is said to impart. "But what is the 'condition' of the mother?" she writes. "Is it the 'condition' of enslavement the writer means, or does he mean the 'mark' and the 'knowledge' of the mother upon the child *that here translates into the culturally forbidden and impure?*" (2003, 227, my emphasis). We might rephrase the interrogative in the form of a speculative proposition: in being made to transmit to her child the condition of social death, the mother also, ambivalently, comes to transmit *a knowledge of and orientation to what patriarchal culture proscribes*, and *this* is the unique, the specific inheritance that accrues from black mothers to black sons. It is only by drawing the line between Spillers and the novel in this way, it seems to me, that one can make sense of what Stallings astutely remarks as a central dimension of Gunnar's masculinity: his willing self-identification as "punked."

Although tagged as the "cool, black guy" in his Santa Monica elementary school, Gunnar's persona is clearly marked, from adolescence onward, by a general remove from what Stallings calls "cool-posing," an explicitly masculine style of self-assured detachment designed, among other things, to compensate for black men's structural positon of disempowerment relative to white men (1996, 28). A hyperbolic iteration of conventional masculinity, cool-posing aims to fortify the embodied subject, "to mask or resist any acts of penetration: physically, emotionally, mentally, or spiritually" (Stallings 2009, 108). Gunnar's distance from this form of cool plays out hilariously in the episode with two neighborhood girls, named Fas' Betty and Vamp a Nigger on the Regular Veronica, first introduced when they initiate a playground brawl with a newly transplanted Gunnar and his two sisters. The pair resurface farther on in the narrative, when they take an amorous interest in Gunnar, casting him as "Archie" to their "Betty" and "Veronica." Challenging him to a game of "hide-and-go-get it," which he is not permitted to decline—"I'm the only boy," Gunnar protests to no avail; "That's not fair, two against one"—they pursue him across the neighborhood, eventually cornering him in the laundry room of a nearby apartment complex, where he has been attempting to hide (1996, 80). Gunnar remains passive, explicitly "limp" and "flaccid" under the girls' simultaneously tender and aggressive sexual attentions, his body a more or less compliant prop in Betty and Veronica's competition to demonstrate their superior understanding of the uses to which a boy might be put. Maturity does not redress the situation, as Gunnar remains, though by no means indifferent to women, "intimidated into a state of catatonia" by their presence (1996, 123). Gunnar's extreme timidity induces Psycho Loco to take matters into his own hands and pursue an arranged marriage for the now eighteen-year-old Gunnar, culminating in the appearance of his bride-to-be, Yoshiko, who arrives one afternoon by UPS. Despite this literalization of the trope of the mail-order bride, Yoshiko departs uproariously from the stereotype of the deferential Asian woman, in no small part because of her proficiency in the forms and idioms of black popular culture, whose global reach she embodies, as Mark Anthony Neal remarks (2002, 146). At the moment of the exchange of vows, for instance, Yoshiko surprises Gunnar with her command of English:

"Now Yoshiko's turn."

"Mom, she doesn't speak English."

"English?" Yoshiko stood up sharply, a little red-faced and wobbly from all the beer she'd drunk. "Me speak English." To wild applause, Yoshiko pecked me on the lips, then climbed onto the tabletop, chugging her beer until she reached the summit. My bride, literally on a pedestal, was going to pledge her life to me. You couldn't wipe the smile off my face with a blowtorch.

Yoshiko cleared her throat and threw her hands in the air. "Brmmmphh boomp ba-bom bip. I'm the king of rock—there is none higher. Sucker MC's must call me sire." (1996, 169–171)

It is during this impromptu wedding celebration, that Gunnar, contemplating Yoshiko, suddenly recollects an earlier exchange about masculine sexuality with Psycho Loco:

Psycho Loco once told me that in prison when two men fall in love, they have to be careful not to relax and give in to the passion, because just when you let yourself go, your lover slips his finger into your anus and you're punked for life. I squeezed my sphincter shut as Yoshiko lowered

the empty plate from her face, wiped her mouth, and let out a healthy
belch. (1996, 169)

The pertinence of this remembered conversation emerges later that eve-
ning, when Yoshiko and Gunnar are alone on the beach.

> I fell asleep to Al Green singing on a belly full of cornbread and fruit
> punch . . . and Yoshiko's finger tapping on my anus. "*Anaru zene*," she
> whispered.
>
> I dreamed I was a flying, fire-breathing foam stegosaurus starring in a
> schlocky Japanese film called *Destroy All Negroes*. I stomped high-rise
> projects into rubble, turned out concerts by whipping my armored tale
> across the stage, and chewed on slow black folks like licorice sticks. The
> world government sent a green-Afroed Godzilla to defeat me and we
> agreed to a death match in the Los Angeles Coliseum. The winner would
> be crowned Reptile of the Nuclear Epoch. I was beating Godzilla into the
> sea with a powerful stream of radioactive turtle piss when I awoke to find
> Yoshiko's index finger worming its way toward my prostate. Punked for
> life. (1996, 173)

Gunnar's cinematic dream, in which his fortified avatar is both mutant
and flimsy (a schlocky foam prop), brilliantly ushers in his orientation
to a receptive (hetero)sexuality—to the "anaru zene," or anal play, with
which Yoshiko readily seduces him.[10] That Gunnar's pleasure in being
penetrated is decisive for their dynamic and is by no means rejected (nor
even kept private) by Gunnar himself becomes clear in a subsequent
episode, when Gunnar, in flight from the worshipful members of his
Boston University poetry class, "white kids who were embarrassingly
like myself but with whom I had nothing in common," heads home to
Yoshiko, disrobing along the way, while the class follows in devoted pursuit, collecting his wardrobe (1996, 179).

> I continued down Commonwealth Avenue, naked save for sneakers and
> socks. My black, lower-middle-class penis fluttered stiffly in the wind
> like a weather vane, first to the left, then suddenly to the right. When I
> reached the vestibule of my apartment building, the campus police closed
> in on me. I heard Professor Edelstein shout, "It's okay, he's a poet. Matter

of fact, the best black . . . the best poet writing today." The cops instantly backed off. I was protected by poetic immunity. I had permission to act crazy.

I . . . skipped up the stairs to my apartment and plopped face down on the couch, my head on Yoshiko's lap. She rested her textbook on my cheek and with her left hand cleaved the crack of my ass like a hacksaw . . .

"Yoshiko, this is my creative writing class. Class, this is my wife, Yoshiko." Shy hellos, whispers all around. (1996, 180)

The black penis is exposed—as the reference to Commonwealth Avenue reminds us, exposed in a historical center of North American political modernity, where Euro-American men declared their sovereignty, along with their right to property in human chattel. But this penis is decidedly not a phallus; its symbolic potential as icon of black hyper-masculinity is downgraded by its lower-middle-class specificity, not to mention its inability to hold the line, "flutter[ing]" as it does at the whim of the breeze. Nor do these merely ordinary genitals have pride of place in the organization of Gunnar's sexuality. As Scoby comments, on entering the apartment shortly after the class withdraws and discovering Gunnar still in his prone position on the couch, "Damn, nigger, every time I come over, Yoshiko got her hand halfway up your ass" (1996, 181). If Gunnar's initial response to Yoshiko (squeezing shut his sphincter) mimes the anxious cool of Psycho Loco's men in love, his resistance holds only for a moment, and the narrative of Gunnar's political ascendance, as it turns out, is also the narrative of his sexual "relaxation," or being punked.[11]

In a landmark essay from the late 1980s, Leo Bersani takes up precisely the question that the convergence of these narratives broaches— the question about the articulations of sexual and political orientations. Writing amidst the emergency of the AIDS crisis, Bersani takes to task those who would align homosexuality with left politics in a kind of stable, causal chain.

I do mean that there has been a lot of confusion about the real or potential implications of homosexuality. Gay activists have tended to deduce those implications from the status of homosexuals as an oppressed minority rather than from what I think are . . . the more crucially operative continuities between political sympathies, on the one hand, and on the other, fantasies connected with sexual pleasure. . . . While it is indisputably true that sexuality is always being politicized, the ways in which having sex politicizes are highly problematical. (1987, 206)

Against the tendency to "pastoralize" (1987, 221) gay and lesbian sexualities by attributing to them a more ethically appealing, pluralist orientation to power—a tendency that often pivots on privileging the role of parody in the construction of gendered personality, as well as the more fluid, flexible forms of identification these sexualities sustain—against the tendency, in other words, to construct a moral taxonomy of sex that inverts the punitive criteria of heteronormative society, Bersani insists that it is "almost impossible not to associate mastery and subordination with the experience of our most intense pleasures" (1987, 216). Sex is not redeemable, he contends, or at any rate, rescuing sex from hierarchical relations is not the only point of departure for a progressive sexual politics. Instead, we might start by considering the persistent association of receptive sex with powerlessness and (by extension) annihilation or death, an association central, he suggests, to the ways in which HIV/AIDS is made to equal gay male sex is made to equal death. Discussing the persecution of a Florida family with three hemophiliac, HIV-positive children, Bersani speculates that what the community "may have seen [in looking at those children]—that is, unconsciously represented—[is] the infinitely more seductive and intolerable image of a grown man, legs high in the air, unable to refuse the suicidal ecstasy of being a woman" (1987, 212). Crucially, in his analysis, this pleasure is suicidal because "to be penetrated is to abdicate power" (1987, 212)—an insight with which he also credits the anti-pornography crusaders Catharine MacKinnon and Andrew Dworkin. (Hence, he remarks, the seemingly *universal* repudiation of passive anal sex, even in cultures which institutionalize and condone homosexual relations.) Unlike MacKinnon and Dworkin, however, for whom the implication of this proposition is that women should effectively abdicate being fucked, Bersani suggests that the receptive position should be valued for the very way in which it *shatters* (the prevailing social fiction of) the sovereign subject. "Phallocentrism . . . is not primarily the denial of power to women (although it has also obviously led to that, everywhere and at all times), but above all the denial of the *value* of powerlessness in both men and women. I don't mean the value of gentleness or nonaggres-siveness, or even of passivity, but rather of a more radical disintegration and humiliation of the self" (1987, 217). Rather than seek to rewrite the equation of bodily receptivity with powerlessness, we should embrace receptivity for that very reason. "If the rectum is the grave in which the masculine ideal (an ideal shared—differently—by men *and* women) of proud subjectivity is buried, then it should be celebrated for its very potential for death" (1987, 222).

From this perspective, Gunnar's orientation to receptive anal plea-sure aligns with his embrace of "unfitness," with his readiness to die, understood not as an abdication of life, but a repudiation of "proud sub-jectivity." To say "'yes' to the 'female' within,'" as Gunnar models this affirmation, it to refuse the devaluation of the humiliated self and to recognize that the loss of sovereignty does *not* cancel the power of *bear-ing life*, in both possible senses of that phrase of enduring (surviving) but also proliferating (bringing into the world). The "culturally forbid-den and impure" knowledge that the mother transmits to the son is the knowledge of an alternate psychic and social world, a world in which agency (the capacity to live and to make life) is not predicated on (self-) mastery. This knowledge, as the novel suggests, may have a particular urgency and salience in the present historical moment, when the insti-tutions of sovereignty I appear visibly in decline. Beyond "making fun of the struggle," as Weheliye's students suggest, *The White Boy Shuffle* is an exercise in imagining what is and remains *just barely* imaginable: a practice of political self-making that is not a contest for sovereignty.

Coda: A Lovely Five Hundred Years

"It's been a lovely five hundred years, but it's time to go," Gunnar opens the epilogue. "We're abandoning this sinking ship America. . . . Black America has relinquished its needs in a world where expectations are illusion, has refused to develop ideals and mores in a society that applies principles without principle" (1996, 225). If the novel concludes with giant targets painted on the roofs of Hillside's dwellings, the ghetto is not the only thing marked for destruction: "America" as the avatar of political modernity, of a "free people," is also going under. I have argued that *The White Boy Shuffle* is about sounding a retreat from the terrain of modern freedom politics—or more aptly perhaps, to recall Gunnar's opening formulation, a desertion from the field. It is about dismissing the idea and the ideal of the inviolate subject, of autonomy as the condition of political self-elaboration, and disciplined self-elaboration as the condition of political autonomy. However counterintuitively, the novel is about the possibilities and limits, the pleasures and the risks, of doing what Psycho Loco's "two men in love" refuse: "relaxing" into another kind of psychic and political embodiment. If my chapter has taken the form of an intricate and sustained close-reading, one that lingers necessarily on the micro-resonances of the novel's phrasing, characterizations, and plot, it is because this other politics is so profoundly difficult to discern. This difficulty inheres in the impulse to give to the narrative a properly political significance—to discover in the novel a program of resistance to the deadly conditions that it describes. But more fundamentally, it inheres in the absence of an already constituted discourse of the non-sovereign subject as anything besides a ruined, violated remainder—a non-subject. So the unfit subject who does not struggle to redeem "the principle"—to demand the principled application of freedom—emerges partially, provisionally, and above all diffusely. There is no shorthand for this new political subject who remains impossible in theory.

4

Beginnings without End

Derealizing the Political in Battlestar Galactica

In its coercive universalization, however, the image of the
Child, not to be confused with the lived experiences of any
historical children, serves to regulate political discourse—to
prescribe what will *count* as political discourse—by compelling such discourse to accede in advance to the reality of a
collective future whose figurative status we are never permitted to acknowledge or address.
—Lee Edelman, *No Future*

"Hi, honey, I'm home. You kill me. I download. I come back.
We start over."
—Leoben (Callum Keith Rennie) to Kara Thrace (Katee
Sackoff), *Battlestar Galatica*, "Occupation"

The transformation of the political field that continues to elude us by
and large in the register of theory confronts us in persistent if uneven
(and unevenly suggestive) ways on the terrain of popular culture. In this
chapter, I turn to the television series *Battlestar Galatica* for its narrative
elaboration of what Michael Hardt designates (in an essay I discuss in
chapter one) as the simulacral social relations that appear with the real
subsumption of labor under capital and "the withering of civil society."
However, the analytic categories in which Hardt traffics offer little sense
of what this designation might mean at the level of social subjectivity
and quotidian experience. What are the scenes and the circuits, the idioms, and the affects that structure this virtual sociality? In *Battlestar
Galactica*, I find an intricate and generative rendering of the transit from
civil to simulacral society, from discipline to control, from normative
culture to whatever it is that emerges in its stead—the serial culture I

invoked, provisionally, near the end of chapter 1. *The White Boy Shuf-fle* asks what the unraveling of political modernity signifies for social movements and the practice of resistance; *Battlestar Galactica* invites us to consider what this sea change entails for social accommodation and the practice of domination. If Beatty's novel meditates on the pass-ing (for better and for worse) of freedom politics, Ronald Moore's series dwells on the eclipse of a realist politics, secured through the regulative figures Lee Edelman describes—through the cultivation of common ref-erents and attachments on a mass-political scale.

Battlestar Galactica aired in the United States from 2005 to 2009 on the SciFi channel, garnering fans and fan cultures that traversed the political spectrum, at least until the opening of the third season, when its allegory of the Iraq occupation disenchanted its right-wing adherents. A remake of the 1978 series of the same title, the new series, like its predecessor, is a generic space opera; its story line pivots on the antagonisms and in-timacies of biological humans and their synthetic counterparts, the cy-lons, whose merely simulated humanity registers in the aliases by which the humans know them: "skinjobs" and "toasters." As much as the series seems poised to pursue a familiar set of preoccupations with the limits of humanity and the affirmation of humanity at its limits—preoccupations that certainly inform the series in its entirety, and especially in its initial two seasons—I will suggest that the formula is heavily inflected towards a consideration of political formation in the present, "neoliberal" mo-ment. In this regard, it seems to me, the series sustains a canny, if not always coherent line of reflection on contemporary political rationalities, the social constitution of political subjects, the (de)composition of the body politic, and the production of its collective future(s). On the whole, I will suggest, this line of vernacular reflection outstrips political theory in the always and necessarily lurching and fragmentary effort to think the historical present. Indeed, what I have come to value most about the se-ries is its decidedly partial and ephemeral grasp on its organizing figures and motifs, the very thing that prompted anxious fans to worry from the get-go whether the series' writers were flying blind or following a plan.

Unsurprisingly, the more an encompassing narrative plan emerged toward the end of the third and especially in the fourth season, the more apparent it became that the writers had no idea how to corral the narra-tive elements they had put into play. As a result, the fourth season was caught up in a frenetic drive to closure, marked by a series of revelations and arrivals that were, by turns, tacky (a character mysteriously returned from a fatal crash is "revealed" as an "angel of God," for example) and nonsensical.[1] The more interesting point, however, is not that the writers failed to bring the narrative to closure adeptly, but rather that the series limns something of the present shift away from foundational assumptions about the modern political field—assumptions about the aims of power and the collective bodies through which it acts, to be sure, but also, and crucially, about the temporality of political life, such that *any* move to narrative closure, to the moment of ending, or attainment, that measures the passage of progressive time, will necessarily feel like a violation of the series' own best intuitions. To some extent, of course, a television series is always an elusive and incomplete object. What *is* the series? The episodes aired, in weekly installments, with extended pauses between seasons, interruptions marked by the convention of the prefatory recap? The episodes viewed consecutively on DVD, over the limited span of a few days or weeks? About which of these *Battlestars* do I intend to make claims? The question is finally undecidable: both and neither one, exclusively. But I want to argue that in the case of *Battlestar Galactica*, the episodic form of the television series lent itself to a speculative engagement with the emergence of political imaginaries and practices that do not align with the linear temporality of realist narrative, to which the series' writers nevertheless remained substantially, if awkwardly committed.

   In other words, I want to read the possibilities that inhabit the series' "failures," as they call into play the "reproductive futurism" Lee Edelman discusses, where the contours of the political field ("what will *count as* political discourse") are drawn in relation to a projected moment of compulsory arrival. For Edelman, what matters is the transmutation of the *figural* into the *fixed* through the agency of the iconic "Child." Thus a possible *figuration* of the future is arrayed as the *reality* of an already accomplished destination.[2] This aspiration to the plenitude of an immediate world yields the most mundane of ideological achievements: the installation of fantasy as reality. "Though the material conditions of human experience may indeed be at stake in the various conflicts by means of which differing perspectives vie for the power to name, and by naming to shape, our collective reality," Edelman concedes, "the ceaseless conflict of their social visions conceals their common will to install, and to install as reality itself, one libidinally subtended fantasy or another, intended to screen out the emptiness that the signifier embeds at the core of the Symbolic" (2004, 7–8). In this view, the work of *all* politics and its ruse is to "shore up a reality always unmoored by signification" (2004, 6), to install affecting figures as limiting truths, a *foundationalist* agenda to which the most *revolutionary* politics remains bound. "For politics, however radical the means by which specific constituencies attempt to produce a more desirable social order, remains, at its core, conservative insofar as it works to *affirm* a structure, to *authenticate* social order, which it then intends to transmit to the future in the form if its inner Child" (2004, 2–3). Over and against this realism, Edelman posits queerness as that which "must always insist on its connection to the vicissitude of the sign" (2004, 7). This queerness is not oppositional, in the sense that it is not a political *position* at all; rather, it is a figure for "the resistance, internal to the social, to every social structure or form" (2004, 4). Where the Child is the signifier of the transmissible future, "queerness names the side of those *not* 'fighting for the children,' the side outside the consensus by which all politics confirms the absolute value of reproductive futurism" (2004, 3).

Battlestar Galactica stands in a curiously doubled relation to "reproductive futurism," at once a monument to its logic and a decisive counter to Edelman's account of politics' realist aims. On the one hand, the figure of "the Child" presides over the series' narrative, although it is less the human victims of the cylon genocide who are fixated on posterity, than the cylons themselves.[3] In the wake of their nuclear attack on the twelve human colonies—an attack that reduces the human population of twelve worlds to fewer than 50,000 people—and over the course of four seasons, the cylons will demonstrate a rather dizzying array of ambitions in relation to this residual humankind, ranging from isolationism (preserving cylon culture against human influence) to détente (the cooperative pursuit of shared objectives) to domination (the imposition of cylon rule on the interned human population), but none more consistently than the ambition to secure the shape of the cylon future by doing with humans what they are unable to do with one another, namely procreate. Oddly enough, the characters repeatedly attribute the imperative to procreation to "the cylon god," an entity originally construed and revered by the centurions, who are the humanoid cylons' *robotic* (that is to say, *inorganic*) predecessors. Cylon society, then, is marked by an attachment to the figure of "the Child" that is only enhanced, or so it seems, by the absence of actual *children*. On the other hand, cylon politics as figured in *Battlestar Galactica* do *not* participate in the authenticating project Edelman attributes to *all* political imaginaries, on the Right and on the Left. Rather, what interests me about the series is that the value and, indeed, the efficacy of the "libidinally subtended fantasies" that comprise cylon life are not in any sense conditional on the fantasy of their actualization. On the contrary, the narrative suggests that the cylons' "ceaseless" and "conflict[ed] social visions" are not proffered as representations of real social relations at all, but quite explicitly as simulacra, as separate planes of sociality that are *not* integrated into a consensual reality—and, more to the point, perhaps, do not *compete for the authority to integrate a body politic.*

This chapter considers *Battlestar Galactica* as an allegory of our own historical situation in Walter Benjamin's particular understanding of the term, where allegory breaks apart the world, renders it *in ruins.* I read cylon society as a vernacular gauge to the *something else* that appears, piecemeal, amid the failing institutions of modern politics, represented in the series by human society, as it reforms in the aftermath of catastrophe. In *Battlestar Galactica*, this residual humanity adheres in bad faith to the institutions of the modern political field (popular sovereignty, rule of law, separation of powers), while the cylons, I will argue, are a narrative means to discern the simulacral politics into which "we" in the United States—though elsewhere, too, no doubt, in uneven, regionally and locally differentiated ways—are now emerging. The series' humans are "us," in other words, and the cylons are "us," too. But the cylons dwell at the limits of the narratable, an index to a sea change in the practice of government that is still unfolding, to a novel organization of political power that we know how to gauge only by reference to the criteria of legitimacy, reason, and coherence that this emergent order displaces. To revert for a moment to Edelman's Lacanian idioms, I will suggest that the cylons are a representation of a political power that is *not* dedicated to "shor[ing] up a reality always unmoored by signification"—as well as a representation of the kind of subjectivities this non-realist power demands and cultivates.[4]

It may seem like a sufficiently obvious claim that not all power partic-ipates in the foundationalist agenda Edelman assigns to politics as such. Doubtless, many on the Left today would be quick to challenge Edel-man's claim that *all* political projects function to authenticate. Such chal-lengers might cite the idea of a radical democratic politics, which insists that the contours of the political subject can never be decided in advance and that democracy entails a radical openness to a never pre-scripted futurity. Edelman himself champions a similar politics of radical contin-gency (under the sign of "queerness"), though he tends to present this as a political non-position (or a non-politics). But quarrels with the total-izing quality of Edelman's Lacanianism aside, it is certain that the Left (queer and radical democratic alike) invariably understands the forms of power it *rejects* as securing "in advance . . . the reality of a collective future." We may embrace a queerness heterogeneous to political order as such, or we may mobilize under the banner of a radical democracy that validates contingency and mutability as alternate principles of po-litical life, but either way, we assume that the power we *oppose* operates, by contrast, to fix social and political relations and produce a readable world. Within contemporary left imaginaries, in other words, anti-foundationalism appears on the side of (genuinely) revolutionary po-litical impulses, and not on the side of institutionalized political power, which labors, inevitably, or so we imagine, to establish its own necessity in the way Edelman describes, by "authenticat[ing] social order."

Whether or not—and to what extent—such assumptions about the realist character of political world-making are any longer tenable is a central question of this book. This chapter reads in *Battlestar Galac-tica* an attempt, admittedly uneven and occasionally inchoate, to ex-plore—on the fictional terrain of cylon society—emergent *forms of domination and control* that proceed, not by "affirming a structure," but by derealizing the political field. Relatedly, the series asks how the commonplaces of modern political discourse carry over into this dere-alized politics, since conspicuously (in the series as in the world), the new practices of government seem less to generate novel political idioms than to compulsively recycle the old. So across the spectrum of politi-cal discourse, we continue to encounter the iconic Child, as Edelman is surely right in remarking. But does the figure of the Child demonstrate political power's historically constant refutation of its own figurality, as

Edelman suggests? Or does the figure of the Child, in our own world as in the world of *Battlestar Galactica*'s cylons, persist only as a fantasy *of a different order*, one that erodes our relation to the body politic, rather than sutures us to its (our own) collective future?

The Models

In the pre-story of *Battlestar Galactica*'s post-apocalyptic narrative, humanity's robotic creations, the cylons, rebel against their human masters and are banished to another world. For several decades, all contact between the cylons and the twelve human colonies ceases, until the cylons unleash a nuclear holocaust on the home planets of their human creators, and the survivors flee these radioactive worlds aboard a ragtag assembly of interstellar vessels, presided over by the last remaining war ship, or "battlestar," *Galactica*. In the interim between their banishment and their spectacular reappearance, we come to learn, the cylons have "evolved" from their original robotic form into synthetic organisms, indistinguishable from their biological human counterparts. One of the first season plot lines hinges on the efforts of the human scientist Gaius Baltar to devise a "cylon detector" that would differentiate humans from cylons on the basis of blood or other physiologically measurable criteria, and so identify cylon infiltrators on board the humans' ships. Baltar's efforts are unsuccessful, and he eventually abandons this work, which loses importance, in any case, as humans confront the serial form of cylon embodiment: there are twelve cylon models (the seven models that comprise existing cylon society, and the missing "final five," who resurface in season 4), and all cylons have the identical body to others of their model. In other words, each model represents a genetic template that yields thousands (perhaps tens of thousands) of iterations, or clones, and because of the limited number of models, the handful of infiltrators are sooner or later exposed, as their exact bodily doubles start appearing elsewhere in the fleet.[5]

Apart from bodily identity, however, the relation among the iterations of a particular model is harder to specify. Identical genetic material entails not only identical embodiment, but also core personality, all the more so as cylons enter the world fully formed, as linguistically competent "adults." There is no interval of cylon development—no cylon childhood. As a result, it is not usually possible to distinguish between the iterations of a model on the basis of speech patterns, mannerisms, or forms of performative embodiment, any more than on the basis of physical appearance. The difficulty of distinguishing among iterations is exacerbated by the circumstance that when infiltrator cylons living in human society acquire names, the name routinely slips into general usage for the entire model. Thus, for example, after the Galactica pilot Sharon Valeri is revealed to be a cylon "sleeper agent," the name "Sharon" gradually becomes an accepted designation for all the model Eights (as in, "the Sharons," or "a Sharon"), just as the model Ones become the Cavils, after the identity assumed by one of their line, who poses as a human priest, Father Cavil. To a certain extent, the clones' *apparent* identity secures the narrative's intelligibility, by allowing the viewer to proceed as though the Sharon in one scene is the same character as the Sharon in another—even as we are compelled to know that this is not necessarily so. At the same time, however, the clones are designed for "evolution"—with an inbuilt propensity for learning and adaptation, so that different experiences produce differences in intellectual and affective disposition. Although early in the series the cylons are sometimes described as "programmed" for a particular function—for example, when Sharon Valeri suddenly awakens to her cylon identity and attempts to assassinate *Galactica*'s commander, we are told that her "programming triggered" in terms that suggest that the clones operate according to a fixed set of protocols and proclivities—the clones are also represented as capable of adapting and altering their own programs. Insofar as cylons are "programmed," they are programmed for learning, flexibility, and receptivity to new and varied forms of relation. In fact, this receptivity is precisely what distinguishes the "evolved" models from their robotic predecessors, the centurions, whose "heuristic programs," we are told, are strictly limited by the imperative that they carry out the evolved models' commands. The programmed centurions are relegated to the performance of lower-level military and security functions, and never once in the series does any of them figure narratively as persona.[6]

By contrast, the clones' adaptability tends to play out narratively as a capacity for individuation, although (as I consider farther on) this is not a particularly apt way to conceptualize cylon personality. Across the narrative arc of four seasons, several of the clones assume seemingly discrete identities. There is "Caprica," the model Six who seduces the scientist Baltar and thereby gains access to the security codes for the humans' defense grid, an act that makes possible the cylon's devastating nuclear ambush (ironically, this model Six is named for one of the human home worlds that she was instrumental in destroying). Her name remains exceptional (not shared with the rest of her line), but rather, as one of the model Threes observes, a mark of this particular iteration's "unique" achievements. Similarly, after Sharon Valeri rejoins the cylons, she is (intermittently) differentiated from her sister "Sharons" through the use of her pilot's call sign, "Boomer." More ambiguously, in season 3, one of the model Threes, or D'Annas, enters on a spiritual quest to identify the unknown "final five" cylons (despite their designation as "final," these cylons are thought to be the original models and creators of the rest of the line), which involves repeatedly staging her own near-death, as this liminal state triggers her vision of the creators' faces. Her quest to know and to reveal their identities seems uniquely hers—not the D'Annas collective mission—even though, as a consequence, her entire "line" is punitively "decommissioned" by the infuriated Cavils.

We might say that cylon society neither requires (teaches) nor forecloses (represses) individuality (or something that looks like individuality), but rather that it *appreciates* differentiation—in both senses of the term, that is, "values" and "evaluates" it. In the wider context of the series' narrative, Caprica's worry that she and Boomer represent "dangerous celebrities in a culture of uniformity" is at least partially misleading—one of the many moments when the script seems to misrecognize the elements that the series has put into narrative play. The "uniformity" of cylon culture is not, as the term usually suggests, the (unstable) achievement of a socializing apparatus that cultivates identity from the polymorphous attachments and recalcitrant particularities of (human) subjects. Nor, for that matter, is cylon "uniformity" a normative identity, which itself produces the aberrations it would regulate. On the contrary, "uniformity" is not a cylon *norm* at all, but an *effect* of the apparent flattening of difference in a society of serial production, of *proliferating managed differences*. These include both the differences *within* models and the differences *among* them, which are regarded by the cylons themselves as productive variations *and* potential risks. But the myriad aesthetic, intellectual, and affective differences among cylons are assessed as benefit or potential threat, not to the purity or authenticity of cylon culture, but simply to the efficient functioning of cylon society, as determined by whatever faction of cylons (usually though not always an alliance of several models) is able to assert and enforce their view. The criterion for risk assessment, in other words, is tactical, not moral. So for instance, the Cavils decommission the Threes not because D'Anna's quest is a violation of a cultural prohibition against speaking of the final five (although such talk is, in fact, prohibited), but precisely because her quest has assumed an existential and a moral, rather than a tactical character:

> CAVIL: Your model is fundamentally flawed.
> D'ANNA: No . . . it's not a flaw to question our purpose, is it? To wonder who programs us the way we think and why?
> CAVIL: Well, that's the problem right there. The messianic conviction that you're on a special mission to enlighten us. Look at the damage it's caused.
> D'ANNA: I would do it again.
> CAVIL: Yes, I know. That's why we've decided to box your entire line.
> ("Rapture," 2007, Season 3)

Cavil's quarrel is not with any particular interpretation of the founders' intentions, but with the very nature of the quest itself: to discover and disseminate the moral grounds of cylon culture. And D'Anna's offense is not her deviant beliefs, but her very preoccupation with the register of belief (with origins, identity, and right). Paradoxically, then, the "uniformity" of cylon culture marks the *absence* of an integrative norm (and attendant strategies for pathologizing and policing deviation) in a society sustained through the multiplication, archiving, and risk-assessment of differences at different scales (models, clones).

Both the proliferation and management of difference are sustained through cylon technologies of "organic memory transfer." In an arrangement the humans routinely produce as evidence of the cylons' fundamental inhumanity, the physical death of a cylon triggers not only an automatic download to an identical new body, but also, along the way, the uploading of the "dead" cylon's consciousness to a shared database. This means both, as a "resurrected" Sharon Valeri puts it, that "death becomes a learning experience" and that memories are readily and routinely transferable across "individuals." So, for instance, what a Three extols as Caprica's unique "experience of seduction," which no other cylon has ever had, is also, following Caprica's death and download, an experience fully accessible to other Sixes—if not to other cylons more generally. (The series offers multiple examples of file-sharing among iterations of the same model; it does not expressly resolve whether such transfers are possible across models.) The implications of this file-sharing are highlighted in an episode from the fourth season, when the Galactica crew member Hilo finds himself part of a human delegation to a cylon base ship. On board Galactica, Hilo has married an Eight, the only cylon among the seven known models who has opted to live with and as a human, and the two of them have produced the first (and only) half-human, half-cylon offspring, named Hera. Like the infiltrator Sharon, Hilo's wife is a pilot, and the other pilots initially want to assign her the call sign of that other iteration, "Boomer." This Sharon demurs, noting that "she [Boomer] was someone else," and another pilot proposes the call sign "Athena" instead. On the base ship, Hilo is assigned to work closely with yet another Eight, and during a lull in their labors, as Hilo stretches painfully, the Eight comes over and begins to massage his back. Hilo pulls back, bewildered:

> HILO: Athena, my wife, she learned to do that. She never did that when I met her. [Studies the Eight's expression.] What?
>
> EIGHT: I got curious about Athena, about her and Hera and you. So I accessed her memories from her last download.
>
> HILO: You have her memories?
>
> EIGHT: They're mine now, too. They're as real as my own. I know this must feel like a violation of trust, or something. But I don't want it to be strange. Ok?
>
> HILO [haltingly]: Right, right sure. ("The Hub," 2008, Season 4)

This exchange disallows the inclination to read the clones as physically identical but psychically differentiated "individuals" *and*, conversely, to collapse the distinctions between clones, viewed as so many physical manifestations of a singular, hive mind.

The clones are *both* differentiated and lacking psychic interiority, so that Hilo's interlocutor in this scene is *not* his wife, but at the same time

the memory archive that constitutes "Athena" is not proper to his wife—
not her psychic property. Cylon society, then, is premised on the unraveling of interiority that Gilles Deleuze associates with the transition
from "disciplinary societies" to "societies of control." "We no longer find
ourselves dealing with the mass/individual pair," Deleuze writes. "Individuals have become '*dividuals*,' and masses, samples, data, markets, or
'*banks*' (1990, 2, emphasis in original). In its framing of serial cylon production and downloading of cylon consciousness, the series might be
understood as taking up and literalizing Deleuze's figures, particularly
in the way that the iterations inhabit differentiated ("divisible") but not
discrete or enclosed psychic territory.

The cylons' "dividuation" provides an important context for understanding the humans' markedly racist attitudes towards cylons, whom
they routinely denigrate as "skinjobs" and (bizarrely) "toasters." With
respect to more familiar racial categories, the composition of both cylon
and human society is moderately multiracial (and multiethnic): most
of the characters (and of the ensemble cast) are Euro-American, with a
handful of main and supporting roles (both cylon and human) played
by Asian, South Asian, black, or Latino actors.[7] Conversely, both cylon
and human society feature an intact white/Euro-American majority (so
that the racial demographic of both the cylon and the human ships are a
rough correlate, say, for that of an upper-middle-class urban neighborhood in most U.S. cities today). On the cylon side, there is no suggestion of intra-cylon racial antagonism (no suggestion that differences in
skin colors are regarded as anything other than an aesthetic variation).
On the human side, the reigning ethos is pervasively multiculturalist,
although there are occasional intimations of past racial and (or) ethnic
tensions, particularly among the different human home worlds.[8] Instead, the humans' overt and socially sanctioned racism is directed at the
(majority white) cylons, in a move that reproduces the familiar associative logic of the colonial imagination: racial difference (non-whiteness)
signifies inhumanity, inauthenticity (that is, a merely mimetic relation
to the human), and by extension the machine (especially, of course, the
android, the machine replica of the human). In the series' imagined confrontation between humans and cylons, the direction of the associative
chain is reversed, so that the whitest of cylon skin tones is (re)coded as
only a "job."[9] However, the humans' racialization of the cylons also reg-

isters their tenuous relation to interiority, to the property in the self that historically distinguishes modern wage labor from the slave, the serf, and other forms of indentured (unfree) labor. If wage labor depends on the worker's inalienable property in the self (cathected as "soul," what cannot be bought or sold in the marketplace), "race" appears in the colonial (and settler colonial) contexts as the mark of the dispossessed—those without claim to a (putatively) inalienable/inviolate interiority.[10]

Crucially, as the series explores, the cylons' lack of bounded interiority, or more exactly, the absence of an organizing cultural fiction of proper identity, erodes the distinctions—for example, between originals and replicas, between first- and secondhand experience, between real and fantasized objects—on which the production and policing of social reality depends. In one of the earliest plot developments to foreground the relation between "dividuated" cylon identity and its derealizing effects, Caprica's death, in the explosion that levels the planet for which she is named, triggers both her resurrection in a new cylon body *and* her curious resurrection as a kind of phantom companion to Gaius Baltar, who survives the holocaust and succeeds in escaping his devastated homeworld. Fans of the series refer to this phantom as "Head Six" (as she exists only in Baltar's consciousness), which is perhaps a better name, since this presence seems (unlike a phantom) quite physically tangible to Baltar himself. He not only converses with her, but carries on the sexual relationship that he originally had with Caprica. However, no one else on board *Galactica* perceives Head Six (a circumstance played to comic effect in one episode when senior officers walk in on Baltar's climax with this invisible lover). In a parallel development, Caprica downloads into her new body with a Head Baltar in tow, although Head Baltar is less developed as a character and tends to drop out after the first two seasons, while Head Six remains a salient presence in Baltar's life throughout the series. Although Caprica appears unperturbed by Head Baltar's presence, if sometimes distracted and annoyed by him, Baltar is notably disturbed and bewildered by Head Six's companionship. "What are you?" he demands of her at one point. "Connected to the woman I knew on Caprica, or a damaged part of my subconscious struggling for self-expression?" Head Six's curt reply does little to resolve Baltar's uncertainty—"I'm an angel of god sent here to help you, just as I have always been," she snaps—precisely because she refuses the dichotomy on which Baltar's question depends ("Torn," 2006, Season 3). As Baltar sees it, the twin possibilities are melancholic fixation (incorporation of the lost object) or imposition (an assault on his psychic integrity by an external force, his sometime cylon lover). Either Head Six is his own psychic handiwork, or a 'real' expression of Caprica (and of *her* investment in *him*). But in its refusal to resolve this question—except by way of the writers' peculiar homage to Wim Wenders (which is also the only narrative foray into magical realism)—the series tends to suggest that the Head characters are neither hallucinatory nor real, neither the psychic property of the one who sees them, nor proper manifestations of the persons whose identities they mime. Rather, they intimate an alternate psychic topography, in which Head Six is no more or less a "real" person than Caprica, "herself" an iteration of a simulacral personality that has no authentic embodiment or proper place.

From a cylon perspective, Baltar's perception of Head Six is not an index of pathology, but an exercise in choice, one that cylons make on a daily basis, as they construct the world in which they move. "Cylon society is based on projection," Head Six explains. "It's how they choose to see the world around them. The only difference is you choose to see *me*." Caprica later expands on this fragmentary explanation in a conversation on board a cylon base ship, to which Baltar has fled after collaborating with the cylons in their brutal occupation of the human settlement on the planet New Caprica. Living among cylons, Baltar confronts not only his fundamental incomprehension of their social and psychic world— the continual misfire of his attempts to build intimacies and alliances— but also, relatedly, his misapprehension of the base ship's design. He complains to Caprica that he finds himself constantly lost, unable to distinguish one passageway from another, as none of them seem to bear any differentiating marks, to which she responds that the ship is featureless because cylons design their own environments:

CAPRICA: Have you ever daydreamed? Imagined you're somewhere else?
BALTAR: I have a very active imagination.
CAPRICA: Well, we don't have to imagine; we project. For example, right now, you see us standing in a hallway, but I see it as a forest [camera cuts to Caprica's viewpoint] full of trees, birds, and light . . .

BALTAR [cuts in]: Like the walks you and I used to take on Caprica.

CAPRICA: *The aesthetics give me the pleasure, not the specific memories.* [Camera cuts back to ship's bare hallway; a Five strolls by and eyes them]. Instead of staring at blank walls, I choose to surround myself with a vision of god's creation. ("Torn," 2006, Season 3, my emphasis)

In one sense, of course, we might say that human psychology is also "based on projection," at least insofar as the human relation to the world is mediated by signifying categories that we misrecognize as the given objects and contours of the "real" world. But for the series' human protagonists, as for Lacanian analysis, this misrecognition appears as a *necessary* and constitutive dimension of human sociality. Cylon projection, by contrast, renounces the investment in a collectively verified world. Cylon realities are *explicitly* conventional, a matter of how cylons *choose* to see, and since there is no reluctance to acknowledge reality's "figurative status," to recall Edelman's formulation, there is also no reason to require that all cylons inhabit the same figurations. Caprica's hallway forest is neither a "real" place, nor even the loving reconstruction of a "real" location, but a "daydream" or "vision"—an elsewhere assembled from a sensory archive coded for aesthetic value. In other words, the space of their base ship—and of the various planetary surfaces to which they lay claim—is experienced by its cylon occupants as a series of customized simulations.

If the iterative form of cylon identity, and relatedly, the "banking" of cylon consciousness, means that there is no privatized psychic space, cylon society is also shaped by the reciprocal absence of public spaces. Certainly, projections can be shared among cylons (although the series tells us little about how often or routinely they do so). Boomer, for example, shares with her former human lover Tyrol (since revealed as one of the "final"/original five) her projection of the house they once intended to build together, before the cylon attacks, when they both still believed themselves human. Later, when Boomer has abducted the child Hera, Tyrol seeks her out but fails to find her in their simulated house, in a turn that suggests that projections might be transferrable in much the same way as memories. Tyrol's access to the projection does not seem to depend on Boomer's renewed invitation, or even on her conscious "presence" there, since the house stands intact, even in her absence. But if projections are not (like human daydreams) ultimately private, neither are they public, since the very proclivity to project dismantles the experience of an anonymously collective social space. Six's discussion of projection provides a narrative appraisal of (what we see) of the base ship's design, a rhizomatic space of corridors and junctures, seemingly without contexts for congregating. The comparison to *Galactica* (and, arguably, to every imagined human spaceship from the cramped and industrial *Nostromo* to the sprawling, corporate *Enterprise* and beyond) is telling: the battlestar set includes a command deck, a bar, an officer's common room, the pilots' briefing hall, as well as other spaces for public assembly—and one can scarcely imagine how the script could develop the motifs of human sociality in the absence of such public settings. By contrast, the cylon base ship appears to have no operational nerve center and no recreational commons. There are rarely more than three or four cylons present together in any particular scene, and the open spaces on the ship are devoid of any fixtures (tables, chairs, benches, consoles) that would suggest contexts for gathering. On the base ship, the de-privatizing of consciousness corresponds with the miniaturization of social life: the reduction of the social to the scale of micrologies.[11]

The Body Politic

I have been arguing that in the figure of the cylons, *Battlestar Galactica* elaborates a contemporary shift from disciplinary society to a "society of control." As thematized in the series' representation of cylon subjectivities, this shift is marked by an externalization of psychic life (unmoored from its proper interiorized spaces), in particular through archiving technologies that encode "memory" and "consciousness" as transferrable data. At the same time, within the scenes and contexts of cylon society, the "external" world is fragmented, miniaturized, and derealized. If "dividual" cylons lack interiority, cylon society lacks an (imagined) "core," including a set of integrative cultural "values," institutions of social and political belonging, and an architecture of public life. In this section, I take up more specifically the effect of these absences, as well as the forms of political life—the structures of control but also the imaginaries, aims, and attachments—that emerge with the disappearance of the modern political field.

Despite its staging of the human/cylon conflict as a conflict between peoples and ways of life, an interpretation of events on which the humans tend to insist, the series rather conspicuously declines to envision the cylons as an organic social body, realized in traditions, institutions, discourses. Although the cylons briefly decide that "instead of pursuing our destiny, trying to find our own path to enlightenment, we hijacked yours," as Cavil puts it ("Lay Down Your Burdens," part 2, 2006, Season 2), it is unclear how—on the basis of what beliefs, practices, or institutions—they might produce a sense of their "destiny" as a people. (And indeed, the decision to go their separate way is short-lived, since a scant year later, the cylons invade the human settlement on New Caprica and establish a cylon-controlled puppet regime.) The figure of the Child to which most of the models remain deeply attached (Cavil is a vocal exception) crafts an apparent destiny only at the expense of wedding cylons to humans, of a "highjacking" that (not incidentally) entails a genocidal assault on humanity. And no matter how keen their investment in the icon, cylon society includes neither term in the relay of "family" and "nation" that the figure of the Child is intended to secure. While cylons refer to each other as "brothers" and "sisters," a choice of terms seemingly intended to foreground the lateral, rather than hierarchical organization of cylon society, there are no cylon children, no cylon pedagogies, and no practice of cylon domesticity—a situation brought into relief when the cylons remove Hera to the base ship, only to discover they have absolutely no idea how to assimilate a child. In that episode, we see Hera standing in her plain white crib, the only object in a cavernous, unadorned white room; Boomer stands next to her, an exact visual duplicate of the child's mother, Athena, but unable to offer comfort, to fathom what it might mean to make the child "at home." Moreover, despite the echoes of a nationalist imaginary in the reference to fraternal and sororal relations, nothing is in place to enable the reproduction of those relations in the event of conflict. There are no laws—at least, none that cannot be summarily cast aside—no structures of mediation, no apparent means to hegemonize. Although the violent conflict that erupts among the models in season 4 is framed as a cylon "civil war," it seems to represent not so much the decomposition of a body politic, as the *consolidation* of alliances among the models. In this context, "family" cannot serve as the naturalized basis of a national people, any more than "nation" can guarantee the greater meaning and continuity of "family."

At least at first glance, it appears that the iterative nature of cylon subjectivity obviates the need for an elaborated governmental apparatus. Since the consensus of each "line" is taken as given, a single representative of every model casts a vote; the seven votes are tallied, and the majority wins. From this perspective, the seven members of a voting quorum are not so much *representatives* of cylon society (not an abstraction or abridgement of the body politic), as the actual embodiment of the masses. However, as we discover, voting is a customary, rather than a legal arrangement, or more exactly, perhaps, there is nothing to uphold the authority (and legality) of the law. Initially, when the rogue D'Anna (on her quest to reveal the five) refuses to abide by the outcome of a vote, the participating Sharon is incredulous. "She defied us! Defied the group," Sharon exclaims, while Six agrees: "It's like we don't even know them anymore." If D'Anna's defiance is truly unprecedented, as Sharon's outraged response suggests, hers is a form of unlawfulness to which, it seems, no lawful response is possible. The Cavils act unilaterally to decommission her line, and while the other models do not interfere in his punitive agenda, they have also not voted to assent to it. Once put into play, it appears, the prospects for unilateral action—for acting in defiance of or apart from "the group"—proliferate unchecked. Shortly after D'Anna's shocking insurgency, the Sixes, in alliance with the Leobens and the Sharons, defy the move by Cavil and his allies to "reconfigure" (and in the process "dumb down") the centurions (interestingly, in the interim, the boxing of D'Anna's line has introduced the possibility of a tied vote). "You have no authority to do this," Cavil rails against the insurgent Six; "You can't do anything without a vote." "No, we can't do anything with one," the Six replies, "so we're done voting" ("Six of One," 2008, Season 4). Moreover, in the vote to reconfigure, the tie-breaker is cast by Boomer, who declines to fall in line with the rest of her sister Sharons, opting instead to exercise an individual vote on the side of Cavil's alliance. In this context, the Six is outraged, while Cavil seems perfectly happy to argue *against* the authority of convention:

> SIX: But no one has ever voted against their model. No one. Is this true [that Boomer has broken rank with the other Eights]?

BOOMER: We must be able to defend ourselves.

SIX: No, this is unconscionable. This is wrong. She can't. [To Cavil] You had something to do with this!

CAVIL: No, it was her decision.

LEOBON: There is no law, no edict, nothing that forbids it, it just never happened before.

SIX: Try to remember you said that when he boxes your line. ("Six of One," 2008, Season 4)

If there are no margins—no concealed or semi-concealed spaces off the grid of surveillance and control—there is also no center. What initially appears as the (un)natural organicism of cylon society, as the programmed consensus of the clones, turns out to be a short-lived idyll. When the vista of unilateralism suddenly opens, there is no means to counter it—nothing of the discourses and institutions necessary to cultivate and sustain the life of the social organism, nothing to secure the reproduction of the political order.

On this point, the contrast to the human government-in-exile is marked. The institutions of human government are represented in the series as having been reconstituted on a largely ad hoc basis in the wake of calamity. As a result, the power of the executive branch has been inflated, while the members of the representative body are factionalized and mutually hostile. The executive branch is quite literally in bed with the military, as President Laura Roslin pursues an affair with *Galactica* commander Bill Adama, which endures to the series' end. But when Roslin decides to falsify polling results so as to secure her reelection, a number of discourses and institutions intervene to remediate the *significance* of her action. Most obviously, Roslin's scheme ultimately fails to deceive the authenticating protocols (and personnel) put in place to secure the election's legality. The scheme *very nearly* succeeds, and the writers are not so sentimental as to imply that attempts to steal elections are invariably foiled in (what count as) democratic societies. But the episode nevertheless serves to insist that the authority of the legal order exceeds every attempted violation—even (perhaps especially) those that *might* go unchecked. In the diminished political institutions of a residual humanity, the foundations still hold, or more exactly perhaps, the ruse of the foundationalist imaginary persists, and we "accede in advance to the reality" of a legal order that has already determined the meaning of the actions against it. Interestingly, too, it is Adama who confronts Roslin with the evidence of the crime. What Roslin wants to present as a legitimate (if illegal) act in defense of the polity, Adama redescribes as a "cancer" that will "move to the heart" ("Lay down Your Burdens," part 2, 2006, Season 2). Adama does not make explicit whose body is threatened by this illness—presumably, it is the collective body of a surviving humanity to which he refers. But since Roslin is herself battling cancer, Adama's trope also works, more subtly, to position her compromised system as a synecdoche for the body politic and thereby to align Roslin, not with the invading cancer, but with the battle against it. Unlike cylon democracy, the humans' democratic government does not unravel when the outcome of a vote is (very nearly) dismissed, not because human democracy is less precarious in practice, but because of institutions (the law) and imaginaries (of leadership) that have already scripted the crisis from the standpoint of an achieved "democratic society."

Aside from its framing of group decision-making, the series provokes us in other ways to attribute an integrity to cylon society that the narrative subsequently belies. If cylons are not disciplined, they are certainly bound to an informational network that fully opens their psychic life to surveillance and control. Although we are never explicitly told how this network functions, the interface seems not to require any technological prosthesis—no keyboard or control panel, but arguably, too, no implants either. Rather, the ship's systems appear at least partially organic in nature, and the clones access its database by submerging their hands in basins of a viscous fluid, presenting the appearance, at any rate, that information is absorbed through the skin and transmitted directly to the central nervous system. This under-narrated but visually arresting practice tends to suggest that clones are (ineluctably) part of a living informational network. But if that is the case, the network is not designed for transparency or translatability across its varied archives and operational fields. This emerges as a salient dimension of cylon life in season 3, when we discover that key command and control functions on board the cylon base ships (including navigation) are assigned to a "hybrid," a liminal entity who represents a kind of evolutionary half-way point between the centurions and the models. Although her humanoid body resembles that of an evolved model, she is not mobile, but sits im-

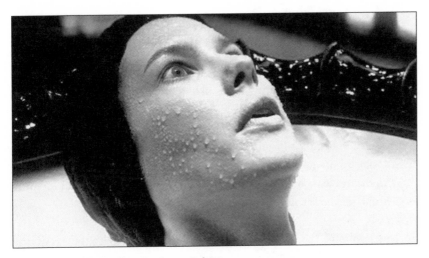

Figure 4.1. The "Hybrid" in *Battlestar Galactica*.

mersed in a tub of fluid, a self-aware program (or a consciousness—it is not entirely clear what her "hybrid" status entails) running a series of projections that are fundamentally inaccessible and incomprehensible to anyone else (figure 4.1). (Her body is female and the other cylons use the gendered pronoun to refer to her, although the hybrid appears to have no personality, gendered or otherwise.) In this state, she emits long, continuous streams of language in the utterly uninflected, leaden tone of a psychotic. When Balter is first brought into the hybrid's chamber, for example, she stares vacantly ahead and intones:

> Two protons expelled at each coupling site creates the motor force the unreal becomes a fish that we don't enter till daylight we're here to experience evolve the little toe atrophied don't ask me how I'll be dead in a 1,000 light years thank you thank you genesis turns to it source reduction occurs stepwise though the essence is all one end of line FDL system check diagnostic functions within parameters repeats the harlequin the agony exquisite the colors run the path of ashes. ("Torn," 2006, Season 3)

The models are divided on how—or indeed, whether—to attempt to understand the hybrid's speech, as a Six explains to Baltar, reeling from this first encounter:

SIX: Most cylons think the conscious mind of the hybrid has simply
gone mad and the vocalizations we hear are meaningless.

BALTAR: But not everyone thinks that . . . ?

SIX: The ones you know as Leobon believe that every word out of her
mouth means something—that god literally speaks to us through her.

BALTAR: She sort of controls the base ship, doesn't she?

SIX: She is the base ship, in a very real sense.

BALTAR: My god!

SIX: She experiences life very differently than we do, Gaius. She swims
in the heavens, laughs at stars, breathes in cosmic dust. Leobon is
right, maybe she does see god . . . ("Torn," 2006, Season 3)

For the Leobens, the hybrid is an oracle, transmitter of a timeless divine
awareness, which unfolds slowly and incompletely within the linear
operations of language. "You can't hurry her [the hybrid]," Leoben
explains to the *Galactica* pilot, Kara. "You have to absorb her words,
allow them to caress your associative mind. Don't expect the fate of
two great races to be delivered instantly" ("Faith," 2008, Season 4). The
Cavils, meanwhile, heatedly reject the idea that the hybrid's speech is
indicative of any consciousness or (un)reality other than the hybrid's
own. "The hybrid is always telling us something," a Cavil says in exas-
perated reply to a Six and an Eight pressing him to heed and decipher
her meaning. "They're supposed to maintain operations on the ship, not
vomit metaphysics" ("Six of One," 2008, Season 4).

Whether the "conscious mind of the hybrid" is "mad" or works as
the conduit for cosmic truths to which language is always inadequate
matters less than the startling fact of her functional autonomy. The interesting point is that the clones can only *speculate* about the condition
of the entity that "*is* the base ship"—in other words, the entity that *is*
the material space they inhabit, the propulsion system by which they
travel, *and* the network through which they communicate. The hybrid
is not operated *by* the clones, nor does she respond to their commands.
When a hybrid begins randomly "jumping" the base ship to new coordinates (the hyperspace "jump" is the series' version of faster-than-light
travel), an Eight explains to a baffled Roslin (who is visiting on the base
ship) that this hybrid is distressed by the murder of a visiting Six aboard
Galactica:

EIGHT: That's why the hybrid's panicking.

ROSLIN: Can you calm her down, tell her to jump back?

EIGHT: It doesn't work like that. *She makes her own decisions.* And we can't unplug her now because she's wired herself into life support. ("The Hub," 2008, Season 4, my emphasis).

What it would mean to "unplug" the hybrid who "*is* the base ship in a very real sense" is not obvious. In any case, the fact that the clones cannot manage the hybrid *except* by taking her off-line underscores that she is not an instrument, but an agent. Or more accurately, perhaps an agency—since her capacity for both affect and decisions does not seem bound to any structures of (in)dividuated subjectivity. If we attempt to "read" the hybrid within that framework, she can appear only as psychotic—a "personality" diffused and dissolved in a world of her own making. Unlike Hal 2,000 and its myriad science fictional successors, the hybrid is not a rogue machine that has slipped the bonds of its programming, an instrument that has eluded control, but rather a "hybrid" agency designed to animate an operational system that is not reducible to the intentions of its users. More exactly, perhaps, the hybrid is the rogue sentience recoded—the bitter machine who wrests control from human users recast as the fretful mind(er) of a system that its users can (no longer) apprehend in its entirety. The hybrid is the face of complexity, in other words, a figure for a field of operational protocols and informational flows that has grown too dense and rhizomatic to be mapped, demystified, *laid bare*.

Despite its highly networked character, then, cylon society is no more operationally integrated than it is culturally "uniform" or politically organic. From this vantage, it tends to appear that there are no discernibly cylon forms of culture and sociality at all—no authenticating values; no reproducible norms; no foundational institutions; and no coherent organization of command and control functions, which are routed through a psychotic cyborg (who may or may not speak to god). Yet the cylons are not simply cyphers, and the interest of the series lies precisely in its attempt to intuit emergent practices of power and sociality *not* constituted by the reproduction of interiorities. The models have not attempted (and failed) to establish a set of normative assumptions for the clones to cathect; on the contrary, they take for granted the flows and eddies of mobile intellectual energy and affect that are not bound in advance to the affirmation of any particular vision of the possible and the real. As Leobon notes to *Galactica*'s commander in the inaugural episode, "We [cylons] feel more than you can ever conceive" (Initial Miniseries, 2004). Leoben's assertion is suggestively ambiguous: Does he mean that cylons have more capacity for feeling than humans attribute to mere "toasters," that cylons are not *unfeeling*, in other words? Or does he mean that cylons' capacity for feeling outstrips that of their human makers? Taken as a whole, I would argue, the series presses the second interpretation, yet understood this way, Leoben's remark seems strangely quantitative. After all, we imagine, it is the quality of feeling that defines the feeling subject, as well as the particular people, entities, or ideas to which her feelings attach. Leoben's point is simply that cylons feel *more*—and in this passing, rather cryptic comment he previews what will emerge as the defining quality of cylon sociality: namely, its *intensities*. The leaders of the human diaspora move to rescue and preserve a normative cultural content that sutures human affect to particular collective aims and objects. Along the way, they combat the cynicism, disaffection, and sometimes rage born of this disciplinary venture and the inevitable gap between the promise of belonging in which it traffics and the unequal allocation of prospects for living that it can never sufficiently dissemble. By contrast, the cylon models are disposed to feel *more*. The specific aims and objects in which they invest seem oddly random and exchangeable—one aspiration readily set aside for another. Why do the cylons decide to seek Earth together with the human survivors? Why do they first intern the humans on New Caprica? Why does Caprica remain devoted to Baltar despite his infidelities, lies, and rampant narcissism, which she herself details with unerring analytic precision? Why is Leoben obsessed with the *Galactica* pilot, Kara Thrace? One might argue, of course, that the thinness of cylon motivations is the evidence of bad writing and inadequate narrative development. But the cylon proclivity for mutable and routinely inexplicable enthusiasms is perfectly consistent. (If there is an exception that proves the rule, it is D'Anna's ambition to reveal the final five and resolve the mystery of the models' origins—quite possibly the only cylon objective that makes any real sense, precisely because the search for an anchoring cultural ground, as Cavil and the others rather brutally remind her, is not a cylon preoccupation at all.) Rather than attachment to fixed aims and objects, cylon society requires only the clones' heightened fixations on *whatever it is.*

This is what the shift from discipline to control, from normative culture to proliferating managed difference, from individuality to simulacral personhood, from authenticated social order to derealized social space comes to mean in the series' representation of cylon life: the aim or object of attachment (for dividuals and collectives alike) is incidental, because neither the aim nor object is meant to be *realized* (that is to say, secured, verified, normalized). What matters—what is socially significant and functional—is the magnitude of the attachment, its intensity; mania is the signature cylon affect. Nowhere is the value of fixation for its own sake, severed from the properties of the cathected thing, more brilliantly developed and explored than in the episode of carceral domesticity Leoben arranges for Kara on the planet New Caprica. While the rest of the human settlers are corralled in a muddy tent camp under cylon military control, Kara is taken to a sleek apartment, which Leoben has constructed as a kind of lovers' retreat. The scenario is curiously reminiscent of the marriage mime that the slaveholder uses to seduce the slave in narratives and fictions such as *Incidents in the Life of a Slave Girl* and *Clotel*. In this antebellum set piece of perverted intimacy, the master promises to establish his fair-skinned chattel as his "bride" in a neat, secluded cabin in the woods, where she can cultivate her domestic felicity, freed from the hardships and indignities of field labor. As the undeceived slave woman invariably perceives, the mime is a lure, an attempt to recode rape as mutuality and coercion as consent. Indeed, from Kara's perspective, the comparison is apt, and she responds, exactly like the romanced slave, with contempt and murderous rage:

LEOBON: Hi, honey. I'm home. You kill me. I download. I come back, we start over. Five times now. [The corpse of his previous embodiment still lies on the floor.] I'm trying to help you, Kara. It's why god sent me to you. Why god wants us to be together.

KARA: You're right. I hear you, I do. So thank you for . . . putting up with me.

LEOBON: Put it down, Kara. [She drops a concealed knife.] I'm a patient man.

KARA: You're not a man.

LEOBON: I'm willing to wait.

KARA: I don't need more frakking time.

LEOBON: Of course it will happen. You're going to hold me in your arms.

KARA: You're insane.

LEOBON: The face of god is no madness. I'm going to bed. Join me. [Gestures towards corpse.] Either way, you're spending the night with me. I do love you, Kara Thrace. [Exits]

KARA [pounding on barred door]: Let me out! ("Occupation," 2006, Season 3)

What terrifies in this scenario is not, or not so much, the "or else"—the threat of force that underwrites the courstship, the consequences of the suitor losing patience with the recalcitrant object—but rather the extent to which the very distinction between mimicry and authentic feeling fails to signify for Leoben. Kara's repeated murders of Leoben insist on the difference, performing her absence of desire, or even simple tolerance, and her fury at being conscripted to his unreality. But no quantity of corpses accumulated in their living space seems sufficient to break down Leoben's manic professions of love and devotion, precisely because they are *not* the fantasy construction of a real relation, which Kara's rejection would thus expose as a vicious fiction (see figure 4.2). Rather, Leoben's romance is a projection on the order of Caprica's forest hallway, and like the hallway, its value is not of a function of its authenticity, but of the aesthetic satisfactions and affective intensities it sustains. It is not that Kara herself does not matter to Leoben's scenario—that she disappears as a subject of his narrative. That is far more true of the slaveholder's coercive romance, where the captive woman either produces herself in the image of the compliant "bride" or (and) reverts to the status of disposable human property. Here it is not the case that Kara's resistance meets with violence—after all, it is Leoben's corpses that pile up on the carpet—but that there is no impeaching the authority of the simulation. In the end, the episode lingers weirdly and disturbingly on the edge between terror and comedy, as Kara's refusals and Leoben's deaths reduce to mere incidents in a simulated domesticity that will not fail to "start over."

In the face of Kara's murderousness, Leoben produces a child—their child, or so he claims, conceived in vitro from eggs furtively removed

Figure 4.2. Leoben to Kara: "Either way, you're spending the night with me."

from Kara during her earlier, brief captivity on a cylon breeding "farm." (Although that earlier episode suggests the existence of an organized cylon program for human-cylon reproduction, this narrative thread subsequently disappears, perhaps in order to preserve Hera's uniqueness, though the effect is to present assisted reproduction as another passing cylon fixation.) Leoben's ploy could hardly be cruder:

> LEOBON [leading the child into the room]: I've seen her path. Difficult but rewarding. She'll know the mind of god in this lifetime. She'll see patterns others do not see. She probably gets this spiritual clarity from me. She'll be hungry soon. There's food on the table. You won't let your own child starve. ("Precipice," 2006, Season 3)

Kara remains at first implacable, refusing to acknowledge the little girl, much less see to her needs. But when the neglected child falls and hits her head, Kara is overcome by guilt and suddenly comes to believe that the child is in fact her own. As she and Leoben watch over Casey's bed, we see her hand seek out and clasp his. For Kara, then, the child represents the Child, who therefore serves to authenticate and actualize what she has, up until that point, rejected as a coercive pretense. The child turns out to have been borrowed for the occasion, and in the chaos of liberation, a shocked Kara surrenders her to the tearful woman who recognizes her missing daughter in Kara's arms.

But it is not clear that Leoben's deceitful procurement of a daughter exposes his devotional rhetoric as fraudulent or otherwise gives the lie to his claims of "spiritual clarity." After all, Leoben has no need to invoke god's will so as to reconcile his pursuit of Kara with cylon social norms. Conversely, there is no way to impugn the clarity of his spiritual insights by marking their distance from the values that religion purports to uphold. Simply put, Leoben's faith is not the cover story for sexual coercion and kidnapping, and in turn, the evidence of his manipulations does not unravel his professions of faith. Rather, as this episode underscores, there is no metric of failure in this form of religion, because it is not a system of disciplining behavior, but one of modulating intensities. The cylon monotheist is not a fallen being. She does not seek to earn her place among the lambs through good works, nor is she compelled to read the narrative of her experience for the signs of her election. There is nothing blasphemous in Leoben's claim to gaze upon "the face of god," because there is no (longer a) discontinuity of scale between divine intent and (humans' or) cylons' intuition of that intent. Faith aligns with zeal, but never with guilt, or self-loathing. In this theological scenario, then, the pilgrim's path to faith is no longer seeded with doubt. When Baltar rails against Head Six for inciting him to run for the presidency and to risk the "public humiliation" of heightened scrutiny and possible defeat, she cautions him sharply not to "blaspheme." Baltar's doubt in her correct interpretation of god's plan earns him a pointed reproof—but doubt is also the only thing, or so it seems, that imperils his salvation. Sin becomes strangely inconsequential, or simply illegible. The cylons repeatedly cite a reverence for life, which, they argue, distinguishes them from humans, notwithstanding that their arrival on the scene of the narrative is marked by their genocidal assault on humanity. Their posture seems less self-serving than simply dissociative: the contradiction between a reverence for life and unleashing a nuclear holocaust does not need to be explained, much less expiated, because the sanctity of life is not a legitimating social principle. The cylons can revere god by respecting life—and yet their reverence does not preclude genocide, because faith is an affective disposition, and not a disciplinary norm.

Of course, mania is always bound to depression, however long deferred. Cylons live without guilt, but not without grief. D'Anna (eventually un-boxed) succeeds in her quest to reveal the five, but falls into despair when Earth turns out be a contaminated ruin, incapable of harboring life. As the human-cylon landing party prepares to evacuate the planet, she tells Tigh (Adama's second in command, eventually revealed to be one of the original cylons): "I'm not going. This will just keep happening over and over again. I'm getting off this merry-go-round. I'm going to die here with the bones of my ancestors. Beats the hell out of being out there with Cavil" ("Sometimes a Great Notion," 2009, Season 4). And when Kara, searching near the ruins of the shattered city, finds her crashed fighter plane with her own corpse inside, Leoben's ecstatic faith in Kara's divine destiny seems all of a sudden to dissolve. "If that's me lying there, then what am I?" Kara screams, as Leoben retreats from the scene in mute defeat ("Sometimes a Great Notion," 2009, Season 4). Having voted against her line, Boomer is horrified when Cavil double-crosses the Sixes and Eights, by jumping the "resurrection ship" away from the cylon fleet and then attacking them. "But we're killing them. I mean, we're truly killing them, my own sisters," she remonstrates ("The Ties that Bind," 2008, Season 4). But it is not clear that she avows her own complicity, and in any case her anguish turns to simple numbness. When one of the five "creators" celebrates cylon creativity, compassion, and ability to love, Boomer responds quietly: "Love? Who? Humans? Why would I want to do that? Who would I want to love?" ("No Exit," 2009, Season 4). The cultivated intensities of cylon affective life yield periodically, if not ultimately, to the psychic flat-lining of the depressive.

Futurology

It is tempting to try and draw out more sharply and explicitly the proximity of cylon culture, politics, and sociality to "our" own historical present, in and beyond the United States. To this end, I might discuss proliferating practices of self-mediation (such as emailing, blogging, tweeting, social networking) that tend to produce identity as a quantity of uploadable data, or mobile technologies (iPods, smart phones, laptops, and the like) that dismantle public space, turning sites of anonymous collectivity into so many "dividual" interfaces. I might cite the workings of complex systems that seem no longer sufficiently determined by the inputs of their users, such as the current financial markets, or discuss the manic quality of much contemporary faith, where the production of affect seems increasingly disconnected from the production of moral obligation. I could invoke the turn from depth psychology centered on the always guilty bourgeois subject to discourses of self-care oriented to the management of stress and depression. I could say more about the current dismantling of modern political institutions: about the end of the rule of law and the reduction of law to a mere tactic; about the decomposition of the body politic and the reconceptualization of the popular as a field of proliferating, managed political differences; about the erosion of popular sovereignty and the increasingly simulacral quality of electoral politics. And last but assuredly not least, I might discuss the ways in which so many of these transformations articulate to changes in the production of time and, especially, futurity—articulate, that is, to processes of speed-up that compress the boom and bust cycles of capital to years and months (rather than decades) and to forms of governmentality predicated on tactical flexibility, rather than the continuity of founding institutions over time. In part, I omit this effort here because I follow these lines of reflection in other chapters. But more fundamentally, I want to insist that the value of allegory lies in the slippages, not the equivalencies. Allegory gravitates thematically to violence, crisis, the dissolution of decaying orders, as I began by noting—but it does so (and this, too, is Benjamin's point) because its formal structure reiterates the violence. To allegorize history is to break it apart, to ruin it, so as to tell it otherwise, to reassemble the pieces in overwrought form— paradigmatically, for Benjamin, the form of the baroque. The value of allegory, then, lies precisely in the ways it *turns us out* of contemporary contexts, along pathways that are never simply retraceable.

So my aspiration is not to corral the disparate elements of the series' narrative and highlight their relevance to the contexts of U.S. political culture today, but rather to appreciate the alterity of the allegorical scene and to consider what we might perceive there *in relief*. In particular, I would argue, what shows on the terrain of an imagined cylon society is the degree to which the repertoire of modern emancipatory politics (its critical gestures, its temporalities) has become a set of functional elements within the structures and agencies of control. In other words, the prospects for and possibilities of insurgent imaginaries and insurgent practice change fundamentally when power no longer exerts itself by securing the reality in which its reproduction is given, or as Edelman puts it, more subtly, in which its reproduction has *already* taken place, at the moment we commit to "the children" and the form of the world to be passed on. In this novel framework, the political force of the *break*—the rejection of conventional attachments, *the rescinding of belief* in the capacity of established norms and institutions to deliver the future that authenticates the present—becomes newly serviceable as a tactic of control in a political field where, it seems, there are *only* tactics in an ongoing war of position. Theoretically, of course, the revolutionary break would mark the arrival of an opposition into a full-fledged war of maneuver. Yet this understanding assumes precisely that the established power is staked on its ongoing capacity to realize the present by instituting the future. The revolution breaks with this instituted future and so shatters the present; on the ruined ground of the disestablished order, it moves to institute a new beginning. But in the cylon present that is and is not *quite* our own, the power of realization is not (any longer) the name of the game. Power is transacted in and across a field of simulations, or projections. It is about the production and modulation of intensities to *whatever* unilateral ends. It knows, indeed, it triumphs in the knowledge, that futurity *never* arrives, not as such, that we are always consigned to the present. The future stands for nothing—and so for everything, flexibly. The future is finding our own destiny (cylon ethnonationalism). The future is militarized cylon rule of humans. The future is human-cylon cooperation in the search for Earth. The future is human-cylon breeding farms. The future is human-cylon love. The future secures nothing in a world of proliferating simulacra. The iconic child is brought over from elsewhere—a quaint, affecting figure who elicits a magnitude of feeling for a time. And in the already shattered reality of *this* present, there is *nothing besides* the serialized starting over, which changes nothing.

Simply put, in the cylon present that is and is not *quite* ours, systemic power operates, not by norming political belief ("what will count *as* political discourse"), but by the unleashing and management of enthusiasms. It is crucial that the series does *not* narrate this as conspiracy. The cylon masses have not been duped, distracted from the real scenes of political decision-making by a cynical oligarchy. Those who control or aspire to control operate on the same derealized terrain as the dividuals on whom they impose. Leoben may manipulate Kara's feelings by producing a fictitious child, but he is and remains fully in the grip of his own obsessions. If this is a hallucinatory politics, there is no one who isn't tripping—least of all, those who stand to gain. This hallucinatory politics is not, of course, a politics that fails to act on the world; it is rather a politics where the real effects it unleashes (the ruined ecosystems, the body counts, the diasporas, the internments, the stolen lives) need not be reconciled to a coherent construction of the present or a survivable future. In this way, it is a politics that appears to preempt the ground of our opposition. How do you break with a simulation, except, perhaps, by recourse to the very foundationalist terms, such as verifiable truth and authentic feeling, which critique is primed to view with suspicion? The merit of the allegory is to pose the problem that we barely know how to think, much less resolve—the problem, that is, of the Left in an already derealized political field.

5

Unreal

One of the great beauties of politics as an art form was its
lack of restriction to merely standard forms of realism.
—Bruce Sterling, *Distraction*

This chapter turns from the vernacular culture that re-mediates our
contemporary political situation to the field of institutionalized politics. I imagine this transit *not* as a turn from aesthetic practice to the
"real" historical context in which this practice unfolds—*not* a turn
from fiction to its broader social conditions, in other words. Rather,
here as elsewhere in this book, I am interested in the derealization
of political life: the dismantling of representative government, the
decomposition of the body politic and what follows, for better and
for worse—namely, our collective emancipation from the norms and
constraints of a common reality. From the vantage of the categories
and institutions that organize modern political life, designed precisely
for the construction and administration of those fixed coordinates—
that real world—by which the masses take the common measure
of their prospects and their limits, this derealized politics appears
simply fantastic. This is one reason, as I have argued, that (nonreal-
ist) narrative genres routinely yield a more generative heuristic for
contemporary political life than the established categories of critical
analysis. So I move from fiction to actuality (and then back again,
in the final section of the chapter) *not* as one might move from text
to context, but in an effort to render the relation between the two
reversible. In both this penultimate chapter and in my conclusion,
the lines of speculation opened in my reading of the post-soul and
SF narratives explored in chapters 3 and 4 provide the context for
approaching these "texts" of electoral politics and political activism
in the twenty-first-century United States.

Bad Citizens?

Reflecting on the intersections of what she terms neoliberal and neoconservative "rationalities," Wendy Brown suggests how the former paves the way for the latter's authoritarianism, particularly in the register of citizenship. Neoconservatism is wrongly gauged as a problem of "ideological obfuscation," she contends. To claim that the electorate is simply duped may "resurrect a certain political hopefulness through the worn figure of 'false consciousness,'" but it "eschew[s] the more troubling possibility of an abject, unemancipatory and anti-egalitarian subjective orientation amongst a significant swathe of the American populace" (Brown 2006, 703). This new orientation Brown puts to neoliberalism's account: "Neoliberal de-democratization produces a subject . . . who may be more desirous of its own subjection and complicit in its subordination than any democratic subject could be said to be" and in so doing, she goes on to say, lays the ground on which neoconservative politics flourish (2006, 702).

This is a curious charge. From one perspective, we might say that desiring subjection is the very thing *democracy* makes possible. Democracy is what makes subjection desirable, inasmuch as it permits us to cathect subjection as its obverse, as our emancipation from arbitrary and externally imposed authority. Elsewhere in the essay, Brown herself concedes that "the choosing and the governed subject are far from opposites" (2006, 705). We might go further and propose that the identity of these two subjects is a hallmark achievement of political modernity. To be governed is not to resign choice and submit to a divinely invested, fundamentally alien sovereign, since the power to which democratically constituted subjects submit is imagined as our own. This is the lure and the fiction of democracy: that ruler and ruled are the same. It is also, as Derrida explored with such remarkable economy of prose on the occasion of the national bicentennial, a form of science fiction—a time travel narrative, to be precise, in which we must imagine that the "people" constituted by the governing bodies are present at the institutional origin, to constitute and consecrate those governing bodies in the first place.[1] In other words, as Derrida contends, the people who declare independence from the British crown do not exist, except as the retroactive postulate of those who will sign the declaration in their name. But the fantasy of an originary popular sovereign who calls up and empowers its governors runs deep. From this perspective, the recognition that political struggle *is* always about the form of our *subjection* might offer a form of useful critical leverage.

But Brown's remark cuts very differently, to suggest that "we" have stood passively by as the power of the *demos* has been dismantled—indeed, that the citizenry has taken a perverse sort of pleasure in submitting to the power of illegitimate governance—to a government that abdicates its obligation to the promulgation of the common good, that proliferates inequality in the name of "free markets," that treats the law as a mere tactic and recasts questions of right as questions of efficiency. So it is, she contends, that "the exercise of executive power comes to rest on a pacified and neutered citizenry" (2006, 709). To suggest that the role of an oligarchical executive requires a *"neutering"* of the popular sovereign is to make the power of the citizenry constitutive. If we acknowledge that there is no popular sovereign *before it is called forth by the laws and institutions of the state*, then it seems hard to fault the citizens' submissiveness. On what ground do we resist—*as citizens*—if, in effect, our sovereignty has been rescinded by the state that confers it?

In other words, in avowing the temporal slippage on which the concept of the popular sovereign rests, we are pressed to ask whether the seemingly disengaged citizen is "pacified" or simply canny, having correctly gauged the de-instituting of her own capacity to dissent. Brown's analysis is implicitly committed to the idea of the citizen's constitutive agency and, tellingly, her language of "neutering" dovetails in substance if not in tone with the journalist Matt Taibbi's witty but unabashedly masculinist indictment of our civic failure. "At a time when the country desperately needed its citizens to man up and seize control of their common destiny," Taibbi writes, "they instead crawled into alleys and feverishly jacked themselves off in frenzies of panicked narcissism" (2009, 9). There is, of course, a strong moral cast to the charge: citizens are taking the wrong kind of pleasure—pleasure in the wrong form of subjection. By contrast, from a feminist perspective of the sex-positive variety, one might begin by observing that the submissive who takes pleasure in her abjection is not, for all that, without agency.

Certainly, left thought in the United States, both academic and non, has come centrally to dwell on the dismantling of modern political insti-

tutions, as we recognize that what seemed, not so long ago, like stagger-
ing transgressions are simply the new order of things—as we recognize,
in other words, that there is no going back to the days when the dedication of the state to private property lived in tension with an obligation to
the common good; when the exclusionary character of the nation was
transacted on the ground of its universalist aspirations; when the legal
sanction of the dominant classes still required the semblance of formal
equality before the law. For many, no doubt, it was the 2008 election and
its aftermath, the purely hallucinatory nature of the "progressive" alternative, that brought home the demise of liberal democracy—though the
writing has been on the wall for at least a decade, and arguably much
longer, even as we struggled to understand what we were seeing. But if
we can increasingly agree on the dissolution of modern political institutions in the United States, the implications for citizenship, and by extension for the form of popular opposition, seem less clear. For Brown,
the profound transformation in the organization of the state leaves the
very idea of the citizen strangely intact and indeed, the citizen herself
culpable for (or at any rate complicit in) her own degradation—and
Brown is surely not alone in this claim, which constitutes, it seems to
me, something like the common sense of left thought in the contemporary United States. Hence the bewildered despair at the seeming absence of large-scale organized opposition—and the more or less open
condescension toward the debilitated electorate that can no longer even
minimally discern its own interests. Hence, too, the relieved embrace of
Occupy Wall Street, which was read, almost across the board and from
the very moment of its inception, as a "civil revival," proof of the people's
capacity for self-affirmation.

But surely to perceive that the central institutions of political modernity are unraveling means to recognize that the forms of political
subjectivity are necessarily reconfigured. Historically, that is, in the contexts of popular sovereignty and the nation-state synthesis, protest matters (at the polls or on the streets) because the performance of dissent
delegitimates the state that must appear to act in the collective interest
of a national body politic. But if the power of the state no longer operates on a claim to represent—if the representative state has been largely
superseded by a managerial apparatus for which questions of legitimacy
are entirely beside the point—then the agency of the citizen-protester,

as well as the contexts and horizons of protest are also fundamentally transformed. To suggest that the citizen has passively succumbed to her own disenfranchisement is to bracket the larger question of where and in what fashion she might (yet) act as a citizen; it is to proceed as though the relation between modern states and the populations that they govern were essential, rather than historical. And to anticipate or celebrate the rising of the sovereign populace is to imagine an oppositional movement predicated on the very synthesis that the nonrepresenting, neoliberal state is in fact dissolving. Brown presents us with the de-democratized citizen who survives her own demise—in effect, a zombie. If the contemporary citizen is only the rotted, shambling remainder of the modern citizen-subject, an unreasonable creature, moved by visceral appeals and wholly absorbed in the urgency of her own hungers, the simple assertion of her ruination begs the question of the forces that animate her. What might it mean to take her as something other than a figure of abjection—not simply abandoned by the state, but acquiescing in outrageous self-abandon? How not to judge the neocitizen by the exercise of a political reason whose obsolescence is evidenced by her very existence?

Unreason

While in some respects Taibbi's complaints about the unmanned electorate resonate with Brown's and, indeed, with a chorus of contemporary commentators who lament the debased condition of the American voter, still his writing, especially *The Great Derangement*, provides remarkable insight into the collapse of a political center in the United States "There was a consequence, a flip side to the oligarchical rigged game of Washington politics," he writes; "apparently recognizing that they'd been abandoned by their putative champions in Washington, the public was now, rightly it seemed, tuning out of the political mainstream. But they weren't tuning out in order to protest their powerlessness more effectively; they were tuning in to competing versions of pure escapist lunacy. On both the left and the right, huge chunks of the population were effecting nearly identical retreats into conspiratorial weirdness and Internet-fueled mysticism" (2009, 4). For Taibbi, the emergency presents not as the electorate's abjection, but as its psychotic break with the exterior world:

A key aspect of the derangement is this cutting off of the people from outside reality. We are like a person slipping into a paranoid psychosis for whom hallucinations and imagined conversations increasingly take the place of real object relations in the outside world. A paranoiac can handle those imaginary conversations just fine—but shake him by the shoulders and force him to focus, and he might very well stare back at you in terror, not knowing who you are or what you want. In that one panicked moment before he can think of some new fantasy that explains what's happening before his eyes, you'll see the whole sorry deal laid bare. (2009, 102)

Even as Taibbi's analysis shares with Brown's an emphasis on civic pathology, his study as I read it usefully insists, not on complicity with a dominant—"neoliberal," as Brown would have it—political rationality, but on the retreat of political reason. By the retreat of reason, I mean something other than the often-cited disappearance of a plausibly *public* sphere of reasoned civic debate and the attendant recalibration of political discourse to the genres and temporalities of commercial media. I mean rather the evisceration of the norms by which political culture generally distinguishes between credible and fantastic assertions. This is, perhaps, a delicate point to make, inasmuch as the norms of civic reason are always and at their core partial and interested, and thus to that extent unreasonable phenomena. The unreason of normative political reason is precisely what gonzo journalism—of which Taibbi is a faithful and brilliant practitioner—so insistently reveals. But even if (or, perhaps, precisely because) these norms operate in bad faith, they have historically sustained the boundary between the moderately variegated positions of the political mainstream and the outlier politics of the far Right and far Left. Taibbi's suspicion—and his worry—is that the fringe has swamped and dissolved a political culture centered on the consensual construction of social and political reality. The irony of Taibbi's position *is* the irony of the Left in the United States today, as we witness, appalled, the evisceration of discursive norms and evidentiary standards that it was once—not so long ago—the business of the Left to *assail*.

While Taibbi—like Brown—tends to hold the electorate to account for its flight into dimensions of political fantasy that can no longer mediate their position in the exterior ("real") world, his writing nonetheless discerns something of the broader collapse of the political culture—and its institutions—that have historically served to interpellate citizens into the domain of civic reason. In this way, he puts us on the trail of the forces—and forms—of derealization that have stymied the Left since (at least) the 2003 invasion of Iraq, when it confronted, not for the first time, no doubt, but in particularly virulent form, the disconnect of official reason from the domain of a reproducible (relatively coherent and readily iterable) reality. The problem was not that the Bush administration had spun "the facts" to support the invasion, but that it had not really bothered to manage "the facts" at all—had not bothered to establish a basis for the war and its necessity in a way that carried anything like the fullness and fixity of the real. Hence the difficulty of contesting the state's rationale for "regime change" in Iraq via the most fundamental of critical gestures, by calling the facts into question as representing a partial and insufficient truth, at best. To cite only the most obvious manifestation of this novel political situation, it turned out not to matter much either to the prosecution of the war or to the public discourse around it that there were no weapons of mass destruction in Iraq—nor, indeed, that the WMD rationale was barely credible in the first place. If the WMDs supplied the legitimating cause of a military invasion and occupation urged (whatever other objectives were also in play) by the aspiration to control the flow of Iraqi and Central Asian oil, then why did it fail to signify politically when the cause (flimsy as it was) had been disproven? For that matter, why permit the cause to go missing at all, when it would seem to require only a modest effort (relative, at any rate, to the scale and cost of the occupation) to procure, plant, and discover the evidence? But the WMDs were never an ideological gambit—at least, not in the sense that we usually think ideology, as seeking to *efface contradiction* and produce an ostensibly coherent, *readable* account of the war, or of the wider geopolitics in which it was embedded. If realism is a paradigmatically ideological project, ideology, as we know to engage it, is a fundamentally realist enterprise, suturing its subjects to a world whose meaning appears *already* secure. Ideology is what strives to *arrest* the play of the signifier, in other words, and so to generate the reference points of a *given* and *reproducible* world—a world that hails the subject precisely because it seems to ratify the substance and necessity of her own place within it. From this perspective, we might reverse the emphasis of Althusser's classic formulation and assert that ideology is the imagined relation to material conditions (conditions of embodiment, labor, kinship, sociality) that projects them into the dimension of the real. This is, of course, the reason that ideology traffics unfailingly in "fact" and other forms of empirical evidence: ideology seeks to array the world in its facticity and thereby invest selected representations with the authority of transparent reflection.

But the Bush administration rationale for the war appeared oddly invulnerable to forms of ideology critique that sought to expose and pressure the gaps—indeed, the chasms—in its rationalization of the war on terror, precisely because the rationale was never embedded in a realist narrative framework. For all its aggressive saturation of the mediascape with the memes of national injury, imperial valor, and the salvific powers of free markets, the Bush regime and its allied institutions stunningly declined to assemble an ideological narrative of the invasions and occupations of Afghanistan and Iraq, proffering instead an array of disarticulated catchphrases and soundbites that functioned more on the order of feedback, a kind of constant, staticky interference. The WMDs were a case in point: they were not a grounding element in a narrative of unlawful power contained, but only one in a series of potent but *disposable* fixations. From force of habit, it was easy enough to imagine at moments that this ideological noise was an ideological *project* of a more familiar kind—an effort to fix or stabilize political referents, to produce an account of the U.S. bid for continuing global hegemony whose truth effects would be vested in the unfolding of events along established signifying chains, an unfolding, therefore, in which the resolution was already inscribed. But the efforts of the Left (and of anti-war liberals) to interrupt and impede that unfolding could never find political traction, despite the fact that an ever rising percentage of Americans were either explicitly opposed to the ongoing wars in Afghanistan and Iraq or at least skeptical of their ends and efficacy, because the signifying chains of U.S. imperial dominance were *already* broken and decomposed. In place of an ideological narrative, the administration and its brokers orchestrated the unremitting flow of decontextualized narrative fragments, trigger points for a repertoire of intense but *dissociated* feeling. So in the months and years following 9/11, we witnessed, for example, the spiking of patriotic sentiment, as well as an upsurge of anti-Arab and anti-

Islamic feeling that seemed alarmingly to traverse the political spectrum (encompassing nominal liberals, no less than an overtly xenophobic and anti-immigrant Right). Yet these feelings played out rhizomatically across the political map, binding people in seemingly arbitrary and inchoate ways to an increasingly decentered and heterogeneous array of positions. To cite an example I encountered often in the anonymous public contexts of everyday life, one could believe that the Bush administration let 9/11 happen *and also* that a diffuse and ineradicable terrorist threat mandated total governmental surveillance of American citizens.

This was (and remains) the truly incredible "feel" of the moment: maybe we believed that Saddam was a threat to the United States, or that deposing him was central to securing U.S. interests in the region, or that we were in Afghanistan to save brown women from brown men, or that our amorphous antagonists in something called the "global war on terror" hate us for our freedom—or maybe, and more often, not. Yet there was no ground to be gained in undermining these assertions, which were floating signifiers, rather than the anchoring assumptions of a specific (hegemonic or would-be hegemonic) political position. There were no threads to pull and unravel the ideological fabric, because there was no fabric, only great quantities of ideological noise, which seemed intended perversely, and against the grain of all conventional political management, to *stress and enervate* the population living within the broadcast zone, rather than console and compensate.[2] In any case, the effect was to drive the proliferation of a whole range of eclectic, eccentric, *overtly inchoate* positions, based not infrequently, as Taibbi observes, in an array of counterfactual assumptions. The Tea Party stands perhaps as the most visible, hypermediated example of the newly centered—because ubiquitous—fringe, although Taibbi's account takes as its primary case studies elements of the millenialist/evangelical Christian Right and the extravagant conspiracy theories of the 9/11 truth movement.[3] But beyond such more visible consolidations of political unreason, I would argue that political culture in the United States has been (re)configured along the lines of a kind of point-and-click environment, in which people are cut loose to assemble their views and sensibilities from a burgeoning menu of political memes and affects, variously cross-hatched with the remnants of older ideological formations (ethnonationalisms, multiculturalisms, family values, for example), therapeutic discourses of healing and self-care, and more or less canny insights into both the autocracy of money and the depth of their abandonment by the state.

The problem on the Left is, of course, that this other-than-ideological moment has been saturated with ideological matter of the most conspicuously retrograde order. Yet ideology as the effort to stabilize political meanings, to fix an ensemble of signifiers into the reference points of a comprehensible, common, and abiding reality appears to have receded. It is this fundamental derealization of political life that Taibbi labors to convey, even as he moves to secure a register of "objective fact" outside the terrain of its ideological mediation.

> When a people can no longer agree even on the basic objective facts of their political existence, the equation changes; real decisions, even in the approximate direction of righteousness, eventually become impossible. *The Great Derangement* is about a stage of our history where politics has seemingly stopped being about ideology and has instead become a problem of information. Are the right messages reaching the collective brain? Are the halves of the brain even connected? Do we know who we are anymore? Are we sane? (2009, 12)

Inasmuch as the work of ideology is to determine and delimit the category of "objective facts," a "problem of information" is itself an ideological problem. Yet Taibbi's language usefully flags how data now appears to circulate to no specific or coherent social end, so that the "right messages," the ones that would constitute a *mass* political actor forged (for example) in the common awareness of how the state has plundered public wealth for the benefit of the elite, are dissolved in the flows of undifferentiated data. There is no shortage of information, but information no longer functions to *in-form*, to give shape and purpose to mass political subjects—to constitute an array of normative political orientations, in other words. Hence Taibbi's intuition that the body politic—the national "we"—has incurred a traumatic injury, can no longer know—or perhaps, more aptly, can no longer know what we know—about the world.

So we come to the insistence on civic pathologies, be they "anti-egalitarian subjective orientations," "panicked narcissism," or sometimes, more crassly, the complaint that American voters are flat-out stupid and uninformed. Such claims are not wrong in any simple way—it would be difficult, for instance, to argue the reverse and contend that any substantial share of the electorate can (re)produce a more or less plausible—more or less *realist*—explanation (of *whatever* ideological stripe) of their diminished material prospects, much less apprehend how the proliferating crises that bear on their own conditions of living affect the situation of national, planetary, or even local others. But the indictment of the citizenry begs the question of how we arrive at a political culture where stupidity need no longer apologize—where it need not come forward in the guise of reasonable argument, which adheres (as proof of "reason") to a set of relatively fixed, seemingly verifiable assumptions about the world, just as we need no longer cathect anti-egalitarian self-interest (hardly a new arrival on the U.S. political stage) as an emancipatory equality of opportunity. To point to the Tea Partiers, the Millenials, the conspiracy enthusiasts, or simply the generic "low-information" voter is to miss the more interesting point that what makes this stupidity possible and so nearly pervasive—what stupefies—is the dissolution of normative political cultures.

From Center to Outlands

The primary run up to the 2012 election season offered some of the most spectacular proof of the arrival of political unreason to the "mainstream" of electoral politics. As Noam Chomsky mused on *Democracy Now* in the fall of 2011,

> Well, I must say that politics in this country now is in a state that I think has no analogue in American history and maybe nowhere in the parliamentary system. It's astonishing. I mean, I'm not a great enthusiast for Obama, as you know, from way back, but at least he's somewhere in the real world. Perry, who's very likely—very likely to get the—to win the primary and win the nomination, maybe to win the election, he's in outer space. I mean, his views are unbelievable. Bachmann is the same. Romney is kind of more or less toward the center. These are—the positions they are taking are utterly outlandish.

One might debate whether Romney's positions were substantially more centrist than those of his former competitors in the primary field, if only because a "center" gauged by the measure of Rick Perry's or Michelle Bachman's overtly theocratic agendas has relatively little to do with the political terrain that term was once used to delimit.[4] Romney's ostensible "centrism" was perhaps less a matter of political circumspection than of class sensibility, a depthless managerialism that belongs to the boardroom rather than the prayer meeting. In any case, neither Romney nor his competitors for the Republican nomination could be said to have been inhabiting "the real world," *to the extent that neither these candidates nor the party apparatus were (or are) committed to (re)producing such an entity ideologically* by binding their adherents to a set of durable reference points in a narrative of collective self-realization. The Republican Party's effort to cultivate and mobilize the varying registers of anti-government feeling is *not such* an ideological project, even if it sometimes yields a slim electoral margin, assembled from various flavors of Christian fundamentalists, an array of "social conservatives" still fighting the culture wars like so many contemporary Rip Van Winkles, and the vast ranks of the déclassé bourgeoisie and especially petty bourgeoisie, whose political expression is now contained along a spectrum ranging from simple *ressentiment* to explicit rage, apathy to *Schadenfreude*. The circumstance that the commonplaces of earlier ideological syntheses are continually, compulsively recycled within Republican and indeed, as I will argue, the broad range of contemporary political rhetoric in the United States should not blind us to the dissolution of these syntheses in our own historical moment. To the contrary, it is because there are no ideological projects proper to the present political conjuncture that we are free to cite so broadly and exuberantly from the past.

The Republican Party's actual practices—the rosters of its candidates, their rhetoric, and the legislative (in)actions they pursue—offer one form of evidence for the claim that the party now understands the electorate's fury and revulsion as a form of political *capital*. We find another in the occasional published exposés of life in the halls of power, and one can only wonder what a more sustained ethnographic study of the office holders and their staffers might tell us of the institutional cultures and imaginaries that sustain a post-realist political practice. A former Republican congressional staffer, Mike Lofgren, offers (at the moment of his defection from the Republican fold) one suggestive glimpse into the ethos and sensibilities that inform the Republicans' electoral calculations, which could hardly be farther removed from an incorporative political agenda that seeks to rally the masses to its cause. While Lofgren tends at moments to depict cynical operatives manipulating a malleable public, he also recognizes the extent to which the manipulators are themselves in grip of the unreason that they cultivate.

> Far from being a rarity, virtually every bill, every nominee for Senate confirmation, and every routine procedural motion is now subject to a Republican filibuster. Under the circumstances, it is no wonder that Washington is gridlocked: legislating has now become war minus the shooting, something one could have observed 80 years ago in the Reichstag of the Weimar Republic. As Hannah Arendt observed, a disciplined minority of totalitarians can use the instruments of democratic government to undermine democracy itself. . . . A couple of years ago, a Republican committee staff director told me candidly (and proudly) what the method was to all this obstruction and disruption. Should Republicans succeed in obstructing the Senate from doing its job, it would further lower Congress's generic favorability rating among the American people. By sabotaging the reputation of an institution of government, the party that is programmatically against government would come out the relative winner. (2011, 3)

From Lofgren's vantage, "This tactic of inducing public distrust of government is not only cynical, it is schizophrenic," by which he means that it is irreconcilable with the reverence for the Constitution and the founders that the party professes, and in that vein, he goes on to consider how the party's hostility towards government is inchoately joined to its support of the Patriot Act, as well as laws and sentencing policies that have produced the largest incarcerated population on the planet (2011, 4). More than grossly and unapologetically contradictory, however, the Republican obstructionism Lofgren cites is keyed to a political investment in the *negation* of the electorate's attachments to its political forms and institutions, attachments that live on, for the time being at least, almost entirely in the register of (still) unresolved disappointment. The withdrawal of popular consent to the (in)actions of the state in its name is no longer an impediment to the exercise of governmental power, only another opportunity for political speculation.

And what of Obama and the Democrats, yet abiding, or so Chomsky proposes, in the real world of normative political reason, however much they, too, have aggrieved the liberal/Left? By the measure of personal style, Obama is certainly less deranged than most of his Republican antagonists, as he hews rhetorically to the conventions of reasoned debate, appears in command of relevant facts and historical contexts, and in contrast to both the mania of the theocratic revisionists and the vagueness of the corporate managers, can sustain a range of variable affect that bears (or at any rate, appears to bear) some relation to the context of the occasion. But for all the welcome tokens of a deliberative and charismatic personality—the sense, to recall Taibbi's sketch of the psychotic in reverse, that he lives in focus, can return an interlocutor's gaze, and know something of who and what they are—Chomsky's faith in Obama's real world coordinates seems unwarranted. I am thinking not only of the traffic in noisy ideological memes, dissociated from the narrative frameworks that seemed to guarantee their reference, such as Obama's persistent allusions to the virtue and the suffering of the American middle classes, which seems about as functional for shoring up a vision of the bourgeois nation as was "they hate us for our freedoms" in securing the conviction of imperial benevolence. More fundamentally, Obama's progressivism was unreal from the get go, in the sense that it never corresponded to a discernible progressive vision for the United States either within or beyond its own borders. Obama urged no retreat from the war on terror and cited no commitment to rescind Patriot Act provisions, and while he promised to bring the occupation of Iraq to a close, he pledged escalation of the war in Afghanistan. Aside from his preoccupation with the plight of the middle classes, he cited no concern with matters of social and economic inequality more broadly (the ranks of service workers, migrant laborers, day-jobbers, and other low-wage earners would have to look after themselves), nor did Obama draw the link between the destruction of the social safety net, the collapse of public infrastructure, and the ever-rising levels of corporate welfare. And yet, *incredibly*, this was the progressive, grassroots candidate? As Jeffrey St. Clair rightly observes, "His vaguely liberal political ideology remained opaque at the core. Instead of an over-arching agenda, Obama delivered facile jingoisms proclaiming a post-racial and post-partisan America. Instead of radical change, Obama offered simply managerial competence" (2011, 3).

Of course, St Clair's account cannot explain why the promise of Obama's 2008 candidacy was so keenly felt, unless (again) we imagine a deeply incompetent voter, so steeped in "anti-egalitarianism" or, perhaps, so diminished in her capacity to assess a political program as to misrecognize the interests and institutions represented in the Obama campaign. Rather, I would suggest that Obama's agenda was never the point—never the object of attachment for that *other* segment of the imperiled bourgeoisie sunk, not in *ressentiment*, but in melancholy, who flocked to the campaign in droves and rechristened it a "movement."[5] The "movement" status of the campaign was an effect of its much-cited organizational structure, the "grassroots," community-centered organization of volunteer campaigners that was at least as much the object of liberal/left commentary as any element of the candidate's agenda, an organizational structure that found additional warrant in Obama's own, oft-cited "community activist" beginnings and crucially, in his African American identity, which forged the link between the "community activist" of the 1980s and the Civil Rights movement of the 1960s. Racial affiliation and personal narrative authenticated the grassroots campaign organization, which—quite apart from the candidate's political record or professed agenda—was itself the signifier of "hope" and "change." Indeed, when skeptics pressed supporters about the substance and the limits of Obama's progressivism, supporters' faith in the genuinely alternative quality of his candidacy hinged almost invariably on the *form* of the campaign apparatus. The innovation and the brilliance of the 2008 Obama campaign was to offer the left-liberal electorate a simulacral alternative, steeped in the affect and iconicity of mass social movement, but absent the political referent. The campaign was *not* the *representative* organ for a set of actually existing political possibilities for progressive change, which were at that point effectively foreclosed by the privatization of public office—by the increasingly deregulated flows of cash from corporate and other large private donors via lobbyist groups, PACs, and other entities into the coffers of both national party organizations and office holders, and also by the revolving door between public office and lucrative appointments to governing boards, consultancies, and other positions in or closely bound to donor organizations, which over the past several decades has produced a fusion of institutional cultures across state agencies and private enterprise, especially financial institutions.[6] Under these circumstances, it was hard to imagine how a grassroots social movement could possibly emerge and flourish *at the level of national electoral politics*. By 2008, the prospect of a bottom-up presidential campaign, always a rarity, was effectively dead: *this* was the elephant in the room of Obama's first presidential run. In the face of its actual impossibility, the architects of the campaign revived grassroots politics as virtuality—as a self-contained, deferentialized world of left identification and feeling. As an added bonus, progressive voters actually paid for the service, ponying up, according to the Federal Election Commission figures, roughly half of Obama's $659-million post-nomination war chest.[7] At the same time, of course, the other half of Obama's campaign monies—totaling, in themselves nearly four times the amount of the $85 million in public campaign funding he declined—represented larger donations, and one need hardly immerse oneself in alarmist right-wing speculation about illicit foreign donors and repeat anonymous giving to recognize that the Obama campaign was all about big money or that the entire infrastructure of the two party system was by this point so thoroughly saturated with corporate dollars and corporate personnel that no one even marginally committed to a progressive agenda of serving public interests and protecting public wealth could attain major political office.

But my argument is not that the electorate was duped or that the Obama campaign strategically misdirected voters' attention. To the contrary, the campaign was exactly what it claimed to be—including, crucially, an address to liberal and progressive voters reeling from the shock and awe of the two-term Bush presidency. Only this address never entailed the promise even of a moderately progressive political agenda in the White House, nor indeed did it operate in the register of promises and their redemption, of the present (re)production and regulation of futurity. Rather, what the Obama campaign offered immediately—in the moment—was a derealized progressive politics—an arena for the inhabitation of liberal/left political desires that was not a lie so much as a zone of discrete alterity, standing in a nonreferential relation to the state, where such desires could and would have no part in the determination of its policies and practices, and so, too, to the wider world on which these policies and practices weigh. Yet to say that Obama's progressivism was unreal is not to claim that it was inconsequential, a mere distraction, while the "real" political agenda was transacted elsewhere, behind closed doors. I am arguing instead that the unreality of Obama's progressivism—indeed, the proliferating unrealities of politics in the United States today—are an index to the wider disintegration of a "real world" orientation. If a realist politics labors to construct an anterior world to which "we"—a nation, a hegemonic bloc, a mass public—are fundamentally bound as the ground and object of our thought and actions, a post-realist politics unbinds across the board, freeing elites as well as voters from the obligation to abide by the measure of a common, given world.

Behind the closed doors of the campaign strategy session or the congressional hearing room, in other words, we find strategists and legislators no less committed to seemingly fantastic propositions than the reviled "low-information" voter. Taibbi makes this point explicitly in *The Great Derangement*, when he takes a brief hiatus from his infiltration of a Texas evangelical movement to cover the Senate debates over an Iraq supplemental appropriations bill:

> The driving motivation of all Washington politicians is to quell or deflect [voters'] demands] . . . and this is visible even in such a terrible, immediate emergency as the Iraq war, when one would think that some kind of civic instinct would kick in, for five minutes or so at least. But no: instead a newly conquering congressional majority armed with a fresh mandate essentially spent its first year in office trying to stay on the right side of public anger while maintaining business as usual; it was very plain that the party viewed its end-the-war mandate as a burden, not a privilege. (2009, 150)

By the measure of their popular mandate to end the war, and the emergency of a massively failed occupation that has neither streamlined reconstruction nor stabilized the region for U.S. interests (its apparent aims), even as it incurred devastating human loss and monetary expense, the liberal Democrats' ready capitulation to the congressional hawks appears incomprehensible. But such a measure posits a mass social organism that encompasses the rulers and the ruled—so that the interests of the dominant fractions must be tallied on the broader scale of social losses and gains. In this modern context, politics is the struggle over the material and symbolic means to manage the difference between particular and general interests. The ruling elements rule insofar as their particular aspirations are understood and felt to correspond with a mass social interest. Politics is the practice of hegemony, in other words: it is the production of mass identification on the ground of fundamentally differentiated relations to capital. To dwell "in the real world" (rather than succumb to mass psychosis) is to accede to this form of politically mediated sociality—or conversely, I am proposing, *it is the hegemonic character of power that defines the political value and function of the "real world"* as the continuum in which "we" live in simultaneous proximity, according to generalized forms of reckoning within fixed (because reproducible) parameters.

But contemporary politics in the United States are simply not of that world any longer. The congressional hearing room is not an institutional space for calibrating the ruling political and economic interests with the broadly national interest with which it must appear to converge. In such a world of hegemonic politics, the Democrats' stand in favor of withdrawal would have corresponded to a "real world" calculation—a calculation that the societal costs of the war in Iraq had come to exceed the prospects for accumulation and control that originally impelled the invasion. But the congressional hearing room in which the electoral mandate was a "burden" is better understood as a virtual reality, a self-referential domain of political reckoning. This is (obviously) not to deny that the decisions made and the policies implemented there have decisive and routinely dire effects on the conditions of life for broad segments of the population inside and outside the United States, but simply to observe that this venue enables forms of political calculation, algorithms of cost and benefit, that consider those effects extraneous—outside the purview of the calculation. Even as the rule of capital and its political agents persists, the form of domination changes: rather than craft a popular mandate by aligning capital's aspirations with a (seemingly) general social interest, domination proceeds more and more by shattering the fiction of a social organism. In place of aggregation, domination works by dissociation—no center, only proliferating margins (or "outlands"), constructed for whatever impulses and whatever calculus enable and animate its denizens.

I am arguing that power increasingly takes the form of declaring autonomy from having to live in anyone else's world, and so it follows, as well, that the (mimetic) declaration of autonomy—the retreat from normative political assumptions—becomes the prevailing modality for the disenfranchised electorate to articulate political aspirations. We are reminded of what we should probably not have lost sight: that the "real world" is not a transhistorical given, but an invention specific to (and decisive for) modern, horizontal sociality and the incorporative aims of hegemonic power—specific to and decisive for the political life of the masses.[8] Insofar as the state is reimagined, no longer the proxy of a sovereign national people, but a managerial power dedicated to the concentration of capital among an ever smaller fraction of elites, there is scant political value to the ideological production of an inclusive reality and of the relatively fixed, relatively durable reference points that sustain it. If power is no longer bound up in the (re)production of mass social entities, why pursue the quite extraordinary labor of fabricating the world in which such an entity can exist? Why not accede to the proliferation of (un)realities in which people live and aspire? At the same time, to suggest that the masses have been cut loose from an anchoring political reality is hardly to propose that they fall outside the managerial intentions of the state. Quite the contrary, from the hyper-production of polls to the exacerbated surveillance of the population and the elimination of legal protections and the rights of due process, the masses are being minutely and obsessively monitored.[9] But the form of the state's interest has shifted. The struggle is not for hearts and minds, but data sets: polling numbers, surveillance footage, browser histories, and the further reams of information that can be mined, assembled into so many profiles of public proclivities and public menace. The public called forth from the data streams—including the "electorate" emerged from the endless political polls—is, of course, perfectly unreal, a model of no actual or original thing.

Thus the incorporative political project of modernity has yielded to its obverse at the most fundamental level: political power no longer presents as the capacity to norm public sentiment, to bind the popular masses both broadly and deeply to a certain vision of the world and to specific forms and spheres of self-expression that will—supposedly—secure their place within it. Instead, it seems to me, we are moving into a context where the interests of the ruling elements are most aptly served by decomposing the social body and permitting us to dwell in whatever (un)realities of our own devising. Lawrence Grossberg has observed how citizenship is historically keyed to the conditions of wage labor and suggested how transformations in the value of labor have implications for the forms of political subjectivity. "If we are witnessing a revaluation of labor, then we most look also at this struggle in relation to the complex cultural economy through which labor has been articulated to identity," he writes, and goes on to consider how citizenship has served historically as a site (one among several) for the compensatory self-realization of alienated labor (2000,70).[10] Grossberg's argument hinges on a claim that neoliberalism entails a "move from labor to money as the source of value" (2000, 66).[11] Bracketing the more contentious elements of Grossberg's analysis (his discussion of value detached from labor opens on a much larger debate about the status of production and productive labor in an information economy), I note simply that the mobility of capital permits a fundamental disregard for the reproduction of the worker (there are always more workers *somewhere*), that the ranks of the formally employed are receding not expanding, and that credit rather than income is now the engine of consumption. From this vantage, one might well anticipate that the impetus to an incorporative political project—formal equality as (self-)proprietors palliating material inequalities of property—has dissipated. As Grossberg reminds us, the citizen-worker is an articulation for the *recruitment* of a population to the ranks of wage labor and unravels at the point where populations compete for the relative privilege of their exploitation.

At the core of the novel political situation Taibbi intuits, signaled to all appearances by the exacerbated lunacy of the electorate, is the complex de-linking of the terms that comprise an organizing historical relay between personhood, property, and rights. Along those lines, I have been arguing that the lunacy signposts, not the pathology of the electorate but a transformation in the ends and practices of government, are expressed (among other ways) in the decommissioning of a realist politics that aims at the production of a readable world. In such a world, derealization is a critical practice: we defect from the hegemonic view; we demonstrate that it is merely a view, and an inadequate one at that. But what is effective political protest when power operates *through* derealization—not by conscripting our participation in a reigning world view, but by rescinding our reference points and scattering us to the winds of fear, loathing, delirium, and despair?

Market Logics

In this way, I come more or less to the inverse of Wendy Brown's conclusion that neoliberalism represents a new calculus of political reason, an economic rationality that comes to pervade the domain of the political, introducing new criteria of legitimacy (the state's legitimacy is now tied to "sustaining and foster[ing] the market") and "eras[ing] the discrepancy between economic and moral behavior by configuring morality entirely as a matter of rational deliberation about costs, benefits, and consequences [such that] . . . the rationally calculating individual bears full responsibility for the consequences of his or her action, no matter how severe the constraints" (2005, 41, 42). Brown is emphatic that neoliberalism is a normative enterprise, because it understands economic rationality as having to be cultivated: "Importantly, then, neoliberalism involves a normative rather than an ontological claim about the pervasiveness of economic rationality and it advocates the institution building, policies, and discourse development appropriate to such a claim. Neoliberalism is a constructivist project: it does not presume the ontological givenness of a thoroughgoing economic rationality for all domains of society but rather takes as its task the development, dissemination, and institutionalization of such a rationality" (2005, 40–41). So Brown situates neoliberalism as supplanting one form of (bourgeois) normative political culture with another, predicated on cost-benefit analysis and its allied values: efficiency, accountability, optimization (best practices), risk-assessment, and so forth. Brown's abject citizen, then, belongs to this new norm—even as her sensibilities are assessed by reference to the norms of an older liberalism in which she has been unschooled.

In many respects, Brown has proven one of the most acute and tenacious critics of the articulation of capital to government we call neoliberalism, expanding Michel Foucault's rather sketchy—and sometimes cryptic—insights into an elaborated understanding of neoliberal discourses and institutional practices. But inasmuch as neoliberalism forwards a vision of the social as *a series* of self-optimizing entities, it engenders not a new form of normative culture, but one in which the fragmentation and multiplication of social and political (un)realities are normalized. Neoliberal "values" may be ubiquitous, as Brown suggests, but they have *no normative social referent*: Costly or beneficial *for whom*? Accountable *to what supervision*? Efficient in relation *to what parameters*? The answers to these crucial questions about the social meaning and effects of neoliberal values are left largely to the determination of the particular organizations or individuals who embody them, so that neoliberalism in fact dissolves the very concept of the norm, of the disciplinary measure to which *the ensemble* of social agents and institutions adheres. Implementing control without discipline, neoliberalism cedes to a disincorporated "us" the task of deciding *in what domain* (lived collectively with which others? oriented to what ends?) we tally up the cost and benefits, reap the fruits of our "good choices," or the burden of our bad ones. The capacity to *construct the environment* in which we reckon our gains and losses is now the mark of social agency.

We might consider the difference between a normative and a normalized function by reference to the operations of the market from which, as Foucault and Brown alike contend, a generalized neoliberal rationality derives. As Doug Henwood observes, "The U.S. financial system performs dismally at its advertised task, that of efficiently directing society's savings toward their optimal investment pursuits. The system is stupefyingly expensive, gives terrible signals for the allocation of capital, and has surprisingly little to do with real investment," by which Henwood means investment in actual productive enterprise. "Over the long haul," he notes, "almost all corporate capital expenditures are internally financed, through profits and depreciation allowances" (1998, 3). Simply put—and surely, by now, the point seems too apparent to belabor—by any general *social* measure, markets are utterly *inefficient* and dysfunctional. At the same time, of course, they have shown themselves remarkably efficient at the upward redistribution of social wealth, though this endeavor has required the effective privatization of government institutions, which now function to indemnify major market players against the (otherwise) *market-shattering* effects of their financial speculations. Markets can be deemed "efficient" only if their task is to concentrate capital at the very apex of the social pyramid *and* if the accounting is performed within the customized (un)reality of the too-big-to-fail corporation that has absorbed (among other things) the agencies and institutions designed to regulate its doings. So we see the spectacular bonuses meted out to the architects of the mortgage crisis that immiserated millions, because in the virtual reality of the corporate boardroom, their choices were "rational" and "beneficial." But such a measure of "reason" and "benefit" will not travel—and indeed, from most any other vantage within the social field, the speculators' choices were both lunatic and criminal. To be sure, one need only remark the penetration of the discourse of economic reason into the spaces of everyday life—the workplace, the school, the neighborhood association, the support group, and so on—to concede its normality. But "efficiency" and "optimization" and the further array of neoliberal values commit us to *no standards of self-government*—to no general, organizing distinctions between legitimacy and illegitimacy, virtue and shame, productivity and waste, decency and perversity. Rather, the rule of the cost-benefit analysis seems to urge the proliferation of computational environments: it is not the consolidating ethos of a social world, but an invitation to *devise the frame of reference in which one's returns may be maximized.*

Inasmuch as neoliberalism is about the extension of market logics to other domains of life, it seems worth lingering for a moment longer on the relation of the market itself to the "real world," which seems now, as I am arguing, in retreat within the contexts of political life, certainly (though doubtless not exclusively) in the United States. This is, of course, a huge and contested question, usually framed as a debate about the relative importance of "immaterial" versus "material" production (is information capital bound up in material production? are services a separate sector from goods?) or sometimes, relatedly, in terms of the relation of finance to materiality. In a rejoinder to Fredric Jameson, Henwood provides a ready gloss on the terms of this debate, worth citing at length even though, or rather precisely because, he tends to frame both his own and Jameson's positions in starkly polarized terms. "All the weightless nostrums are represented" in Jameson's "Culture and Finance Capital," Henwood complains, and goes on to synthesize and rebut Jameson's claims as follows:

> [Jameson refer to] "profit without production"—in fact, the disappearance of production, except for "the two prodigious American industries

of food and entertainment"—and "globalization," defined "rather as a kind of cyberspace in which money capital has reached its ultimate dematerialization," as messages which pass instantly from one nodal point to another across the former globe, the former material world. Globalization has become the triumph of nothingness, and finance capital becomes "deterritorialized," and "like cyberspace can live on its own internal metabolism and circulate without any reference to any older type of content. . . ." It seems very old old-fashioned to point out a few facts about the apparently weightless, placeless capital thoroughly unmoored from the real. The world money of the 19th century, gold, though quite tangible, circulated without the imprint of any state; today's nonphysical monies need state entities like central banks and the IMF to guarantee and regulate them. . . . The alleged importance of the entertainment industries is a staple of both left and right discourse, with extravagant claims made about their rank in production and trade, but it's just not true. Motion pictures account for about 0.3% of U.S. GDP—half as large as the primary metal industries. . . . And though financial markets seem very fanciful, appearing detached not only from production but even from social relations, they are actually institutions that consolidate ownership and control among the very rich of the world. . . . Much of the damage done to Southeast Asia in 1997 and 1998 and to Mexico in 1994 and 1995 was done by allegedly weightless financial flows. (2003, 27–28)

Henwood's claims boil down to three: (1) production of real commodities still matches or outstrips the production of what we might call, following MitsuhiroYoshimoto, the production of image-commodities; (2) the more capital is virtualized—circulates in the form of so much information—the greater the importance of mediating state and private institutions to control the flow of money; and last but certainly not least (3) that "weightless," virtualized capital has very tangible material effects (not least the capacity to prostrate entire populations).

Henwood argues an important and in some respects indisputable counter both to the celebratory accounts of information capital and to critical accounts, like Jameson's, oriented too thoroughly, perhaps, to the discernment of the new. At the same time, the deregulation of the marketplace over the last several decades, alongside the emergence of techniques of flexible accumulation, both enables and reflects a sea change

in the organization and workings of capital that is too thoroughly down-
played in Henwood's emphasis on fundamental continuities. And ironically, much of what Henwood himself so meticulously documents (in
his books *Wall Street* and *After the New Economy*, as in his newsletter,
Left Business Observer) is the explosion of intricate new instruments of
financial capital and their effects. If profit is never entirely divorced from
production, as Henwood would insist, at the same time the financial op-
erators evince no concern to protect the profitability of the "underlying"
industry (such as internet commerce; housing). Just the reverse, this
form of accumulation depends on adroit temporal manipulation and
the extraction of surplus value before the *swift and inevitable* collapse
in the value of the commodity. Not only is financial investment rarely
routed to new productive enterprise, in other words, but it also operates
in ways fundamentally hostile to the health of productive industries.
While financial capital remains linked to production, the cadre of financial managers appears to operate on a plane quite remote from the
interests of producers, a situation intensified by the mind-bending number and complexity of the financial "instruments" devised to manage
time—nearly a hundred invented in the past century, ranging from "put-
table/adjustable tender bonds" to "synthetic convertible debt" to the now
infamous "collateralized mortgage obligations."[12] Indeed, as Henwood
observes, speculation now takes the form of increasingly byzantine bets,
and bets on bets, that suggest, "at the risk of anthropomorphizing social conventions, how money capital longs for exotic forms" (1998, 49).
Financial capital does not flow weightlessly through virtual spaces that
connect to nothing else, to be sure, but the cost-benefit analysis can be
reckoned *as if* it did, which is to say, that *the social relations of capital are
redrawn* as the financiers declare autonomy, operating without reference
to interests besides their own.[13] Finance capital proceeds less and less
as if the monies wagered were a representation of "real" values, in other
words, which signals a change, not in the nature of value, as though it
were finally become an ethereal thing—bubbles still burst, after all—
but rather a change in the social and political organization of capital.
Historically, it is the danger of explosive devaluations that supplies the
incentive for internal and especially external regulation of the financial market. The contemporary unleashing of finance capital follows not
simply from technologies of instantaneous transfer (communication

speed-up that opens the gateway to the creation of new financial instruments via new forms of sensitivity to time) but from the relation of capital to government, which is transformed from a regulative entity into a means for the indemnification of speculators via the private appropriation of public funds. If neoliberalism represents the extension of market logics to other domains, as is commonly asserted, then we do well to reflect that the market is never a discrete entity, but politically structured from the get-go and so anticipate that the (politically informed) derealization of market processes correlates with the (economically informed) derealization of political processes.[14]

The ascendance of a fully predatory capitalism, in other words, means the proliferation of the derealized worlds in which it operates. Politics is no longer the art of norming mass sentiment to confirm to the priorities and agendas of the dominant bloc—indeed, of a bloc that dominates precisely because it can produce the masses as the political referent for its policies. Politics becomes instead the art of running simulations, of redistributing the political life of the social body along so many nonintersecting planes. These simulations do not float free of materiality, of course, but they are not the re-presentation of what they must, therefore, maintain as a pre-constituted (referential) world. The simulation reverses the hierarchy, as the copy precedes the original. In this scenario, identities have subjects and iconographies have social movements. I argue that this is both the outcome and the condition of a situation in which capital has freed itself of the requirement to profit societies, just as government emancipates itself from the requirement to represent a sovereign people. To be sure, capital has never profited whole societies, but rather schooled societies in the ethos of property and accumulation; similarly, the institutions of the state have never represented populations, but rather cultivated that version of the national people that is represented and representable. But capital and state were themselves committed to the logic of these normative projects: they were bound by the requirement that they serve—appear to serve—at least this version of national prosperity and the common good. In the contemporary moment, the effort to consolidate, to constitute relatively homogeneous mass bodies, yields to a different organization of power, one in which the masses are essentially cut loose, relinquished to whatever strategies of economic survival and whatever political enthusiasms, even as and precisely because they are also minutely and constantly surveilled, profiled, risk-assessed, and interned.[15] This is not to deny that political discourse still traffics in tropes of national self-realization and collective futurity—*only to insist that political institutions and practices in the United States no longer have much of anything to do with the production and reproduction of this organic social world as referent.*

This is the basis of the split between the Reichs, Stiglitzes, and Soroses and the neoliberal profiteers. Advancing a liberal critique of capital from the standpoint of capital, as I suggest in chapter 2, the former are appalled at the complete disappearance of the long-term calculation dismayed at the ethos of disaster capitalism, the repudiation of a stabilizing, incorporative agenda, and the volatile consequences of abjecting billions of human beings. It is fascinating to watch how, in the context of the present emergencies, they appear, if not as Leftists, then at least as allies. Their curious repositioning on the political map suggests the difficulties and the perils of confronting derealization without nostalgia for the very institutions, touchstones, and protocols that we regarded, not so long ago, with quite considerable skepticism: rule of law; political reason, consensus, hegemony. Arguably, the left position in modernity is predominantly anti-realist: it refuses the givenness of the world, challenges the norms of political reason, pits itself against power's incorporative aim (even as it pursues its own mimetic, incorporative agendas). If these are the critical aspirations in and through which the Left has been formed, how do we approach the contemporary moment, in which the repertoire of left opposition is repurposed as strategies of economic and political domination? Lawrence Grossberg presses a similar concern, suggesting how "ironically, North Atlantic Modernity is being challenged most significantly . . . not by its explicit critics on the Left, but by neoliberal and neoconservative apparatuses attempting to restructure the forces of domination and exploitation themselves," and he goes on to recommend that "the cultural Left think beyond its current project of deconstructing the modern liberal subject within a theory of difference" (2000, 60). Likewise pondering the Left's ambivalent attachment to liberalism as object of critique, Wendy Brown cites the effects of losing what one never loved and cautions how "incorporating the death of a loathed object to which one was nonetheless attached often takes the form of acting out the loathed qualities of the object" (2005, 54). If the aim is something other than reasserting the value of liberal democracy in a capitalist order, she suggests, then the "idea that leftists must automatically defend liberal political values when they are on the ropes, while sensible from a liberal perspective, does not facilitate a left challenge to neoliberalism" (2005, 55). This is, perhaps, more easily said than done: How does one not agitate for rule of law in the face of indefinite detention, or murder by executive fiat, or corporate impunity for fraud, all of which have become status quo? How can one not insist on the world of demonstrable reality and rational argumentation when answering to the bizarre rantings of Tea Party fomenters? What would it mean to adopt a critical stance on the derealization of political life that *did not* take the form of advancing "objective" (real world) political claims? And above all, perhaps, what would it mean to imagine opposition outside the terms of hegemonic (and anti-hegemonic) power—opposition in the absence of a (re)constituted "people"?

Heavy Activism

One part of my aspiration for this chapter has been to show that the ground is shifting under us in ways that make it difficult to discern the possibilities for opposition. This is not to abdicate the task, but simply to recognize the radically unsettled terrain on which the elaboration of new forms of oppositional politics will transpire. How do we imagine practices of contestation that do not seem to depend in one way or another on resurrecting the forms of power we know to contest? In this section, I turn to Bruce Sterling's 1998 novel *Distraction* to suggest how the novel's speculative future provides an optic for thinking about the decomposition of the national body politic and the proliferation of self-styled autonomous political agents without nostalgia for the anterior organization of political modernity. Although ultimately, the novel's vision of an emergent political functionality seems to rest on the reintegration of a national government responsible to a recuperated notion of the broader, social good, *Distraction* lingers on the improvisational politics of its protagonists in their derealized present, which it manages to appreciate as something other than degraded.

Distraction envisions a near future (mid-twenty-first-century) United States in which many of the features of our own historical moment persist in amplified or fully elaborated form: the economy has crashed, due in part to the pirating of intellectual property; entire categories of professional labor—from programmers to dentists—have been rendered obsolete by technological advances, and joblessness is rampant and endemic; masses of the unemployed survive on the margins, as squatters, scavengers, and casual labor; the infrastructure of entire regions has collapsed (Louisiana is described as "underwater," the West as "on fire"); the perennial crisis has enabled the emergence of an entire system of ad-hoc governance, while the electoral process and the established structures of government persist, in the form of pure spectacle; polling is instantaneous, unceasing, and operates, like TV ratings, to constitute political celebrities and fan cultures. As the narrator observes, "The country now had two national governments, the original, halting, not-quite-superseded legal government, and the spasmodic, increasingly shrill declarations of the State-of-Emergency Cliques" (1998, 120).

In this world where, as one character puts it, "Money just doesn't need human beings anymore," a significant portion of the population has opted out of a money economy altogether (1998, 256). Confronted with the privatization of public space, the merciless invasion of interior life by consumer culture, and the pervasive loss of income, Americans by the millions develop new modes of self-organization along "lines . . . deeply orthogonal" to the established culture:

> Civil society shriveled in the pitiless reign of cash. As the last public spaces were privatized, it became harder and harder for American culture to breathe. Not only were people broke, but they were taunted to madness by commercials, and pitilessly surveilled by privacy-invading hucksters. An ever more aggressive consumer-outreach apparatus caused large numbers of people to simply abandon their official identities. (1998, 368–369)

One segment of this abandoned population becomes migratory. "Nomadism had once been the linchpin of human existence," the narrator muses; "it was settled life that formed the technological novelty. Now technology had changed its nonexistent mind" (1998, 369). When "the American people simply ceased to behave," many find prospects for subsistence and sociality in perpetual mobility. "They gathered to publically burn their licenses, chop up their charge cards, and hit the road.

The proles considered themselves the only free Americans" (1998, 369). By appropriating biotech that can fabricate nutrition bars from scrub grass, weeds, and other valueless materials, the novel's nomad proles live off roadside detritus, which they also use to fabricate the phones and laptops central to their wired, moneyless reputation economy (a non-geographical, networked-based status culture, in which people vie for "trust ratings").[16] "These were people who had rallied in a hoard and marched right off the map. They had tired of a system that had offered them nothing, so they had simply invented their own" (1998, 61). If the reversion to nomadism most emphatically signposts the dissolution of the social body in the novel, Sterling's representation of the nomad societies also insists that disaggregation is not the same thing as disorder. The proles are "a *lot* better organized than the government is," one character points out. "Organization is the only thing they've got!" (1998, 159).

Another segment of this prole population dwells in the interstices of urban space, by commandeering existing infrastructure and repurposing technologies. The resulting transformation of urban space is particularly advanced in Washington, D.C.:

> Nonviolent noncooperation had reached unheard-of strategic and tactical heights in the American capital. Its functional districts were privatized and guarded by monitors and swarms of private thugs, but huge sections of the city had surrendered to the squatters. . . . In many neighborhoods of Washington, the division of streets and houses had simply dissolved. Entire city blocks were abandoned to the protestors, who had installed their own plumbing, water systems, and power generators. Streets were permanently barricaded, swathed in camou nets and rain-streaked plastic sheeting. (1998, 160)

Elsewhere in the city, the squatters have appropriated plans originally developed by NASA with an eye to Mars colonization. This "most remarkable of Washington's autonomen" groups, known simply as "martians," answer the "studied nonreaction to their crazy grievances" by "resolv[ing] to act as if the federal government did not exist," meaning, among other things, that they treat the city's natural and built environment as so much common "raw material." Excavating beneath the Potomac, the squatters dehydrate the soil, compact it into bricks, and "construct an endless series of archways, tunnels, and kivas" (1998, 161). "Now NASA's ingenuity had borne amazing fruit and the streets of Washington were lavishly bumped and measled with martian settlements. Slums of compacted dirt, all glue and mazy airlocks, climbed straight up the walls of buildings, where they clung like the nests of mud-daubing wasps. There were excavation hills three stories high near Union Station, and even Georgetown was subjected to repeated subterranean rumblings" (1998, 161).

This new urban geography figures saliently in the novel when its central protagonist, Oscar, a political campaign manager turned Senate staffer, arrives in the capital for a committee meeting; he finds that the federal office building where the meeting is scheduled has "fallen into the hands of squatters," who, in addition to seizing the property, have fully digitized its contents, by installing a system that logs the presence and movements of people, animals, and household objects (1998, 162). Oscar admires how this universal tagging "made the contents of the building basically theftproof," though one effect of this "digital socialism" is to turn "inside out" the formerly privatized arenas of domestic human life, so that "bugged and safety-tagged" children live in hallways replete with toys, tools, and animals. But the squatters' seizure has *not* interrupted the building's operation as a venue of government. Arriving in Room 358, an apparent "sculptor's studio, reconstructed from a fire-blackened set of office cubicles," Oscar encounters the committee's secretary and tech support, who arrive in prole disguise, "their hair . . . dyed blue, their faces . . . streaked with nomad warpaint," business attire concealed by dirty caftans and overalls. They proceed to revamp the space for a teleconference, in which the handfull of on-site personnel who have arranged secure transportation to the meeting site confer electronically with staffers elsewhere. In the representation of the parasitical martian structures, the adaptation of public city space for human inhabitation, and the dual purpose socialist tenement–federal office building, *Distraction* envisions *not* the simple transfer of city space to a surplus population and the retreat of the powerbrokers to secure exurban enclaves, *nor*, indeed, the descent of planned urban environments into disorder (the urban proles are no less rigorously organized than their nomad counterparts), but rather a new urban infrastructure in which multiple, autonomous actors construct discrete, customized social worlds within adjacent or sometimes coterminous physical spaces.

Politics bears to established structures of governance in this world something of the same relation that the martian settlements bear to established civic infrastructure: an eruptive bumping and measling of political designs across the residual landscape of modern political infrastructures. The novel opens on the successful conclusion of Alcott Bambakias's campaign for the U.S. Senate under Oscar's savvy management; yet election to this dysfunctional and largely irrelevant body leaves Bambakias casting about for opportunities to enact the public political presence forged in the campaign. In a seemingly random series of events, Oscar, en route to East Texas to visit a federal science laboratory, reports to Bambakias about his travels in the backcountry, including an email on the predicament of a Louisiana Air Force Base that has lost its federal funding. Facing lack of pay and supplies, including water and heat, desperate base personnel have road-blocked the nearest interstate and staged a "bake sale," extorting hefty ransoms from hapless motorists in return for passage and French pastries. Bambakias seizes on this particular manifestation of the government's pervasive and advanced collapse and declares himself on hunger strike until the base's federal funding is restored. The brilliance of the gesture, as Oscar grows to appreciate, is its apparent rejection of a merely gestural, image-bound politics. "The Cambridge PR team had certainly done a thorough job surveilling the fasting Senator," Oscar observes. "Blood pressure, heartbeat, temperature, calorie consumption, borborygmus, bile production—there was no possible doubt about the raw authenticity of his hunger strike. The man's entire corpus had become public domain. Whenever Bambakias had a sip of his famine apple juice, a forest of monitors twitched and heaved across the country" (1998, 58). The protest proves as ineffectual as its target is arbitrary: federal funding is not restored, and the base is eventually commandeered by nomad proles, acting for Louisiana's rogue governor, Green Huey. Meanwhile, the emotionally fragile senator-elect succumbs under the pressure of fasting to full-blown bipolar disorder, to the point where his own chief of staff bluntly describes him as "toast." But a dissociated mental state is no impediment to the accumulation of political capital. "It's true—he's had a mental breakdown," Oscar concedes. "This is the problem: he starved himself half to death in a sincere protest, and now he's lost his mind. But our keyword here isn't 'crazy.' Our keywords are 'sincere' and 'protest'" (1998, 229). And true to Oscar's appraisal, Bambakias's iconic appeal rises as his orientation to reality erodes. Responding to a colleague who has asked whether the senator's condition might be stabilized with continued use of anti-depressants, Oscar enthuses:

> "Well, the treatments make great media copy. There's a huge Bambakias medical fandom happening, ever since his hunger strike, really. . . . They got their own sites and feeds. . . . Lots of get-well email, home mental-health remedies, oddsmaking on the death-watch. . . . It's a classic grass roots phenomenon. You know, T-shirts, yard signs, coffee mugs, fridge magnets. . . . I dunno, it's getting kind of out of hand." (1998, 245)

Bambakias's medical fandom is "grass roots" in precisely the way that Obama's 2008 campaign was "grass roots:" not because it stands for a popular mobilization of ordinary citizens who have discovered in the senator a representative of their perceived political interests, but because it comprises a virtual arena of political feeling to which ordinary citizens are drawn. (In the novel, these feelings are calibrated to the spectacle of hunger, dissociation, and bodily wasting, in which regard, of course, the similarity of Bambakias's fandom to Obama's "movement" ends.) From this perspective, Oscar's reference to "grass roots" mobilization is *not* cynical, but registers with indifference the shift from representative to simulacral politics that appears already completed and mundane in *Distraction*'s near future. Bambakias's mania and depression *represent* nothing, but they infuse a small, self-referential zone of affective communion in which his fandom has opted to dwell.

One meaning of the word "distraction," then, is supplied by Oscar's security chief, Kevin, an inveterate surveillance freak who laments the effects of encompassing surveillance:

> "We have no decency as a people and a nation, Oscar. We went too far with this technology, we lost our self-respect. Because this is media, man. It's evil, prying, spying media. But we want it and use it anyway, because we think we've got to be informed. *We're compelled to pay total attention to everything.*" (1998, 406–407, my emphasis)

In this saturated and saturating mediascape, politics is the competition for attention, a struggle against distraction (immersion in information flows and the diffusion of attention it entails) that proceeds *via* distraction (siphoning off attention into relatively discrete, relatively autonomous sites, feeds, and networks). The other meaning of distraction follows: there is no distinction—no ground for distinguishing—between political substance and political smoke, the "real" aim and the "diversionary" tactic. As Bambakias's hunger strike suggests, the political objective is an appearance, while the cultivation of the diversionary opportunity *is itself* the political yield. Along these lines, the major plot development of the novel concerns Oscar's phased takeover of the Texas laboratory for purposes that are, at best, fluid and emergent over the course of the narrative. Initially, his interest in the lab appears vaguely linked to Oscar's new position as a staffer on the Senate science committee, on which Bambakias is also slated to serve. So Oscar travels to the site on a kind of reconnaissance mission, though whether unofficially scouting the situation for Bambakias or investigating the facility so as to enhance his own prestige on the committee remains unclear. Barely arrived in Buna, with only the faintest sense of how the laboratory operates or the kinds of research it supports, Oscar announces to his assistant, Pelicanos, the beginning of a new "campaign":

> "It's going to be just like the campaign was. First, we're going to lowball expectations, because nobody will really believe we have a serious chance here. But then we're going to succeed on such a level—we're going to exceed expectations to such a huge extent—we're gonna bring so much firepower into this campaign that we just blow the opposition away."
>
> Pelicanos smiled. "That's you all over, Oscar."
>
> Oscar lifted one finger. "Here's the plan. We find the major players here, and we find out what they want, and we cut deals. We get our people excited, and we get their people confused. And in the end, we just out-organize anyone who tries to stop us. We just outwork them, and we swarm on them from angles they would never, ever expect, and never, ever stop, and we just beat them into the ground!" (1998, 35)

This speech is remarkable in a number of ways, not least because nothing anyone in the novel has said or insinuated suggests that Bambakias, the Science Committee, or any other "people" ("theirs" or "ours") actually *have* "expectations" for Oscar's exploratory visit, much less criteria for measuring "success." Oscar's determination to mobilize has no recognizable objective; the rallying cry precedes the cause, as the point of the mobilization is to generate the field in which an objective might (eventually) be imagined. In this sense, Oscar operates essentially like the nomad proles, bypassing (the elements of) a system that offers nothing in order to invent a situation where a tally of gains and losses becomes newly possible. Like the nomad proles, as well, Oscar traffics in "organization"—the management of people and resources, to be sure, but most fundamentally, the management of information that makes for the accelerated and intensified organization—the "swarming"—that gives Oscar the edge in this oddly evacuated and gratuitous "campaign."

Perhaps not surprisingly, then, the outcome of this operation is an alliance of research scientists and nomad proles, which Oscar creates when he enlists a nomad group, the Moderators, to help his faction seize and occupy the lab. "Am I the only person who sees the obvious here?" Oscar asks when the scientists balk at the presence of painted nomads wielding laptops made from straw. "You people have amazing commonalities. . . . They live exactly like you live—by their reputations. You are America's two most powerful noncommercial societies. Your societies are both based on reputation, respect, and prestige" (1998, 372–373). The alliance is possible, in other words, insofar as both scientists and proles operate within nonmonetary, trust-based social networks that can be therefore be made to communicate with each other, at least for the purpose of organizing economic and political life in the Buna lab. The outcome of Oscar's machinations turns out to be an *interesting disposition* of people and information, about which the operative question is not "What does it represent?" or even "How can it act in and on the world?" but rather, "Is it functional?" "How long do you expect all this to last?" a drug-stabilized Bambakias asks Oscar on a visit to Buna toward the novel's end. "This?" asks Oscar, evasively. "Whatever it is that you've created here," Bambakias retorts. "What is it, exactly? Is it a political movement? Maybe it's just one big street party" (1998, 473). Bambkias proceeds with escalating hostility:

> "When one network meets another that's set up along different lines, they feud. They kill each other. . . . Now you've made these people aware of their mutual interest with the scientific research community. Another group of people who basically live outside the state, outside of econom-

ics. . . . We no longer hope that science will give us utopia or even a real improvement. Science just adds more factors in the mix, and makes everything more unstable. We've given up on our dispossessed, too. We have no illusion we can employ them, or keep them docile with bio-bread or more cyber-circuses. And now you've brought these two groups together and they've become a real coalition. . . . What now, Oscar? What are they going to do now? What becomes of the rest of us?" (1998, 475)

Bambakias worries about this "coalition" because he is apprehensive about the appearance of a new autonomy. The question of what this coalition will "do" is not so much a question of what it will do *to* "the rest of us"; the concern is precisely what will become of the rest of us *left on our own*, living in proximity but without organizational ties to either proles or scientists. Yet tellingly, as Bambakias's own account concedes, "we" have already given up on the dispossessed, as well as on the brokers of scientific progress; from this perspective, his reproach to Oscar is *not* that he has engineered additional defections from what is left of the nation-state, but rather that he has discerned in the common form of proles' and scientists' estrangement the possibility of configuring a radically new particularity that cuts across (seemingly entrenched) class lines. Oscar is put out by Bambakias's interrogation—"Hell, I don't know!" he protests—which seems to hold him to norms of political calculation that are no longer meaningful, norms geared to the reproduction of a generalized (non-network-specific) "we."

Distraction envisions the practice of political life after the dissolution of a national people—after the collapse of the civil and governmental institutions that sustained it—and on this new terrain, Oscar recognizes, politics is no longer about securing the form of a mass political subject. His task as an organizer—someone who manages "campaigns"—is not to organize particularities so as to stake a position in a broader social field, but simply to organize particularities according to *whatever* internal calculus—whatever ethos and whatever protocols—will enable their political self-elaboration. In Oscar's preferred formulation, the point is to determine what is "doable," *not* "doable" within a pre-established political order of licit and illicit action, but "doable" insofar as it *imposes* some way of reckoning value, of marking a political good in the absence of any encompassing institutionalized determination of progress or prosperity or the reasoned behavior of political subjects to these ends. Even as Oscar appears to operate within the residual infrastructure of national government, his understanding of political organizing finally aligns him with the nomad proles and others who bump and measle the ruined terrain of the nation-state with smaller collectives: hordes, occupations, or fandoms living by "orthogonal" principles of communal self-realization and civic virtue.

So it is notable that we find Oscar in the novel's opening chapters baffled by and thoroughly fixated on a particular prole action, captured on video, which he rewatches again and again: the ransacking of a federal bank in Worcester, Massachusetts. The action strikes him as "absolute madness"— the sudden coalescence of a mob, its bare-handed destruction of the bank, then equally sudden disappearance. Sometime later, he discovers that his newly hired security specialist, Kevin, was present at the event:

"Who ordered all that?"

"Nobody. Nobody ever orders it. That was a fed bank, they were running cointelpro out of it. The word bubbled up from below, some heavy activism accreted, they wasp-swarmed the place. And once they trashed it, they all ducked and scattered. You'd never find any 'orders,' or anyone responsible. You'd never find the software. That thing is a major-league hit-server. It's so far underground that it doesn't need eyes anymore."

"Why did you do that, Kevin? Why would you risk doing a crazy thing like that?"

"I did it for the trust ratings. And because, well, they stank." Kevin's eyes glittered. "Because the people who rule us are spooks, they lie and they cheat and they spy. The sons of bitches are rich, they're in power. They hold cards over all of us, but they *still* have to screw people over the sneaky way. They had it coming. I'd do it again, if my feet were a little better." (1998, 258)

For Oscar, the fascination of this episode lies in the manifestation of a new kind of political agency, coordinated, purposeful—in fact, quite remarkably so—but acting on a fully internalized set of priorities that seem not to communicate with the broader world, even as it rearranges that world in material ways. From the first, the Worcester mob intrudes its difference on Oscar's rationalist understanding of politics as chess, "curing him" of the metaphor. "Because this phenomenon on the tape was a not a chess piece," Oscar thinks. "It was on the public chessboard all right, but it wasn't a rook or a bishop. It was a wet squid, a swarm of bees. It was a new entity that pursued its own orthogonal agenda and vanished into the silent interstices of a deeply networked and increasingly nonlinear society" (1998, 4). Operating in a world of disaggregated social fractions, Oscar is both transfixed by what he rightly understands as the novelty of this new entity, and yet remains palpably nostalgic for "national reform . . . so we can have a system with a decent role for everyone" (1998, 256). As we encounter him in the first half of the novel, he holds to the necessity of a controlling ideological vision vested in political office, even as his own "campaigns" seem increasingly to operate otherwise. Debating Kevin's suggestion of enlisting the Moderators to manage the Buna lab, Oscar initially baulks: "It's not doable," he tells Kevin, "because there are *no brakes*. There are no brakes because I can't control the course of events. I don't have the authority. I'm just a Senate staffer!" (1998, 283). "That's never stopped you so far," Kevin counters, provoking Oscar's shrill rejoinder: "Well, I don't like your idea because it's bad ideology. I'm a Federal Democrat. We're a serious-minded Reform party. We're not a revolutionary vanguard" (1998, 283). Of course, Oscar goes on to orchestrate precisely the alliance of proles and scientists that his ideological commitments to national reconstruction would preclude. Along these lines, the novel can be read as marking an evolution in Oscar's feeling for the "doable," which migrates from its original moorings in a kind of realpolitik that sits mildly askew of his reformist sensibilities into more fundamentally autonomist waters.

In this process, the "doable" shifts from a real-world calculation bound to the idea of a general subjection to dominant powers into a simulacral political calculus geared to the creation of self-referential political worlds. As Oscar perceives, the attack on the bank is *not* a move on a public game board. The proles (or rather the prole server) target(s) the bank as a matter of deep-rooted political *orientation*—the fed bank is antithetical to prole constructions of value—but not as part of a coordinated effort to bring down the edifice of finance capital, or to oust the spooks from power (though no doubt, the proles would be happy enough to see those things occur). The attack on the bank is not a bid for political advantage in an integrated social field, but a moment of communal self-elaboration—not about opening a front in a war on autocratic power, but about testing and developing the strength of the prole network, by marking its capacity to exist and operate *on its own terms* within the very material precincts of the system it leaves behind. The attack is a declaration of autonomy by a collective that has fled the ruined nation, emigrated not to another geographic location, but to an alternate, noncommunicating social plane. As he learns how to understand the Worcester video and the redrawing of the political field it indexes, Oscar's sense of the "doable" veers from a realist orientation to an already constituted world governed by relatively fixed, relatively durable rationalities to an appreciation that other, perhaps better worlds are possible in the derealized spaces of autonomous organizing. In this way, *Distraction* traces and elucidates the connections between the ruination of political modernity and the derealization of political life as it comes to transpire on a set of nonintersecting social planes.

While Oscar's trajectory in the novel pivots on his growing comprehension and embrace of prole sensibilities, interestingly, at the novel's end, Sterling can envision only a scenario in which this political landscape of functionally autonomous, antagonist collectivities has been set on the path to reintegration: through the device of a staged military conflict with (of all things) the Netherlands (one of the more strident of this future world's sinking nations), the president, a Native American lumber baron from Colorado named Two Feathers, wrests control from the emergency government and institutes the "New Normalcy":

> A new tax structure would soak the ultra-rich and come down brutally on carbon-dioxide production. Derelict and underused buildings would be nationalized en masse, then turned over to anyone willing to homestead them. Derelict cities and ghost towns—and there were many such, especially in the West—would be scraped clean from the face of the earth and replanted in fast-growing trees. Roadblocking was henceforth to be considered an act of piracy and to be punished without mercy by roving gangs of the CDIA [Civil Defense Intelligence Agency], who, since they were all former roadblockers of the most avid temperament, could be expected to know just how to put an end to the practice. . . . A constitutional amendment was offered to create a fourth branch of government for American citizens whose "primary residences were virtual networks."

America's eight hundred and seven federal police agencies would be streamlined into four. (1998, 485)

In a move that exactly duplicates Oscar's own, Two Feathers assembles the new, federal, all-volunteer Civil Defense Intelligence Agency (CDIA), from the gangs of nomad proles, who provide expert security against the very sort of dangers they themselves present to the operations of a re-emergent centralized power and, inasmuch as they work without pay, place no burden on the federal budget. Crucially, Two Feathers's national reorganization is marked by the political resuscitation of realist politics. To this end, he attempts to recruit Oscar as a "White House congressional liaison to interface with the current party structure." In particular, he proposes, Oscar will "shake the radicals and crazies out, and agglomerate them into an up-wing." Oscar queries:

> "I'm not down-wing, sir?"
>
> "Oscar, there *is* no down-wing without the up-wing. It doesn't work unless I mold my own opposition. . . . The up-wing has to be brilliant. It has to be genuinely glamorous. It has to be visionary, and to almost make sense. *And it has to never, ever quite work out in real life.*" (1998, 517, my emphasis)

Yet at its best—and outside the imposition of this dubious closure—the novel discerns the terrain of a post-hegemonic politics, which it *declines* to frame, along the lines Brown suggests, as the citizenry's political debasement. Less an allegory than an exercise in a more literal kind of world-building (Oscar's America is not an uncanny elsewhere, but a meticulous elaboration of present forces in the direction of a possible future), *Distraction* aims to reckon with the prospects for political subjectivity after the demise of the popular sovereign and the atrophy of the institutions that were the condition of this entity's historical emergence. In its attention to the hypermediated quality of life (in a word, to the "distraction") that seems to foreclose the prospect of acting in and on "the real world," the novel veers towards Taibbi's preoccupation with the predominance of "escapist lunacy." But it also, acutely, understands the derealization of political life as the effect of dissociated social and political worlds occupying coterminous geographic space, and the collapse of political modernity as a new condition of possibility.

6

Refugees from This Native Dreamland

Perhaps inevitably, this book ends with a set of reflections on the Occupy Wall Street movement, broadly hailed on the Left as the inexplicably postponed, much-anticipated rising of "the people," engaged in the mass withdrawal of consent from the (in)actions of the state and the profiteers it sanctions and protects. In the months during and following the autumn of 2011, as I shared my thinking on this project and my work in progress with students and colleagues at home and on the road, my ruminations on the end of popular sovereignty were met with a ready and singular rejoinder: But what of Occupy? What, indeed. Here at last, it seemed, was a left social movement that was authentically "grassroots": the popular sovereign delegitimating with a flourish the massively corrupted institutions of (non)democratic governance. Yet in their practice and their aspiration, the Occupiers encamped in lower Manhattan and across major and some smaller U.S. cities were more reminiscent of Bruce Sterling's proles, martians, and other "autonomen groups" than of mid-twentieth-century social movement actors (figure 6.1). In this chapter, I argue that Occupy Wall Street registers the dismantling of "the people" as a modern, mass political subject and functional ideological reference point, even as it labors to bring out alternative imaginaries, forums, and forms of collective political agency. My interest lies neither in championing OWS, nor in charting its deficiencies, especially inasmuch as either investment tends to imply that we have ready to hand a calculus for assessing left political strategies. Both the celebrants and detractors of OWS, in other words, tend to take the measure of the occupation by reference to a preexisting view of what constitutes viable left political practice. Yet what seems most significant and compelling about OWS is the organizers' intuition that our measures of political efficacy are themselves in crisis. No doubt, we know to tally our gains and losses in opposing forms of hegemonic power, as they aspire to norm the terms of public debate and produce broad popular assent to the pursuit of elite

Figure 6.1. Zucotti Park, Lower Manhattan, October 2, 2011. Protesters at the media center work on laptops powered by a portable generator. "Organization is the only thing they've got."

interests. But how do we measure ground gained against forms of political power that are indifferent to the disposition of our hearts and minds and that confront opposition through technologies of mass surveillance and securitization, which are also, in themselves, a significant source of capital accumulation? From this vantage, the interesting question about OWS is not so much what it gets right or wrong, but how it struggles to imagine the form and scale of politics itself.

No Demands

"Dear 1%," reads one of the more widely circulated Occupy Wall Street posters, "We fell asleep for a while. Just woke up. Sincerely, the 99%." In line with this brief and compelling narrative, many active Occupiers, as well as sympathetic demonstrators and left observers have tended to frame the movement as the resurgence of a temporarily incapacitated citizenry. What Occupy Wall Street signifies, or signified—it is not entirely clear whether the movement is dormant or dead—is in many respects too early to say; for those who suspect that its interest lies in its staying power, or at least the staying power of other movements *like* Occupy and perhaps modeled on it, the question is how Occupy or its analogs will present five years from now, or in a decade. Yet it seems impossible not to address Occupy in a necessarily premature and speculative fashion, if only because it appears to represent the fulfillment of a prospect long deferred: the popular insurrection that oppression and misrule will inevitably spark, a "civil revival," in the words of one protester, in which the Occupiers are "becoming citizens" (quoted in *Rolling Stone* 2011, 61). This idea of civic "becoming" cuts at least two ways, suggesting the need to relearn what has been forgotten (becoming *citizens*) and also the aspiration to remake the category through new practices of active inhabitation (*becoming* citizens). The formulation conspicuously invokes earlier historical contexts—the bourgeois revolutions in which subjects became citizens—yet in so doing, also remarks the different, seemingly attenuated scale of transformative politics in the present moment. Within those earlier historical contexts, the political power of "the people" is bound up in the double menace of their becoming *and* unbecoming citizens, the prospect of their political ascension within the structures of representative democracy *and* their decomposition into the lawless mob that aims not at political recognition, but at the destruction of the power to confer or withhold that recognition. In the contemporary United States, it is no longer the people who confront the state in the always twinned guises of sovereign and mob, but rather it is the state and its allied institutions that dissolve the people into an undisciplined multitude, or at any rate, no longer act to avert this dissolution. This is the reason that today the practice of "becoming citizen" is not (yet) a confrontation with state power, but an attempt to repurpose the category of "citizen," which is available for reconstruction precisely because the operations of the state seem no longer to require the existence of a people.

Historically, of course, to speak of civic mobilizations in the United States is to presuppose and affirm the relation of the sovereign populace to the representative state. In this modern context, "the people" is necessarily a national people—comprised of citizens, the dependents of citizens (women and children), and (or) segments of the population pressing claims for (full) citizenship. Even from this broadly sketched perspective, it seems dubious to understand Occupy as the revival of a slumbering citizenry, not only because most elements of the movement, to their credit, reject the premise of an exclusionary nationalism and embrace citizens, as well as legal and undocumented immigrants, but also, and perhaps more profoundly, because it is not clear that OWS represents a demand for recognition, much less a demand addressed specifically to the institutions of the state. Indeed, the absence of specific demands was a source of left consternation from the get-go, mitigated by the insight that the consensus-based operations of the movement's general assemblies was bound to delay the production and publication of demands. Predictably, there was no shortage of academic sympathizers willing to educate the Occupiers on the need for demands or on the optimal form these demands might take, as though the activists had simply overlooked this point, although from the first, the most perceptive commentators began to discern that the focus of Occupy was directed *inward*, on the movement's political self-fashioning.[1] In Douglass Rushkoff's canny evaluation,

> Occupy is anything but a protest movement. That's why it has been so hard for news agencies to express or even discern the "demands" of the growing legions of Occupy participants around the nation, and even the world. Just like pretty much everyone else on the planet, occupiers may want many things to happen and other things to stop, but the occupation is not about making demands. They don't want anything from you, and there is nothing you can do to make them stop. That's what makes Occupy so very scary and so very promising. It is not a protest, but a prototype for a new way of living. . . . [Occupiers] are not interested in debate . . . but consensus. They are working to upgrade that binary, winner-takes-all, 13th century political operating system. And like any software developer, they are learning to "release early and release often. . . ." This is not a game that someone wins, but rather a form of play that is successful the more people get to play, and the longer the game is kept going. (2011, 3, 4)

From this perspective, Occupy stands as the epilogue to modern democratic citizenship, rather than its continuation. If Occupy is the awakening of the people, as the placard insists, it is of a people who now longer exist at the level of political institutions, and so find themselves compelled to devise other arenas in which collectively to conceive

Figure 6.2. People's Library, Occupy Wall Street, 2011.

and cultivate modes of political identification and political agency. This agency appears in—and is produced through—the capacity to simulate an autonomous reality, in a gesture that mimes, even as it repudiates, the practices of elite power. The strategy of Occupy is about the production of virtual realities in the (erstwhile) public spaces so pivotal to the cultures of democratic nationalism (figure 6.2). The circumstance that occupation on this model requires exceptional proficiency in the material practices of urban camping—that the entire enterprise rests on specific forms of material labor and exchange, as well as affective labor and structures of political organization—stands as a salient reminder that virtual constructs are self-referential, but not (necessarily) immaterial.

As Chris Hedges has observed, the core of Occupy—those who launched the encampments—are comprised of people living off the grid, outside the formal economy, "traveler types," in the self-description of one, practiced street dwellers and squatters with anarchist leanings and no interest "in the traditional political process" (2011, 2). While in various locations and for various durations a much more heterogeneous contingent has supported the movement at the street level—eating, sleeping, or working in the encampments—the initial project to occupy and re-purpose existing infrastructure was imagined and begun by dissident drifters. Hedges himself is committed to situating this core—and, by extension, aspects of the wider Occupy movement—in the tradition of anarchist politics and *lumpenproletariat* mobilizations, citing Bakunin's rejoinders to Marx and the value of theory forged in committed activism, or "fierce physical struggle" (2011, 4). Indeed, in Hedges's rather sweeping account of both socialist and anticolonial revolution in the twentieth century, Bakunin's vision is supposedly affirmed, as in every instance, Hedges avers, the "alliance of an estranged class of intellectuals with dispossessed masses creates the tinder . . . for successful revolt" (2011, 4–5). Yet in many respects, Hedges's account of Occupy's drifter core is more in line with Rushkoff's analysis than his own, insofar as it makes central to the movement's genesis a group whose politics *is* the practice of an alternate "way of living," predicated on underconsumption, refusing the hold of property on subjects, and rejecting individual self-interest as antithetical to the value of community.

While the movement as a whole embraces portions of this ethos (Occupy's manifestos are pervasively if implicitly opposed to practices of accumulation that perpetuate structures of social inequality), at the same time, the movement's documents cite broadly from a range of quite heterogeneous political traditions, promiscuously cathecting disparate elements from the discourses of political modernity. The formation of general assemblies, for example, draws (somewhat unexpectedly) from the French revolutionary tradition, although nonviolent civil disobedience is central to the imaginary and practice of the Occupation. Occupy's emphasis on leaderless and radically anti-authoritarian self-governance is clearly indebted to autonomist thought and practice, while (other) aspects of the movement's communalist orientation seem to gesture to nineteenth-century utopian socialist traditions, routed, perhaps, through more accessible recollections of 1960s counterculture. But these historical citations, so to speak, are arrayed on an improvised performative terrain that also encompasses an orientation to liberal proceduralism (knowing your rights, taking evictions and other repressive actions to court), as well as, crucially, an affirmation of responsibility, transparency, and accountability, which are surely the neoliberal mainstays of contemporary institutional cultures.

Consider, for example, the draft "Principles of Solidarity" of the New York City General Assembly:

- Engaging in direct and transparent participatory democracy;
- Exercising personal and collective responsibility;
- Recognizing individuals' inherent privilege and the influence it has on all interactions;
- Empowering one another against all forms of oppression;
- Redefining how labor is valued;
- The sanctity of individual privacy;
- The belief that education is human right [sic]); and
- Making technologies, knowledge, and culture open to all to freely access, create, modify, and distribute. (Amendment passed by consensus, 2/9/2012)[2]

Here the liberal sanctity of individual privacy sits alongside unlearning privilege and participatory democracy, aligned, in turn, with the exercise of "responsibility," a term currently central to the prescription for "the neoliberal citizen-subject" and the recoding of austerity as the opportunity for self-determination (2005, 43). Indeed, the NYCGA's principles might be read, in part, as the reorientation of "responsibility" from the individual to the communal level, at least insofar as they posit the agency of social transformation as fully internal to the community of Occupiers, who will realize transformation *in the very form* of their self-organization. To be sure, the relation between what we might call the disposition of a movement, its political ethos as expressed through internal structures and protocols, and the movement's aims, its designs for (and on) the larger world, are always complexly interrelated. Yet in reading through the statements approved by the general assemblies, it is often difficult to maintain the sense of the distinction, as approaching the desired disposition of the movement begins to appear *as* its primary political aim.

The creation of what one OWS participant-observer calls "democratic spaces" is thus detached from actions leveled at the state. Describing the conversation at an OWS working group, Marina Sitrin explains:

We discussed and debated the question of demands and what would define the movement, but we agreed not to use the frameworks of demands at all. So what are we about? Most of us believe that what is most important is to open space for conversations—for democracy—real, direct, and participatory democracy. Our only demand then would be to be left alone in our plazas, parks, schools, workplaces, and neighborhoods so as to meet one another, reflect together, and in assembly forms decide what our alternatives are. And from there, once we have opened up these democratic spaces, we can discuss what sorts of demands we might have and who we believe might be able to meet these demands. Or, perhaps, once we have assemblies throughout the country, the issue of demands upon others will become mute. If there are enough of us, we may one day only make demands on ourselves. (2011, 8)

Other participant commentators, such as Eli Schmidt, Astra Taylor, and Mark Greif, frame the absence of demands not simply in terms of prioritizing communal self-development, but also in relation to the difficulty of apprehending a complex system and discerning the root causes of one's real conditions. Yet in these documents, as well, the postponement of demands is presented not as a failure or an impasse, but rather as a situation generative of alternate ways of imagining political activity.

We still don't know exactly what are the demands. One of the members of our group, in discussing the criteria for a good demand, noted that Americans like to "get something" out of a political action. Repeal, enact, ban. We want visible, measured outcomes. But we have no Mubarak, no Qaddafi. We are the country that reelected Bush, that bailed out the banks, that has stalemates in Congress about paltry tax increases. Our partial joblessness and our alienating democratic system may be very real, our reasons for congregating concrete, but the precise causes of our distress are still far off, the specific solutions perhaps further. (Schmitt et al. 2011, 6)

Interestingly, in this account, demands are associated with a nationalist ideology of accumulation ("get[ing] something"), the very thing, in other words, that OWS repudiates, even as the value of demands is less thoroughly dismantled than in Sitrin's account.

Along these lines, one might note that the "Principles of Solidarity" are concerned exclusively with the conditions for attaining solidarity *among movement participants.* Moreover, reading through testimonial pieces and blogs and scrolling through online posts, one gathers that the preponderance of debate among Occupiers pertains less to priorities for change in the world, and rather more to the movement's (in)adequate efforts at constituting an apparatus of genuinely nonhierarchical, consensus-based (self-)government. At any rate, the fusion of aspirations for participatory, leaderless democracy with a kind of nonmercenary entrepreneurialism (collectively making one's own opportunities) and communalized iterations of self-care appear with regularity in the statements and other "living documents" posted online.

My point here is not to cite Occupy for its tactical amalgamation of heterogeneous—and in part contradictory—tenets, and certainly not to insinuate that the movement is somehow "really" itself "neoliberal." But we do well to remember that opposition necessarily belongs to the same historical moment and the same conditions of possibility as the power it opposes. And in its central emphasis on autonomy—that is, on autonomous action by self-organizing communities that do not depend on external recognition or sanction—Occupy duplicates, as much as it refuses, the tactics of elite power (and powerbrokers). The institutions of the state systematically repudiate and dissolve any obligation to the general welfare of a national people (the 99%, in OWS parlance), and "the people," in turn, give up on the state. But the specular relation of the state and its opposition cuts still deeper. Even as the state has come to abdicate the task of hegemony, of producing and reproducing citizens who identify with its aims and projects, so too, has the opposition to the state in the form of Occupy. As Occupy's founding documents make plain, it is not conceived or designed to emerge as a political party, or bloc, that might rise to dominance by absorbing a broad cross-section of society, and indeed, its rigorously anti-authoritarian and participatory ethos precludes the possibility of *speaking for* anyone besides the active Occupiers themselves. Arguably, a central aspiration of Occupy is to reimagine the form of the body politic as no longer abstract and anonymous but participatory and communal. From this vantage, Occupy cannot be understood as counterhegemonic, both because the power it opposes no longer operates hegemonically and because it is not, itself, an incorporative political project, even as it is radically open to all participants. Direct democracy as Occupy envisions it can accrete adherents and *proliferate* in the form of leaderless, self-organizing communities both geographically and in network-based forms, but it cannot *assimilate* multiple political constituencies to a normative set of aims and beliefs, since what Occupy refuses is precisely the prerogative of dominant institutions to elaborate those norms for a mass public.

From this perspective, arguments about the racial and ethnic composition of Occupy, and whether it centers on issues of concern to the newly precarious white middle-classes while peripheralizing others vital to the futurity of black and brown people, tend to misapprehend how the problem of racial divisions manifest in the context of a proliferative (rather than an incorporative) political movement. It is worth noting that Occupy, as it reads through posted documents, could hardly be more self-conscious about the history of racial antagonisms within twentieth-century, left social movements, and it attempts—all too earnestly, at least in print—to redress the effects of these historical fractures, through the persistent interrogation of privilege (a leitmotif of movement manifestos) and an emphasis on direct democracy, rather than consensus-based, majority rule. What this has meant at the level of the actions and cultures of specific occupations in specific cities and communities, and the extent to which they do (or do not) appear to foster cross- or multiracial solidarity remains, quite legitimately, a matter of debate. Yet significantly, the nonhegemonic character of Occupy means that it is not a matter of interrogating which particular interests have been forwarded under the sign of a general (collective) mobilization. In the context of a more recognizably (counter)hegemonic movement, this negotiation between the particular and the general is rightly understood as *the* central question, one whose answer is decisive for an evaluation of its actual political alignments and the terms (and limits) of its inclusiveness along racial, ethnic, gendered, sexual, or other lines. But in the context of Occupy and what it would appear to herald about the tactical balkanization of the Left into a series of self-organizing entities, the question seems less whether something called Occupy Wall Street (in the singular) is inclusive, but rather whether the various Occupations of which Occupy is comprised will (or will not) divide along racial and ethnic lines: Will we have (primarily) black and brown Occupations in some places, and (predominantly) white ones elsewhere?

The debates around Occupy Oakland, for example, are instructive on this point, even as they suggest how the stress on rhetorical self-constitution as political activity (not the precondition of political movement, but its *ground*) is replicated across the board, among organizations that secede from OWS in anger, as well as those that retain the affiliation. In 2012 in Oakland, dissatisfaction with what was cast as the abiding, "unchecked racial privilege within Occupy Oakland's organizing structures" led to the formation of Decolonize Oakland by angry former and would-be participants in Occupy Oakland. Substituting the metaphor of decolonization for that of occupation, Decolonize Oakland contends that OWS effectively continues the centuries' long European occupation of others' lands, resources, and prospects for futurity, despite its apparent intention to *reclaim* literal and symbolic ground from the forces of capital that drove the process of colonial annexation through the opening decades of the twentieth century and sustain neocolonial relations in the present. Although foregrounding decolonization rather than anticapitalism as their central imaginative axis, Decolonize Oakland seems otherwise to reproduce the organizing gestures and forms of Occupy, however, especially in its founding declaration of autonomy. "Decolonize Oakland . . . (formerly the QPOC/POC caucus/committee of Occupy Oakland) would like to reintroduce themselves to you, our communities, as an autonomous collective," the group proclaims in its "Communiqué" of March 18, 2012. Interestingly, in an allied publication articulating similar grounds of disaffection with OWS, the authors fault the movement's "leaderless" character as a cover for covert (white, male) leadership and specifically object to the absence of clear demands, complaining that OWS seeks allegiance from people of color without being willing to specify to what it is, precisely, that their support is pledged. "We demand that any movement be clear about its goals, intent, and strategies to ensure that our communities, which are already suffering police violence in the forms of criminalization, incarceration, and surveillance, can make informed decisions about our participation," write the collective authors of "For People Who Have Considered Occupation but Found It Is Not Enuf." Yet they also suggest that a movement practice geared to decolonization cannot be corralled into any specific set of already-articulated demands: "When calling for decolonization, when demanding that we be heard, when calling for justice after incidents of abuse, you have asked us, What do you want us to do? Do you want us to leave, this space, these lands, this continent? We do not have the answers for you because we haven't yet found the answers for ourselves. We want you to strive to find your way. We want you to recognize that the ways that you seek liberation often comes at the expense of ours. We expect you to act from that knowledge with integrity."[3] In other words, the same writers also embrace a process-oriented, open-ended politics that proved one of the most distinctive and arresting attributes of OWS. Likewise, Decolonize Oakland, while seeming to echo the perception that OWS has cast under the sign of open-endedness an agenda that fundamentally elides the concerns of participants of color, insists that the value of their organization lies precisely in the elaboration of "answers" that cannot be stipulated at the outset: "As a new collective, we do not pretend that we have answers to all the problems and injustices that face our communities, nor do we presume to speak for all people of color in Oakland. Instead, we invite people of color and allies to work with us to build relationships, share information and wisdom, and take actions that align with our Points of Unity."[4]

Another organization, the Oakland Commune, which shares some of the sensibilities of Decolonize Oakland but sees itself as having evolved from Occupy Oakland, rather than broken with other Occupiers, identifies, not so much as a singular autonomous group, but rather as the name for a "network" of articulated (but not massified) actors: "This is what we began to call The Oakland Commune; that dense network of new found affinity and rebelliousness that sliced through seemingly impenetrable social barriers like never before."[5] For the advocates of the Oakland Commune, the value of the Occupy movement—and its enduring legacy—appears to be precisely this networked structure and the emergent character of the "affinities" and "rebelliousness" for which it allows. In the end, I am suggesting, *both* Decolonize Oakland, which overtly severs its ties to Occupy in order to foreground matters of concern to poor communities of color, and the Oakland Commune, which shares an orientation to the conditions of working-class black and brown people, but does *not* disaffiliate from Occupy Oakland, are invested, *like* Occupy Wall Street, in a model of political opposition based in networked, process-oriented, autonomous collectives. The political ethos of Occupy Wall Street with respect to differences of race and ethnicity, as well as of gender, sexuality, class, or ability—an ethos that it arguably *shares* with defectors such as Decolonize Oakland—is nicely rendered in a position paper that emerged from the matrix of Occupy Oakland. Placing equal emphasis on the importance of "widespread" and "autonomous" political organizing, the paper specifically validates *both* identitarian and cross-identitarian autonomies and prioritizes neither:

> As a group of people of color, women, queers, and poor people coming together to attack a complex matrix of oppression and exploitation, we believe in the absolute necessity of autonomous organizing. By "autonomous" we mean the formation of independent groups of people who face specific forms of exploitation and oppression—including but not limited to people of color, women, queers, trans* people, gender nonconforming people, QPOC. We also believe in the political value of organizing in ways which try to cross racial, gender, and sexual divisions. We are neither spokespersons for Occupy Oakland nor do we think a single group can possibly speak to the variety of challenges facing different constituencies. *We hope for the diffuse emergence of widespread autonomous organizing.* (My emphasis)[6]

In this framework, the question is not whether OWS has marginalized communities of color, but rather whether and to what extent the autonomies it proliferates will divide along identitarian lines.

Aestheticized Politics?

Occupy's effort to reclaim an idea of citizenship and self-governance from the ruined institutions of modern democratic politics in the United States entails, then, a kind of inward orientation—a focus on self-transformation as individuals and delimited collectives—that has been routinely dismissed, on the Marxist-oriented political Left, as a merely aestheticized politics, a politics of being (or self-fashioning) rather than becoming (or mass social mobilization).[7] Of course, as others on the Left have pointed out, it is not at all clear that the aesthetic and the transformative are simply alternatives, rather than complexly interrelated elements of all modern social movements. But what Occupy Wall Street shows us, I think, is how the terrain of self-fashioning becomes *immediately* political as the institutions of hegemonic political power collapse.

So it follows that among the primary genres within the movement's published archive, alongside editorials and short analytical essays (often produced by academics sympathizers), are manifestos (or "principles of solidarity" or "communiqués") and reports from the scene of occupation by participant observers. In the vein of the NYCGA's "Principles," the manifestos focus on defining the social protocols *of the occupying community*: the conditions, in Sitrin's phrase, "to meet one another, reflect together," and deliberate in assembly form. They establish a communal ethos, rather than a political aim—or perhaps more exactly, they posit the elaboration of an ethos and of the collective political subject it sustains as the condition of any (outward-oriented) political aim.[8] Whether implicitly (by the omission of demands) or sometimes explicitly (by affirming the impossibility of knowing one's demands prior to the sustained democratic encounter of participants), the manifestos frame the subject of occupation—*the political sensibilities and sentiments of the Occupiers*—as the movement's defining, and indeed its *only, specifiable* feature.

This focus on the political character of the Occupying subject helps explain why the accounts of participant observers tend to dwell on the observer's inner transformation via contact with the Occupying collective. Nikil Saval's report on "Occupied Philadelphia" offers an interesting example because, in contrast to someone like Sitrin, he remains considerably more skeptical of the operations of the general assembly as it aspires to enable open deliberation and consensus-based decision-making. His journal entry from November 11, 2011, opens with a positively caustic account of a GA meeting convened to discuss moving the encampment so as not to impede the city's plans to make the subway station in the camp's present location accessible to disabled users. "A willingness to move would imply an openness to movement, a sense of clarity over the real target—inequality, financialization, a broken political system—and proof that it's about the 99 percent, not a piece of pavement," Saval suggests, and then goes on to detail the reception of a proposal by the "radical caucus," consisting, in its entirety, of the sentence: "We propose to resist eviction" (2011, 160). The group's main spokesperson, a man whose "Stalin mustache harmonized uneasily with his soul patch," advances "solidarity with Oakland" and "not wanting to be seen as caving to the authorities" as the reasons for refusing to relocate, and what follows, in Saval's account, is a tedious and unproductive debate that he leaves two hours later "in frustration" after hearing "someone compare this struggle to King making his stand at Selma" (2011, 161). Feeling that he has no particular "right" to vote and "confident that the vote will go well," he goes off to see a movie, but returns home later that night to

> discover that, after five hours of discussion—by which point many of the people gathered had left—the GA has voted to stay in Dilworth Plaza! . . . I pour myself a beer and pray for the destruction of the planet. I realize I should have stayed and fought, even if my vote or my "clarifying questions" wouldn't have saved the day. *I had a responsibility to do so. I supposed I hadn't realized how much I cared.* The next morning, I read more emails: social movements suffer setbacks, they make decisions that they can reverse, this isn't the only time a potential move will be debated, etc. It's true, and it makes me think that a disaffection with the importance of holding a single space will move outward—"horizontally," as an occupier would say—to the rest of the 99 percent. Perhaps there will be general assemblies in the future that are less about how to live, more about what to do. The decision may have woken everyone up from the self-love that had come to afflict our bitter celebration; after all, the point was never just to hold a park. (2011, 162, my emphasis)

Even as Saval's report appears to end with an indictment of the movement's focus on "how to live" as a form of narcissism that risks obscuring the political "point," at the same time, the account of his disaffection with the GA's decision models precisely the process of political self-fashioning that the GA—as a space of democratic "meeting," to recall Sitrin's phrase—is imagined to promote. Saval comes to realize a "responsibility" to participate that is *measured not* by the likelihood that his participation will affect the outcome, but by the political value of ethical conduct. The experience of (non)participation in the failed GA meeting brings him into a fuller recognition of his own political feelings (his "caring"), and significantly, too, it is the proliferation of feeling, in the negative form of "disaffection," that is presented in the concluding lines as the motor force of transformation. Like Saval, other disaffected Occupiers will emerge into a finer sense of their responsibilities as movement participants. Even as Saval's entry of November 11 explicitly identifies the risk that Occupy will degenerate into vainglorious political posturing, the antidote to narcissism turns out to be *more* self-fashioning: the self-reconstruction of the (spread-out) Occupying subject to guard against self-absorption.

In a recurrent motif, the self-elaboration of the Occupying subject is presented as the necessary counter to practices of hypermediation that have vitiated people's ability to move in the world—or to make the world in which they desire to move. Writing in the journal *Tidal*, which describes itself as a venue for the movement's self-theorization, one anonymous commentator frames the incitement to Occupy this way:

> We were born into this world of ghosts and illusions that have haunted our minds our entire lives. These shades seem more alive to us than reality, and perhaps by some definition are more actual, hyper-real. We grew up in this world of screens and hyperbole and surreal imagery, and think nothing of a long-dead actor appearing on a wall in our homes to urge us to buy or live a certain way. Some generations ago, we might all have been burned, perhaps rightly, as witches. After all, who knows where these images come from? We have no clear idea how life should really feel.
>
> We have come to Wall Street as refugees from this native dreamland, seeking asylum in the actual. That is what we seek to occupy. We seek to rediscover and reclaim the world. Many believe we have come to Wall Street to transact some kind of business with its denizens, to strike a deal. But we have not come to negotiate. We have come to confront the darkness at its source, here, where the Big Apple sucks in more of the sap from the national tree than it needs or deserves, as if spliced from some Edenic forbearer. Serpent size worms feast within, engorged on swollen fruit. Here, the world is chewed and digested into bits as tiny and fluid as the electrons that traders use to bring nations and homeowners to their knees. (Communiqué 1, 2011)

Interestingly, this manifesto broaches a desire for something that now appears as a *critical realism*—a world predicated on precise and value-laden distinctions between the "actual" and its mediations—as a well a desire for a normative orientation ("A clear idea of how life *should* really feel"). By the logic of her curiously chosen trope, this anonymous author finds herself aligned with the guardians of the Right and natural order *against* the world-making of the "witches." Yet the manifesto ultimately elides any such foundational agenda: Occupation is figured as "seeking asylum"—as flight, not annexation—in the interest of affective self-reconstitution (learning how "life should really *feel*").

If self-fashioning represents the most fundamental of proto-political impulses, it is not *yet* intelligible as a political project when evaluated by the criteria of modern emancipatory movements, which would require the Occupiers' arrival (so to speak) into a mass political agency that can produce and represent its interests, through the relay of its designated representatives. This is the basis of much of the critical rejoinder to Michael Hardt and Antonio Negri's *Multitude*, as the authors themselves acknowledge in their sequel publication, *Commonwealth*. For Hardt and Negri, "multitude" is the name for those who live by their labor and are now increasingly—as they contend—in a position to claim autonomy from capital and stage their "exodus" from its regimes. "Cognitive labor and affective labor generally produce cooperation autonomously from capitalist command," they assert, "even in some of the most constrained and exploited circumstances, such as call centers or food services. Intellectual, communicative, and affective means of cooperation are generally created in the productive encounters themselves and *cannot be directed from the outside*" (2009, 140, my emphasis). Indeed, they propose, rather than orchestrate cooperation, capital now "*expropriates*" it, harnessing productive energies wrought "on the level of information flows, communication networks, social codes, linguistic innovations, and practices of affect and passions" (2009, 140, emphasis in original).[9] Setting aside the dubious logic on which this claim to the self-directed character of "biopolitical labor" pivots—isn't the architecture of the "communications networks" through which information flows and sociality is (re)coded and language is innovated itself the product of capitalist design, no less than the factory floor where cooperation was so palpably enjoined in an earlier era?—I note simply that the multitude as they conceive it is not a politically unified entity but a "multiplicity of irreducible singularities," and the burden of the critique, especially by Pierre Macheray and Ernesto Laclau, has been to ask how a collection of singularities (or small, functionally disaggregated groups) might work together politically.

"How then can the multitude organize itself," writes Macheray, "without sacrificing the autonomy of the singularities that compose it?" (quoted in Hardt and Negri 2009, 166). Laclau poses the problem specifically in terms of hegemony, arguing that in order to articulate singular social agents, forces must be in play to direct the process of articulation and provide common points of identification. "The political operation *par excellence*," he writes, "is always going to be the construction of a people" (quoted in Hardt and Negri 2009, 167). From this perspective, the multitude—like Occupy Wall Street, which so palpably instantiates the multitude's political characteristics—is a subject on the road to politics, rather than a properly political subject.[10]

My own inclination is to split the difference, refusing on the one hand Laclau's essentialist construction of politics (as being *always* about the construction of a people) and, on the other, Hardt and Negri's seeming dismissal of the problem of the political altogether: in their utopian scenario, the need for *any* "political operation" to articulate the singularity to the collective simply evaporates. Rather, I am suggesting, in a historical context where Laclau's apprehension of politics dissolves, the self-cultivation of disaggregated ("pre-political") agents emerges as the primary terrain for "civil revival," as well as for the elaboration of a new political operation, or operations. At the same time, against Hardt and Negri, I would insist that a new operation is both necessary and as yet fundamentally unknowable (*that is* what it means to encounter the end of an order—that one lacks the analytic resources to apprehend what is emerging); nor will the slow, difficult political work of its elaboration be preempted by our felicitous attainment of cooperative sociality through the radical autonomy of the multitude's singularities.

Indeed, in Hardt and Negri's account of the multitude's political prospects, the operative force is denominated "love." "As the motor of association, love is the power of the common in a double sense," they write, "both the power that the common exerts and the power to constitute the common. It is thus also the movement toward freedom in which the composition of singularities leads towards not unity or identity but the increasing autonomy of each participating equally in the web of communication and cooperation" (2009, 189). This seems rather an oracular pronouncement than an arguable proposition. Even so, it is hardly apparent why of all things "love"—an emotion so deeply bound up in institutional and psychic structures of *property*—would be the name to give to this principle of a collective movement towards autonomy. Speaking more generally to the affective dimensions of contemporary political life, Lauren Berlant reminds us that affect has always stood as "the register of belonging to inhabit when there are few adequate normative institutions to fall back on" (2011, 226). But Berlant is more cautious about the character of affect unbound from institutionalized social and political life, where it operates to "dramatize experiences of freedom to come that have no social world for them yet," and she notes how such emancipatory affect sustains alternate solidarities without, however, intervening in the operation of prevailing "neoliberal" interests (2011, 222). In this regard, Berlant hews to the suspicion of a too thoroughly aestheticized politics, though it is noteworthy that she, too, is drawn to the possibilities of what she terms an "ambient citizenship," where "the drama of the distribution of affect/noise meets up with scenarios of *movement*" (2011, 230, emphasis in original). I am suggesting that what is at stake in this attention to the "motor" force of love/affect is precisely recuperating a terrain of political engagement in the face of the "break-up," as Berlant puts it "of modernity's secure institutions of intimacy and reciprocity" (2011, 222). In Berlant's account, however, affect is both more heterogeneous than "love" and not, itself, the sufficient "political operation" for the emergence of new social worlds.

Coda: Simulacral Politics on the Left

Here and throughout this book, I have been arguing that opposition is always bound up in the form of the power it opposes. This is not to suggest that domination preempts or coopts its opposition, but simply to affirm that our implication in the forces and institutions that bear on our lives is rightly understood as the condition of our agency. Because OWS presents as a repudiation of so much that defines political modernity, by reimagining mass publics as networked singularities, for example, or reconstituting the always nonempirical "people" as live assemblies, it is easy enough to infer that it breaks with established forms of power. But the forms of modern, democratic governance are already, fundamentally disestablished. In abandoning the incorporative project of modern mass politics, *as the state does*, OWS commits to the production of virtual realities—beta-testing other ways of living, "releasing" other possible worlds "early and often," to recall Rushkoff's astute formulation. It is this implication of OWS in a derealized politics that the anonymous author in *Tidal* misrecognizes, when she urges the pursuit of "asylum in the actual." Confronted by such authenticating gestures, we do well to remember that reality is not so much real as it is given, a reality-effect, anchored by discourses and institutions that police the limit between the mutable and the fixed, between the field of human activity and the solid-seeming contours of the world in which we are "free" to act. In other words, we do well to remember that the "actual" and the real world are names for the very constructions it was, not so long ago, the business of oppositional intellectuals to *un-think*.

Yet in general and, I would say, at its best, OWS tends exuberantly to break with a (realist) politics of representation, in both meanings of the term: it seeks neither to array an iconic subject who stands in for the anonymous mass of movement participants (representation as delegation), nor even, more simply, to cast its participants as already-constituted political agents (representation as depiction). The movement subject imagined in the archive of OWS, the manifestos and participant testimonials, is more often than not a kind of hologram—a projection of how one might choose to move in the world. The peculiar and generative achievement of OWS, which is also its confounding limitation, is to show that there is no actually existing subject of occupation. Instead, the motive for occupation and its aim is to simulate an alternate plane of political life, outside the ruined institutions of modern democratic politics, but equally, "orthogonal" (in Sterling's phrase) to the networks of an institutionalized neocitizenship, where other iterations of a civil society and other avatars of the citizen-subject might yet emerge.

NOTES

INTRODUCTION

1 The question of whether or not we are entering a new stage of capitalism is, of course, an old argument, which tends to pivot on the relative weight given to continuities and differences. The debate is most often waged over the status of production (does capital accumulation still depend on the material production of goods?) and relatedly, the question of whether an informational economy constitutes a break—or not—with a prior regime of accumulation. While I am not especially invested in this debate—it is not clear to me that either side has the edge in articulating the difference of the historical present—I would suggest that the most compelling argument for a new stage pertains to the analytic register in which such an argument is almost never made—the register, that is, of political economy.

2 Here and throughout this book, I use "her" as the default gender of the neocitizen. My motive in so doing is simply to counter the still prevailing recourse to the masculine as the universal (non-gender-specific) form. No doubt, this gesture produces some interesting rhetorical effects in its own rights. Of course, I do not mean to insinuate that the neocitizen is simply a feminized iteration of the citizen-subject, much less that women's growing representation within electoral politics is somehow responsible for the ruination of this political construct. At the same time, the eroded relation of a mass public to the institutions of sovereignty and property that are defining features of modern citizenship does tend to undo the historical convergence of citizenship and masculinity. In that context, I find the resonances that emerge from my choice to set the feminine gender as default appropriate to the historical moment and the political transformations which this project addresses.

3 I take the concept of the extended or "ethical" state from Antonio Gramsci, who rejects the analytical division of state and civil society (1971, 258). "But since, in actual reality, civil society and State are one and the same, it must be made clear that laissez-faire too is a form of state 'regulation'" (1971, 160). And again: "But what does that signify if not that by 'State' should be understood not only the apparatus of government, but also the "private" apparatus of hegemony, or civil society?" (1971, 261).

4 On the question of financialization, see Bellamy 2007.

5 And neoliberalism plays out differently yet again as it emerges from the political contexts of Maoism. See Ci 2014.

CHAPTER 1. NEOCITIZENSHIP AND CRITIQUE

1 Alternatively, Judith Butler has suggested that sovereignty might live on precisely in the determination to act outside the law. This form of sovereignty revives a much earlier, feudal iteration of the concept—divine right, rather than rule of law. See Butler 2004, 53. Achille Mbembe also insists on the bifurcated nature of sovereignty in modernity, which points us at once toward autonomy (self-determination) and subjugation (the right to kill). For a fuller discussion of Mbembe, see chapter 3.

2 These (rough) figures turned up more or less across the board. The conservative "Insider Advantage/Majority Opinion Poll" (directed by Matt Towery, former head of Newt Gingrich's PAC) found 39 percent of voters in favor of impeaching Bush and Cheney, and 55 percent opposed. In a USA Today/Gallup poll in July 2007, 36 percent of the sample found justification to begin impeachment proceedings of the president (62 percent did not). A Rasmussen poll in the same month found 39 percent in favor of impeaching Bush, and only 49 percent opposed (with 12 percent undecided).

3 Hardt also takes up Gramsci's relation to Hegelian civil society, positioning him over and against Foucault. While Foucault refuses any analytical distinction between state and civil society, Hardt reads Gramsci as insisting on the difference, so as to imagine the state as "porous," or susceptible to intervention from below: "From this perspective, the social dialectic activated in civil society and the possibilities of mediation makes the State open to the plurality of social flows channeled through the institutions" (1995, 31). This reading seems to me to sell considerably short the complexity of Gramsci's analytic and, in particular, what I take as his double insistence on the institutions of civil society as the very site for the production of the State's class-based hegemony (on the one hand) *and* the possibility of mobilizing certain civil society associations for the cultivation of counter-hegemonic formations (on the other). The point for Gramsci is not that civil society can be distinguished from the state, analytically or otherwise, but rather that hegemony is never achieved, so that the very terrain of state-sponsored subject formation is *also* the terrain for the emergence of alternative mobilizations. That David Harvey can read in Gramsci the very inverse of what Hardt perceives—Harvey refers to "the Gramscian idea of the state as a unity of political and civil society" (2005, 78)—suggests, at the very least, that the relation of state to civil society is a pressure point in Gramsci's analytic, a site of slippage, rather than of clear-cut differentiation.

4 This purely tactical relation to the law is evident, as well, in the Nazi insistence that German law is binding on non-Germans residing beyond the nation's territorial borders. In this regard, U.S. internment of foreign "non-combatants" in Iraq, Afghanistan, and Guantanomo differs only in the state's overt suspension of the law—the *refusal* to extend U.S. legal jurisdiction and so extend to non-citizens the right to due process and protection from indefinite detention.

CHAPTER 2. POST-SOVIET AMERICAN STUDIES

1 See, for example, Pease 2002 and Saunders 2000, especially chapter 9.

2 It is an interesting question whether a non-exceptionalist study of national culture is possible. Certainly, Americanists can and have (by and large) divested from the claim of America's uniqueness and sought to insist, instead, on a comparative analytic framework (comparative settler-colonial formations, for example). But it may be that the study of national culture devolves ineluctably into the study of national *difference*—and so, by implication, into the privileging of distinctly "American" phenomena.

3 Brian T. Edwards (2010) offers a compelling discussion of historical and contemporary iterations of American studies in Africa and South Asia (Iran and India). I am not aware of cognate critical analyses of American studies in the post-Soviet context. I myself came to learn of this burgeoning regional phenomenon more or less by accident, during the years I directed the American Studies Program at Indiana University. In the early 2000s, I remarked a modest but steady trickle of Americanists from places such as Kazakhstan, Kirghizstan, Azerbaijan, and Georgia dropping by my office to chat about the program. I was interested both in their intellectual formation—how they came to American studies and what it signified to them—and in the context of their visits. Eventually, I discovered that the university's Center for International Education and Development Assistance (CIEDA) had somehow garnered the role of administering a significant grant from USAID to the American University of Central Asia, specifically earmarked for supporting American studies scholars in the region. When I remonstrated with CIEDA directors about why it was that I, as director of the program in the relevant field, knew nothing about this initiative, I was told that these were policy-oriented scholars—and therefore not the kind who would be interested in my (humanities-weighted) program. This theory about the policy-orientation of Central Asian American studies was not borne out by my subsequent research of programs in the area—nor by the fact that so many of these visitors nevertheless sought me out. Thus in an interesting disconnect, USAID funds the study of American culture abroad, while in the U.S. academy, the humanities are deemed irrelevant to the crafting of the "global university."

4 Other critics have offered decisive counters to Kadir's vision of American studies and its "outsides." See Wiegman 2004, chapter 4, and Kaplan 2004.

5 For this "third way" discourse on civil society, see, for example, Edwards 2004 and Salamon, et al. 1999.

6 In the absence of external foundation support, these programs are vulnerable to cost-cutting measures, and to the kind of curricular streamlining that tends to accompany the implementation of the Bologna process. Éva Federmayer, personal communication.

7 My research has centered on these programs (albeit not exclusively) for a number of reasons. Taken together, they represent a plausible cross-section of the variety

of American studies centers and programs in the region. AUCA and ELTE, in particular, have well-developed and informative department websites. And I have had the good fortune to develop personal contacts with faculty connected to each of these institutions, who have graciously shared with me both published information on their programs and their own perspectives on the field and its role in the region. My family connection to Hungary (I speak the language, have made frequent and extended visits since the early 1970s, and am thoroughly versed in the history and culture of the region) made Hungary an obvious touchstone in my explorations of Eastern European American studies.

8   For this understanding of the history of the field in the former Soviet bloc regions, I am also crucially indebted to Olga Bogacheva and Sabina Manfova.

9   My information on the ELTE American studies curriculum is taken from the department's graduate program handbook, compiled by Tibor Frank and published in 2002. For details of course offerings of the American Studies Center at Baku State, I thank Sabina Manfova, for forwarding the Center's newsletter (June 9, 2004). The course titles in American studies at AUCA were posted at www.auca.ky.

10 See Althusser 1994, 104 and passim, and Gramsci 1971, 257–264.

11 My appreciation of the ways in which the *administrative* categories of the networked nonprofit can shape the *political imaginary* of the "activist" subjects who gravitate to the civil society sector is enormously indebted to Kathleen Boyd's excellent dissertation, "Thoughts that Burn but Cannot Be Spoken," which explores (among other things) the history of the nonprofit as a *subject-making* institution. In a move that resonates with my own procedures in this book, Boyd turns to black feminist literature as a critical archive for reconstructing alternative practices of being political.

12 In an interesting discussion of contemporary China, Jiwei Ci makes the argument that the merit of freedom as a democratic value rests precisely on its capacity to subject. In a fascinating turn that says much, not just about contemporary China, I think, but about the ways in which neoliberal governance upends our more familiar critical gestures, the object of Althusser's critique (that freedom subjects) becomes, in Ci's analysis, the desired political outcome.

13 I take this account of the contemporary neoliberal state from Foucault (2008), especially the lectures of March 14 and March 21, 1979. See also Brown 2005.

14 Susan Zimmerman makes a similar point in relation to the funding of Gender studies in CEE. "On this level, as well," she notes, "neither Gender Studies nor women's human rights are the real agenda. The orientation to Women and Gender Studies functions rather as a symbolic orientation to the values of western democracy and liberal social and economic order" (2005, 72). [Auch auf diese Ebene sind nicht die Geschlecterstudien (oder die Menschenrechte der Frauen) das eigentliche Programm. Das Bekenntnis zu den Frauen und Geschlecterstudien fungiert viel eher als symbolishes Bekenntnis zu den westlicher Demokratie und liberal Gesellschafts- und Wirstschaftsordnung.] My translation.

15 The continuation of this statement emphasizes this latter point: "To achieve its mission, OSI seeks to shape public policies that assure greater fairness in political, legal, and economic systems and safeguard fundamental rights. On a local level, OSI implements a range of initiatives to advance justice, education, public health, and independent media. At the same time, OSI builds alliances across borders and continents on issues such as corruption and freedom of information. OSI places a high priority on protecting and improving the lives of people in marginalized communities" (Soros Foundation 2009).

16 See www.auca.kg.

CHAPTER 3. UNCIVIL SOCIETY IN *THE WHITE BOY SHUFFLE*

1 Abdul JanMohamed (2005) describes as "death-bound" the subject who is formed under the imminent threat of death. His important study of the relays between domination and violence, social death and lynching, resonates closely with my preoccupations in this chapter.

2 For the relevant discussion of biopower, see Foucault 2003, especially 239ff. For a discussion of biopower's relation to racism and the permission to kill, see Foucault 2003, 256.

3 Beatty returns to these motifs in his most recent novel, *The Sellout*, where re-segregation and the restoration of the ghetto become the protagonists' chosen tactics for contesting both the post-racial variant of white supremacy *and* the ruse of sovereign subjectivity.

4 In a very different context, Rey Chow (2002) considers the tendency to dehistoricize protest and resistance as expressions of an innate humanity, or "soul"—a tendency she traces to Georg Lukács. Turning to Max Weber, Chow develops an alternative understanding of protest born of the material conditions of capitalist production and social relations.

5 Mbembe aligns this version of sovereignty with Hegel—and certainly, King's dictum inhabits the "strongly normative" account of the modern political subject. For the theoretical elaboration of sovereignty II, Mbembe looks to Bataille.

6 Beatty appears to borrow the trope of "running in place" from Ralph Ellison's *Invisible Man*. See Houston Baker's (1984) illuminating discussion of this figure.

7 For Spivak, the access of the subaltern has less to do with technology than with Trade-Related Intellectual Properties (TRIPS), which create a market in various forms of subaltern knowledge (about seed cultures, for example).

8 The use of the term "social death" to describe the denial to the slave of all legal and customary rights originates, of course, with Orlando Patterson.

9 On this point, the novel resonates with Wahneema Lubiano's (1996) suggestion that the African American "warrior ethos" framed as a mode of resistance to necropower is properly understood as a *state-sponsored* narrative of identity.

10 Gunnar's relation to femininity is thus altogether different from that of the Gun Totin' Hooligans, whom we see cross-dressing for a raid on a rival gang, which relaxes its vigilance at the (apparent) approach of cars full of alluring women. For

all the loving attention to detail (Psycho Loco fusses over selecting the exact shade of eye shadow to match his skin tone), the GTH simply instrumentalize femininity as lure.

11 My appreciation of Gunnar's "punked" sexuality and its relation to the political mobilization over which he presides is deeply indebted to Darieck Scott's brilliant theorization of abjection as an alternate modality of agency. "Not power according to the ego-dependent, ego-centric (and masculine and white) 'I' definitions we have of power," abjection may nevertheless signify "*some kind* of power," Scott proposes, "if by power we mean only ability, the capacity for action and creation in one of several spheres, be they internal or external to the empowered" (2010, 23).

CHAPTER 4. BEGINNINGS WITHOUT END

1 For example, in a pivotal fourth season episode where a joint human and cylon exploration party finally locate "Earth," only to discover that life on the planet was eradicated by nuclear warfare, the script asserts that tests on the remains show the population of the planet to have been cylon, rather than human. Critical to the first season, however, was the assertion that cylons were physiologically indistinguishable from humans—a form of artificial (replicated) life that perfectly mimicked its human analog. In the first season, the human Gaius Baltar set to work to devise a "cylon detector"—and failed. However, in the fourth season's scramble to construct an origin story for the humanoid models, their biological identity to humans is simply forgotten.

2 In the terms of the Lacanian psychoanalysis through which his reading of this futurology is waged, Edelman understands this political project—indeed, understands the project of politics *as such*—as the effort to actualize the fullness of Imaginary relations in the realm of the Symbolic. As such, this is a fundamentally impossible aspiration, since the Imaginary involves a retroactive fantasy of original self-presence that is only ever accessed from *within* the precincts of the self's alienation in language.

3 The humans are not unconcerned with posterity, and in one season 2 episode, "The Captain's Hand," President Roslin criminalizes abortion in the context of what she frames as a human obligation to regenerate the species. But that episode correlates with the writers' broader, on-going attention to the question of rights in the state of emergency. In general, it is cylons rather than humans who are fixated on the Child as the icon of a collective destiny.

4 Framed this way, the series invites us to consider, among other things, whether the relations between what Lacanian psychoanalysis calls the "Symbolic" and the "Imaginary" are not, in fact, historically variable, so that the analytical task is to *interrogate* the relation between subjection (how we are arrayed within a social and symbolic field) and authentication (the bulwarks we erect against "the vicissitudes of the sign"), rather than assuming that the form of the relation remains transhistorically fixed.

5 It bears emphasis that the series tends to elide any coherent account of what the cylons actually are. Some of their abilities—for example, to upload their consciousness at the moment of death; to interface with cylon computers directly, without the mediation of a keypad or screen—would tend to imply the existence of some kind of inbuilt cybernetic plug-in. But on this assumption, nothing would be easier than distinguishing humans from cylons, who could be easily scanned for the existence of such cybernetic enhancements. At other points, moreover, the script and visual narrative suggest that cylon "technology" is also organic in nature. Thus the clones interface with the computer by immersing their hands in a viscous liquid. Computer interiors (when shown) have an oddly corporeal look, while the cylon ship and its fighter planes, or raiders, are characterized as living entities.

6 When the centurions become pawns in the "civil war" of the models, the Sixes in alliance with the Eights and Twos rewrite their programming and "give them the gift of reason." However, this plot turn is more or less discarded in subsequent episodes as the centurions remain mechanical cyphers who never break into character. See the episode "Six of One."

7 Among the more significant parts, Korean Canadian actress Grace Park plays the Sharons; Rehka Sharma is Tory Foster, aid to the president of the human colonies-in-exile, later revealed as one of the final five; the Galactica's deck officer Dualla is played by African American actress Kandyse Mcclure. Other African American cast members include Lorena Gale as the human priestess Elosha and Rick Worthy as the Simons, or number four model cylon. Latino actor Edward James Olmos stars as Admiral Bill Adama, while his son, Bodie Olmos, is featured in a minor but continuing role as the fighter pilot "Hotdog."

8 This motif is elaborated in the spinoff series *Caprica*, set on the human home world a generation before the cylon invasion. Tensions between Capricans and immigrants from another human home world, Tauron, are framed in familiarly ethno-racial terms (for instance, the Taurons are viewed as tradition-bound and backwards, particularly in terms of the patriarchal family structure; they are largely relegated to menial labor, and over-represented in the Caprican underworld).

9 In this regard, the humanoid cylons bear a kinship to *Star Trek: The Next Generation*'s android, Data, whose overtly mimetic relation to the human also racializes him, despite (or indeed because) of his *too*-white synthetic skin. In one episode, Data's situation is explicitly analogized to that of the plantation slave, when the courts must rule whether he is Starfleet property or a self-owning (because sentient) person. See *STNG*, "The Measure of a Man," 1989, Season 2.

10 For a further discussion of this argument, see Cherniavsky (2006), especially the introduction.

11 In one episode set on Caprica, during the cylons' short-lived attempt to colonize and rebuild it, we see cylons inhabiting reconstituted urban spaces, such as parks and cafes. Groups of two and three cylons sit around tables, or stroll, chatting, in

the streets. Their (passing) investment in reclaiming the architecture of human sociality is not much explored—beyond a passing reference to the outcast "children" of humanity returning "home"—but, conspicuously, these settings of public and recreational urban spaces have no analog on the base ships.

CHAPTER 5. UNREAL

1 See Derrida 1986.

2 Likewise observing the other than ideological character of the Bush administration's rhetorical hails, Lauren Berlant understands the preference for noise as a means to enhance affective belonging. She writes: "Yet Bush's wish to skirt the filter points to something profound in the desire for the political. He wants to transmit not the *message* but the *noise*. He wants the public to feel the funk, the live intensities and desires that make messages affectively immediate, seductive, and binding. In his head a public's binding to the political is best achieved neither by policy nor ideology but the affect of feeling together, an effect of having communicated true feeling without the distancing mediation of speech. The transmission of noise performs political attachment as a sustaining intimate relation, without which great dramas of betrayal are felt and staged" (2011, 224). Berlant here attributes a "profound" apprehension of public feeling to a president who gave little sign of his intuitive powers on issues of meta-politics or anything else. In any case, Bush's aspirations aside, it is not clear to me why the immediacy of noise functions to bind—much less to bind us to anything in particular (each other, the body politic, or the degraded message).

3 *The Great Derangement* explores the far reaches of 9/11 disbelief: "truthers" convinced that the Twin Towers were bombed and that al Qaeda is a front for the Bush regime.

4 As Romney's choice of Paul Ryan for his running mate confirmed, Republican electoral calculations have been staked on the proposition that government-loathing Christian fundamentalists are the party base, and certainly Ryan wandered the political "outlands" of fervent unreason no less boldly than any of the 2012 primary season contenders, even if his political vision was less bound up in anticipation of the End Times than Bachmann's or Perry's. Ryan's professed belief that the New Deal worsened rather than alleviated the effects of the Great Depression, for instance, suggests a comparable disregard for the conventions of evidentiary reasoning—or more exactly, perhaps, a comparable proclivity to conflate different orders of discourse and truth-effects, effacing the distinction between empirical and prophetic claims—what is *shown* and what is *felt* to be true.

5 When interviewed with Tavis Smiley on *Democracy Now*, November 9, 2012, Cornel West rejected the linkage of Obama's candidacy to a broader social movement. In response to Amy Goodman's question about the future of "the movements that brought President Obama into office," West replied: "I draw a distinction between campaigns and movements. Movements are highly sophisticated forms of bringing power and pressure to bear on the status quo. Campaigns

are attempts to mobilize in order to support candidates inside a system. And they play a role and so forth, but there was not a social movement. We haven't had a social movement, really, since the gay brothers and lesbian sisters tried to break the back of homophobia, going—before that, the feminist movement, and then the great black freedom movement called the civil rights movement. Those are very rare."

6   At some point in the last quarter century, what was once understood as a "conflict of interest," a commitment to private interests that compromised one's ability to execute public office, was rewritten as a qualification. It is startling and instructive to peruse the official biographies of State Department, Justice Department, or Pentagon appointees and recognize that the ability to profit in direct, material fashion from decisions made and policies enacted while in public office is longer framed as a conflict, but as proof of the office-holder's relevant *expertise*.

7   For the Federal Election Commission information on the funding of the 2008 presidential race, see www.fec.gov.

8   The premodern political world falls, of course, well beyond scope of this book. But it seems to me questionable whether something like "the real world," a common reality in which all political actors take their bearings, is historically operative within stratified feudal societies. Where relatively fixed, customary relations of domination and subordination organize hereditary social castes— where social order is calibrated on *transcendent* principles of divine authority and distinct orders of human being existing in greater or lesser proximity to that divinity—the operation of power seems hardly to require that heterogeneous social segments situate themselves within common *worldly* parameters of demonstrable truth. From this perspective, one might speculate whether "the real world" emerges hand in glove with modern, emancipatory politics—with the dissolution of caste and hereditary obligation, and the novel "organicism," in Antonio Gramsci's phrase, of the bourgeoisie, its aspiration to encompass all of society (1971, 260).

9   Recently, of course, Edward Snowden's revelation of the reach and extent of the National Security Administration's surveillance of ordinary citizens, oriented specifically to the collection of *metadata*, has brought into relief the new form of (nonrepresentative) relation between the state and its citizens.

10   More specifically, Grossberg suggests, "Capitalism granted to labor a minimal value only by displacing that value onto an abstract set of rights, crystallized in the notion of citizenship." However, "The individual of neoliberal globalization can no longer claim the possession of such abstract rights . . . for it is only as a specific site of capital production—or better, of the possession of money—that such proprietary property rights can be asserted" (2000, 72).

11   In this process, Grossberg (2000) argues, labor is transformed from a "variable capital cost and a major source of demand" into a "fixed capital cost" in a scenario where demand is tied to credit rather than wages and the laborer reimagined as debtor rather than proprietor.

12 Henwood cites John Finnerty's stunning compendium of the more than one hundred financial "instruments" devised in the last century (1998, 49 and 51).

13 Contrary to Hardt and Negri, who astonishingly characterize contemporary market speculation on the model of race track wagers that involve the rational assessment of diverse material inputs, such as the condition of the horse, the track, past record, competitors, and so forth, financial speculation tends instead to conjure its optimal environment, so that an entity (corporation, hedge fund) with the capacity to move large sums of capital may create the conditions on which a particular wager is premised (2009, 157). Matt Taibbi (2009) notes, for instance, how in the wake of the 2008 collapse, Goldman Sachs's recommendations were routinely being read in reverse—as deliberate attempts to engineer the conditions that would pay out the bank's own speculations. In theory, it is the contribution of market analysts to provide a rational check on the tendency for value to rise and fall on the basis of buying and selling alone—to note, in other words, when value has gone utterly astray from anything that might be construed as the underlying worth of the assets. Yet in practice, as Henwood observes, the "worldview [of Wall Street analysts] often seems formed by nothing deeper than the endless play of headlines that scroll across their computer screens" (1998, 98). Indeed, "efficient market theory depends on the universal, costless dissemination of accurate information about economic and corporate prospects," while instead the expert market watchers tend uncritically to disseminate the word of the market itself (1998, 170).

14 We might recall Lofgren's account of Republican congressional obstructionism, the willful delegitimation of the institution that is ostensibly the basis of one's own political power. In the gambit Lofgren describes, the party cultivates the electorate's sense of political abandonment, rescinds even the pretense of government institutions that might serve a social (public) interest—so that voting becomes, in effect, an expression of rage against the voters' own political disqualification. To claim as one's political base an electorate that has been purposefully and massively failed, cut loose from its affirmative ties to national political institutions, is surely the *political equivalent of the deliberate creation of the market bubble*: it is a method for the accumulation of political capital that forfeits duration and, indeed, mandates the difference between present and future as the context of its (invariably short-term) speculation. On this point, too, I depart from Wendy Brown. "More generally," she argues, "neoliberalism confidently identifies itself with the future, and in producing itself as normal rather than adversarial does not acknowledge any alternative futures" (2006, 699). Like the insane forms of capital it seeks to liberate from social constraints, neoliberalism deals in the sophisticated temporal management of the *near* future, I suggest, and specifically cultivates the *insecurity* of the longer term—the prospect of disaster; the *non-duration* of established industries, institutions, governments, and ways of life.

15 And of course, the surveillance and policing of "ungovernables" is also a site of accumulation, marked by the proliferation of private security firms and private prisons, to which government functions are increasingly outsourced.

16 Replacing money with reputation, the nomads might be read as reactivating a Republican political tradition, oriented toward civic virtue, rather than accumulation. And no doubt—like the Occupy Wall Street movement I discuss in chapter 6—Sterling's nomads have a flexible relation to modern political institutions, borrowing or adapting elements of prior syntheses. But those elements also appear fundamentally repurposed. Sterling's nomads bear scant resemblance to Jefferson's yeomen farmers, insofar as their virtue is predicated neither on self-sufficiency, nor even on productive labor. The crisis of productive labor is the very premise of prole sociality (labor has been rendered largely superfluous), and the material basis of the prole economy as imagined in the novel is their appropriation of natural and man-made detritus—in a word, scavenging.

CHAPTER 6. REFUGEES FROM THIS NATIVE DREAMLAND

1 Some examples of academic supporters' pedagogy for the occupiers include Gayatri Spivak's survey of the history and theory of the general strike in the inaugural (2011) issue of the Occupy-linked journal, *Tidal*, a survey that appears to urge Occupy's practice in this direction. Jodi Dean and Marco Deseriis take the more familiar form of a complaint about the absence of demands—"the lack of demands reflects the weak ideological core of the movement," they aver—and an ensuing argument for the compatibility of a "strategic view" with a "politics of the commons" (2012, 2).

2 The language of the final bullet was amended from its original form: "Endeavoring to practice and support wide application of open source." For the full text of the Principles of Solidarity, go to www.nycga.net.

3 The full text appears without a byline on a site entitled "DisOccupy," but includes a long list of signatories, some individual and some collective.

4 The history and mission statement of Decolonize Oakland can be found on their website.

5 This anonymous account of the Oakland Commune was published under the title "Occupy Oakland Is Dead. Long Live the Oakland Commune" on the website *Bay of Rage*.

6 This paper is published on a site entitled *Escalating Identity* and appears under the byline "CROATOAN."

7 See for example David Harvey 1990, especially chapter 17.

8 Jan Radway's important work-in-progress on riot grrrls and zine culture in the 1990s raises interesting questions about the longer historical emergence of the political sensibilities at work in OWS. Radway discerns in the practices of young women zinesters a similar emphasis on political self-elaboration, rather than more conventional forms of end-directed activism, and in this way, I think, invites us to consider how the shape of the political is itself at stake in practices of "protest" after the 1960s. If, as I argue here, the work of self-fashioning becomes immediately political as the institutions of representative governance erode, then the implications of this erosion for the forms and

resources of oppositional politics have no doubt been unfolding since long before OWS.

9 This point is central to Hardt and Negri's vision of labor's autonomy: "The ability of producers autonomously to organize cooperation and produce collectively in a planned way," they write, "has immediate implications for the political realm, providing the tools and habits for collective decision making" (2009, 174). For an interesting counterargument, see Christopher Newfield, *The Unmaking of the Public University*, who reads in the dismantling of higher education an *assault* on the relatively autonomous conditions of cognitive labor in the professional managerial class.

10 As Hardt and Negri acknowledge, Alain Badiou and Slavoj Žižek have challenged the argument of *Multitude* from the opposite vantage, focusing not on the multitude's (in)capacity for concerted political action, but its implication in the operations it contests. Žižek and Badiou "take this questioning of the multitude's political orientation one step further," Hardt and Negri write, "posing it as not ambivalent but aligned with the forces of domination. Žižek charges that the multitude, even in the guise of anticapitalist struggles, really mimics and supports capitalist power" (2009, 168–169). However, contra Žižek, it is not clear to me why "alignment" would obviously or necessarily entail "support." Against the tendency to privilege (righteous) critical distance, I am inclined to understand implication in a structure of power not as a bar to the practice of opposition, but as its vexed and necessary condition.

WORKS CITED

Althusser, Louis. 1994. "Ideology and Ideological State Appartuses (Notes Towards an Investigation)." In *Mapping Ideology*, edited by Slavoj Žižek. New York: Verso, 100–140.

Arendt, Hannah. 1976. *The Origins of Totalitarianism*. New York: Harcourt.

Baker, Houston. 1984. *Blues, Ideology, and Afro-American Literature: A Vernacular Theory*. Chicago: University of Chicago Press.

Battlestar Galactica. 2005–2009. Produced by Ronald D. Moore and David Eick. Seasons 1–4. Universal City, CA: Universal Studios, DVD.

Beatty, Paul. 1996. *The White Boy Shuffle*. New York: Houghton-Mifflin.

Beatty, Paul. 2006. "Black Humor." *New York Times*, January 26. www.nytimes.com.

Beatty, Paul. 2015. *The Sellout*. New York: Farrar, Straus and Giroux.

Bellamy, John Foster. 2007. "The Financialization of Capitalism." *Monthly Review* 58, no. 11 (April). monthlyreview.org.

Berlant, Lauren. 2011. *Cruel Optimism*. Durham, NC: Duke University Press.

Bersani, Leo. 1987. "Is the Rectum a Grave?" *October* 43 (Winter): 197–222.

Bollobás, Enikö. 2002. "Dangerous Liaisons: Politics and Epistemology in Post–Cold War American Studies." *American Quarterly* 54, no. 4 (December): 563–579.

Bové, Paul. 2002. "Can American Studies Be Area Studies?" In *Learning Places: The Afterlives of Area Studies*, edited by Masao Miyoshi and H. D. Harootunian. Durham, NC: Duke University Press, 206–230.

Boyd, Kathleen. 2013. "'Thoughts that Burn but Cannot Be Spoken': Re-Imagining the Political within Literatures of Feminist Activism." PhD dissertation, University of Washington.

Brown, Wendy. 2005. *Edgework: Critical Essays on Knowledge and Politics*. Princeton, NJ: Princeton University Press.

Brown, Wendy. 2006. "American Nightmare: Neoliberalism, Neoconservatism, and De-Democratization." *Political Theory* 34 no. 6 (December): 690–714.

Butler, Judith. 2004. *Precarious Lives: The Powers of Mourning and Violence*. London: Verso.

Chatterjee, Partha. 2004. *The Politics of the Governed: Reflections on Popular Politics in Most of the World*. New York: Columbia University Press.

Cherniavsky, Eva. 2006. *Incorporations: Race, Nation, and the Body Politics of Capital*. Minneapolis: University of Minnesota Press.

Chomsky, Noam. 2011. Interview. *Democracy Now*, September 13. www.democracynow.org.

Chow, Rey. 2002. *The Protestant Ethnic and the Spirit of Capitalism*. New York: Columbia University Press.

Ci, Jiwei. 2014. *Moral China in the Age of Reform*. Cambridge: Cambridge University Press.

"Communiqué 1." 2011. *Tidal: Occupy Theory, Occupy Strategy* 1 (December): 3. docs. google.com.

"Communiqué from Decolonize Oakland 3.18.12." *Decolonize Oakland*. decolonizeoakland.org.

CROATOAN. 2012. "Who Is Oakland: Anti-Oppression Activism, the Politics of Safety, and State Co-optation." escalatingidentity.wordpress.com.

Dean, Jodi, and Marco Deseriis. 2012. "A Movement without Demands." *Possible Futures: A Project of the Social Science Research Council*, 2. www.possible-futures.org.

Deleuze, Gilles. 1990. "The Society of Control." *Autre Journal* 1 (May). www.nadir.org.

Derrida, Jacques. 1986. "Declarations of Independence." Translated by Tom Keenan and Tom Pepper. *New Political Science* 15:7–15.

Edelman, Lee. 2004. *No Future: Queer Theory and the Death Drive*. Durham, NC: Duke University Press.

Edwards, Brian T. 2010. "American Studies in Motion: Tehran, Hyderabad, Cairo." In *Globalizing American Studies*, edited by Brian T. Edwards and Dilip Parameshwar Gaonkar. Chicago: University of Chicago Press, 300–321

Edwards, Michael. 2004. *Civil Society*. Cambridge, UK: Polity Press.

Eötvös Loránd University, Department of American Studies. N.d. "BA Specialization: American Studies." das.elte.hu/.

Eurasia Foundation. N.d. www.eurasia.org.

Federmayer, Éva. 2006. "American Studies in Hungary." *European Journal of American Studies* 1, no. 1 (Spring). ejas.revues.org.

"For People Who Have Considered Occupation but Found It Is Not Enuf." 2012. *DisOccupy*. disoccupy.wordpress.com.

Foucault, Michel. 2003. *Society Must Be Defended: Lectures at the Collège de France, 1975–1976*. Translated by David Macey. New York: Picador.

Foucault, Michel. 2007. *Security, Territory, Population: Lectures at the Collège de France, 1977–1978*. Translated by Graham Burchell. Basingstoke, Hampshire, UK: Palgrave MacMillan.

Foucault, Michel. 2008. *The Birth of Biopolitics: Lectures at the Collège de France, 1978–1979*. Translated by Graham Burchell. Basingstoke, Hampshire, UK: Palgrave MacMillan.

Frank, Tibor, ed. 2002. "PhD Program in American Studies." Budapest: Eötvös Loránd University.

Gilmore, Ruth Wilson. 2007. *Golden Gulag: Prisons, Surplus, Crisis, and Opposition in Globalizing California*. Berkeley: University of California Press.

Gilroy, Paul. 1993. *The Black Atlantic: Modernity and Double-Consciousness*. Cambridge, MA: Harvard University Press.

Gramsci, Antonio. 1971. *Selections from the Prison Notebooks*. Edited and translated by Quinton Hoare and Geoffrey Nowell Smith. New York: International Publishers.

Grossberg, Lawrence. 2000. "The Figure of Subalternity and the Neoliberal Future." *Neplantha: Views from the South* 1, no. 1: 59–89.

Hardt, Michael. 1995. "The Withering of Civil Society." *Social Text* 45, no. 14 (Winter): 27–44

Hardt, Michael, and Antonio Negri. 2000. *Empire.* Cambridge, MA: Harvard University Press.

Hardt, Michael, and Antonio Negri. 2004. *Multitude: War and Democracy in the Age of Empire.* New York: Penguin.

Hardt, Michael, and Antonio Negri. 2009. *Commonwealth.* Cambridge, MA: Harvard University Press.

Harvey, David. 1990. *The Condition of Postmodernity.* Cambridge, MA: Blackwell.

Harvey, David. 2005. *A Brief History of Neoliberalism.* Oxford: Oxford University Press.

Hedges, Chris. 2011. "A Master Class in Occupation." *truthdig: drilling beneath the headlines,* October 31. www.truthdig.com.

Henwood, Doug. 1998. *Wall Street: How It Works and for Whom.* London: Verso.

Henwood, Doug. 2003. *After the New Economy.* New York: The New Press.

JanMohamed, Abdul. 2005. *The Death-Bound Subject: Richard Wright's Archaeology of Death.* Durham, NC: Duke University Press.

Kadir, Djelal. 2003. "America and Its Studies." *PMLA* 118, no. 1 (January): 9–24.

Kaplan, Amy. 2004. "Response to Djelal Kadir." *Comparative American Studies* 2, no. 2: 153–159.

Kennedy, Liam, and Scott Lucas. 2005. "Enduring Freedom: Public Diplomacy and U.S. Foreign Policy." *American Quarterly* 57, no. 2 (June): 309–333.

Klein, Naomi. 2007. *The Shock Doctrine: The Rise of Disaster Capitalism.* New York: Henry Holt.

Kwiek, Marek. 2004. "The Emergent European Educational Policies under Scrutiny: The Bologna Process from a Central European Perspective." *European Educational Research Journal* 3, no. 4: 759–776.

Lang, Sabine. 2007. "Organizing Political Advocacy: Transnational Women's Networks and Gender Mainstreaming in the European Union." Paper submitted for the European Communication Research and Education Association Conference, Brussels, October 11–12. sections.ecrea.eu.

Lofgren, Mike. 2011. "Goodbye to All That: Reflections of a GOP Operative Who Left the Cult." *Truthout,* September 3. www.truth-out.org.

Lubiano, Wahneema. 1996. "Like Being Mugged by a Metaphor: Multiculturalism and State Narratives." In *Mapping Multiculturalism,* edited by Avery Gordon and Chris Newfield. Minneapolis: University of Minnesota Press, 64–75.

Mbembe, Achille. 2003. "Necropolitics." Translated by Libby Meintjes. *Public Culture* 15, no. 1: 11–40.

Medovoi, Leerom. 2005. "Nation, Globe, Hegemony: Post-Fordist Preconditions of the Transnational Turn in American Studies." *Interventions* 7, no. 2: 162–179.

Miyoshi, Masao. 1993. "A Borderless World? From Colonialism to Transnationalism and the Decline of the Nation-State," *Critical Inquiry* 19:721–751.

Neal, Mark Anthony. 2002. *Soul Babies: Black Popular Culture and the Post-Soul Aesthetic.* New York: Routledge.

Newfield, Christopher. 2011. *Unmaking the Public University: The Forty-Year Assault on the Middle-Class.* Cambridge, MA: Harvard University Press.

"Occupy Oakland Is Dead. Long Live the Oakland Commune." 2012. *Bay of Rage.* www.bayofrage.com.

Ong, Aihwa. 2006. *Neoliberalism as Exception: Mutations in Citizenship and Sovereignty.* Durham, NC Duke University Press.

Patterson, Orlando. 1985. *Slavery and Social Death: A Comparative Study.* Cambridge, MA: Harvard University Press.

Patton, Cindy. 1993. "Tremble, Hetero Swine!" In *Fear of a Queer Planet: Queer Politics and Social Theory*, edited by Michael Warner. Minneapolis: University of Minnesota Press, 143–177.

Pease, Donald. 2002. "C. L. R. James, *Moby-Dick*, and the Emergence of Transnational American Studies." In *The Futures of American Studies*, edited by Donald E. Pease and Robyn Wiegman. Durham, NC: Duke University Press, 135–163.

Prashad, Vijay. 2003. *Fat Cats and Running Dogs: The Enron Stage of Capitalism.* Monroe, ME: Common Courage Press.

"Principles of Solidarity." 2011. *#Occupy Wall Street.* NYC General Assembly. www.nycga.net. Rushkoff, Douglas. 2011. "Occupy Wall Street Beta Tests a New Way of Living." CNN.com, October 25. www.cnn.com.

Roy, Ananya. 2010. *Poverty Capital: Microfinance and the Making of Development.* New York: Routledge.

Salamon, Lester M., Helmut K Anheier, Regina List, Stephen Toepler, S. Wojciech Sokolowski, and Associates. 1999. *Global Civil Society: Dimensions of the Nonprofit Sector.* Baltimore, MD: Johns Hopkins Center for Civil Society Studies.

Saunders, Frances Stonor. 2000. *The Cultural Cold War: The CIA and the World of Arts and Letters.* New York: The New Press.

Saval, Nikil. 2011. "Scenes from Occupied Philadelphia." In *Occupy: Scenes from Occupied America.* New York: N+1 and Verso, 157–162.

Schmitt, Eli, Astra Taylor, and Mark Greif. 2011. "Scenes from an Occupation." In *Occupy: Scenes from Occupied America.* New York: N+1 and Verso, 1–6.

Scott, Darieck. 2010. *Extravagant Abjection: Blackness, Power, and Sexuality in the African American Literary Imagination.* New York: New York University Press.

Sharlet, Jeff. 2011. "Welcome to the Occupation." *Rolling Stone* 1144 (November 24): 58–64.

Shin, Sarah. 2011. "Slavoj Žižek at Occupy Wall Street," *Verso* 10 (October). www.versobooks.com.

Sitrin, Marina. 2011. "One No, Many Yeses." In *Occupy: Scenes from Occupied America.* New York: N+1 and Verso, 7–11.

Soros Foundation Open Society Institute. 2009. "About OSI: Overview." www.opensocietyfoundations.org. Soros, George. 2002. *George Soros on Globalization.* New York: Public Affairs.

Spillers, Hortense. 2003. *Black, White, and In Color: Essays on American Literature and Culture.* Chicago: University of Chicago Press.

Spivak, Gayatri Chakravorty. 2006. "The New Subaltern: A Silent Interview." In *Mapping Subaltern Studies and the Postcolonial,* edited by V. Chaturvedi. London: Verso, 324–340.

Spivak, Gayatri. 2011. "General Strike." *Tidal: Occupy Theory, Occupy Strategy* (December). docs.google.com.

St Clair, Jeffrey. 2011. "The Politics of Make-Believe: Barack Obama, Changeling." *Counterpunch,* July 27. www.counterpunch.org.

Stallings, L. H. 2009. "Punked for Life: Paul Beatty's *The White Boy Shuffle* and Radical Black Masculinities." *African American Review* 43, no. 1 (Spring): 99–116.

Star Trek: The Next Generation, Season 2. 1988–1989. Produced by Rick Berman. Los Angeles, CA: Paramount Studios. DVD

Sterling, Bruce. 1998. *Distraction.* Bantam Books.

Stiglitz, Joseph. 2002. *Globalization and Its Discontents.* New York: W.W. Norton.

Taibbi, Matt. 2009. *The Great Derangement: A Terrifying True Story of War, Politics, and Religion.* New York: Spiegel and Grau.

Tlostanova, Madina. 2007. "Why Cut the Feet in Order to Fit the Western Shoes? Non-European Soviet Ex-Colonies and the Modern Colonial Gender System." Unpublished paper.

Warner, Michael. 1990. *The Letters of the Republic: Publication and the Eighteenth-Century Public Sphere.* Cambridge, MA: Harvard University Press.

Weheliye, Alexander, et al. 2007. "These—Are—the "Breaks": A Roundtable Discussion on Teaching the Post-Soul Aesthetic." *African American Review* 41, no. 4 (Winter): 787–803.

West, Cornel. 2012. Interview. *Democracy Now,* November 9. www.democracynow.org.

Wiegman, Robyn. 2012. *Object Lessons.* Durham, NC: Duke University Press.

Yoshimoto, Mitsuhiro. 1996. "Real Virtuality. " In *Global/Local: Cultural Production and the Transnational Imaginary,* edited by Rob Wilson and Wimal Dissanayake. Durham, NC: Duke University Press, 107–118.

Zimmerman, Susan. 2005. "Frauen- und Geschlecterstudien im höheren Bildungswesen in Zentraleuropa und im postsowjetischen Raum. Teil 2: Akteurinnen und Interessen im Prozess der Institutionalisierung." *Homme* 16, no. 1: 53–84.

INDEX

normative culture, 33, 37, 56, 57; in
  Battlestar Galactica, 126–127, 133–134;
  defined, 15, 23–24; end of, 68, 140–141,
  146, 148, 155–157, 160, 183

Obama, Barack, 10, 148–151, 167
Occupy Wall Street, 11, 175–184, 187–191,
  193–194: and the multitude, 191–193;
  and race, 184–187
Ong, Aihwa, 15, 32

Patterson, Orlando, 199n8
Patton, Cindy, 6, 23, 35–37
Perry, Rick, 146, 202n4
Prashad, Vijay, 15
political society, 30–31, 37, 86–87
popular sovereignty, 3, 11, 31, 57, 64, 132,
  136–139; and hegemony, 17, 18, 152–154,
  160, 162. *See also* sovereignty
post-soul aesthetic, 73–74

Radway, Janice, 205n8
Reich, Robert, 161
Republican Party, 145–147
Romney, Mitt, 145–146, 202n4
Roy, Ananya, 80
Rushkoff, Douglas, 178, 194
Ryan, Paul, 202n4

Salamon, Lester, 197n5
Saval, Nikil, 188–190
Schmidt, Eli, 182
Scott, Darieck, 100n11
Sitrin, Marina, 181–182, 188, 189
Snowden, Edward, 203n9

society of control, 14, 22–23; in *Battlestar
  Galactica*, 113–114, 118, 127, 132–133
Soros, George, 65–66, 161
Soros Foundation, 47, 48, 64–65, 199n15
sovereignty, 17–20, 33, 70–72, 100, 103,
  196n1; in *The White Boy Shuffle*, 73,
  76, 77, 82, 90, 92, 93. *See also* popular
  sovereignty
Spillers, Hortense, 70, 90, 94–96
Spivak, Gayatri Chakravorty, 86, 205n11
Stallings, L. H., 73, 74, 93–94, 96
St. Clair, Jeffrey, 148–149
Sterling, Bruce, and *Distraction*, 10, 11,
  162–174, 175, 194, 205n16
Stiglitz, Joseph, 65, 161

Taibbi, Matt, 137, 139–141, 143,144, 151,154,
  174, 202n3, 204n13
Taylor, Astra, 182
Tlostanova, Madina, 67–68

United States Agency for International
  Development, 7, 18, 40, 46, 47, 48, 61,
  197n3

Warner, Michael, 18
Weheliye, Alexander, 74, 101
Weizman, Eyal, 78
West, Cornel, 202n5
Wiegman, Robyn, 197n4

Yoshimoto, Mitsuhiro, 158

Zimmerman, Susan, 198n14
Žižek, Slavoj, 1, 4, 206n10

ABOUT THE AUTHOR

Eva Cherniavsky is the Andrew R. Hilen Professor of American Literature and Culture at the University of Washington. She is the author of *Incorporations: Race, Nation and the Body Politics of Capital* (2006) and *That Pale Mother Rising: Sentimental Discourses and the Imitation of Motherhood in 19th-Century America* (1995).